Histories of Public Service Broadcasters on the Web

This book is part of the Peter Lang Media and Communication list.
Every volume is peer reviewed and meets
the highest quality standards for content and production.

PETER LANG
New York • Washington, D.C./Baltimore • Bern
Frankfurt • Berlin • Brussels • Vienna • Oxford

Histories of Public Service Broadcasters on the Web

EDITED BY Maureen Burns & Niels Brügger

PETER LANG
New York • Washington, D.C./Baltimore • Bern
Frankfurt • Berlin • Brussels • Vienna • Oxford

Library of Congress Cataloging-in-Publication Data

Histories of public service broadcasters on the web /
edited by Maureen Burns, Niels Brügger.
p. cm.
Includes bibliographical references and index.
1. Public broadcasting. 2. Online journalism. 3. Webcasting.
I. Burns, Maureen. II. Brügger, Niels.
HE8689.7.P82H57 384.540285'4678—dc23 2011037361
ISBN 978-1-4331-1175-4 (hardcover)
ISBN 978-1-4539-0232-5 (e-book)

Bibliographic information published by **Die Deutsche Nationalbibliothek**
Die Deutsche Nationalbibliothek lists this publication in the "Deutsche Nationalbibliografie"; detailed bibliographic data is available on the Internet at http://dnb.d-nb.de/.

29 Broadway, 18th floor, New York, NY 10006
www.peterlang.com

This book was published with support from the Department of Information and Media Studies, Aarhus University.

Contents

Part Two. Commercial vs Public

Part Three. A Perfect Match? Ideals, Policies and Practices of Public Service Broadcasters on the Web

Part Four. Local, National, International, Global?

Foreword: Public Service Broadcasters and the Web

Interplay of Convenience, Necessity, and Challenge

Nicholas W. Jankowski

Nearly all individuals and institutions have incorporated the internet and, more specifically, the web into every day, routinized practice. The digital natives in North America are unaware of a life that is not, almost always, online. Small craft fishermen in Malaysia use their mobile phones to navigate towards more plentiful waters; investors in Canada digitally monitor the markets in Japan and China; demonstrators in Cairo rely on myriad social media to exchange strategic information and mobilize support elsewhere in the country and far beyond.

Media institutions around the world have similarly adapted routine practices for gathering, processing and disseminating news and other media products as the web has become a common and taken–for–granted component of the media environment. This story of adoption is well known among a range of media, particularly newspapers that have been struggling for decades to make the transition to a web environment. The story is less well known regarding how one segment of the media environment, public service broadcasting (PSB), has managed in this "New Networked World." This book is about the relation between PSB and the web, a marriage sometimes preceded by long periods of engagement, sometimes by elopement, sometimes enthralled embracement, and sometimes by very rocky times.

PSB, it should be remembered, is far from a single, unified system of broadcasting, but a conglomerate of activities reflecting the particular social, cultural, political and historical contexts of individual nation–states, and a system continually in flux wherever situated. This book represents one of the few scholarly efforts to examine how public service broadcasting situated in a broad range of countries across North America, Europe and Australasia has reacted to the multiple media–related opportunities available on the web. Another feature setting this collection aside from other initiatives, *Histories of Public Service Broadcasters on the Web* takes its cue from a cultural historical approach. The scholarship is rich in detail and conscious of the centrality of historical context for gaining understanding of the relation between PSB and the web.

In this foreword to the volume, I need not summarize the contributions to the book; that task has already been performed in the panoramic introduction following this text. Instead, I will concentrate on a small number of themes, some salient, that overarch many of the chapters. These include:

- Defining PSB across cultures, times and places;
- PSB in the Digital Age;
- Further research: social, cultural, historical.

Each of these themes is addressed globally in the contributions, and sometimes in poignant detail. I would like to illustrate some of these themes as reflected in the chapters and, on occasion, draw from other literature. Perhaps a suitable starting point is the term public service broadcasting: what it has been and what it is becoming in a web environment.

Defining Public Service Broadcasting

Many efforts have been undertaken to define and elaborate on the term public service broadcasting (e.g., Price & Raboy, 2001; Hooper, 2002); most relate to specific broadcasting systems, but a few cross the boundaries of nation states.[1] Almost all discussions of the characteristics of PSB, however, pay at least nodding respect to the "holy trinity" of "entertainment, education and information" as formulated by the first director of the BBC, John Reith, in 1926 (House of Commons, 2004, pp. 23–24). Much has been added to this formulation in subsequent decades, in part as response to technological developments (e.g., introduction of television, cable and satellite program delivery, recording and replaying equipment) but also as response to changing political and cultural climates (e.g., Hills & Michalis, 2000). Should programming be locally, nationally or internationally oriented? What should the relation be to commercial interests regarding programming sponsorship, advertising, and merchandising? What should the relation be to community and nation building, and to special groups within a society such as ethnic minorities and economically underprivileged? What should the relation be between programming primarily considered entertainment and that with mainly educational or service objectives?

These concerns have, in fact, often been formulated as tensions within the groundwork of PSB: commercial vs. non–commercial, local vs. national, national vs. international, service vs. advocacy, professional vs. amateur. One of the striking initiatives regarding the tension between commercial and non–commercial activity is documented in Chapter 6, analyzing the about–face policy decision by the Norwegian Broadcasting Corporation to first institute banner ads on its web site and then a decade later prohibit such commercial activity. The BBC also considered commercial options for its online news operation, as detailed in Chapter 1, but a clear policy decision was taken not to do so even though there was substantial pressure to embrace such sources of revenue during lean times.

Regarding geographic orientation of PSB programming, a standard policy position is that PSB stations are to serve their communities and contribute to nation–building. How a community is defined, however, varies considerably. For the public radio station *Vocalo* in Chicago, described in Chapter 10, community is defined along the lines of impoverished neighborhoods. For the PSB station Al–Jazeera English, community is global in scope with a programming palette intended for viewers throughout the Middle East as well as North America, Europe and Asia; see Chapter 15.

The role of professional programming staff, particularly journalists, is being redefined by those PSBs experimenting with incorporation of contributions from the lay public such as amateur filmmakers and other versions of citizen journalists. On the one hand, some PSB services, such as BBC News Online, have come to be recognized for their pioneering contributions to developing online journalism. Parallel to this strain of innovation, interestingly, is experimentation initiated by the same organization in establishing an editorial department to handle user–generated content, appropriately called UGC Hub; see Chapter 1. Not all of the initiatives at incorporating user–generated content, however, have been equally successful; at the Chicago PSB station *Vocalo,* it seems that too much of that "good thing" may in fact be contributing to declining listenership.

PSB Initiatives within a Web Environment

In almost all instances presented in the chapters in this book, initial initiatives at utilizing web–based platforms were taken by technical staff on the work floor interested in exploring the possibilities of using the potentials of the web. How innovation transpires within large organizations has been a serious topic on the agendas of management scholars for decades; here it is interesting to note that many of the public service broadcasting organizations portrayed were blessed with management personnel willing to allow programming and engineering staff to experiment, to "think outside the box" as termed in relation to the BBC News Online crew (see Chapter 1). At NPR Online, described in Chapter 3, it was in fact the technical–savvy engineers that initiated such exploration, with little involvement or interest from editorial staff.

Prediction is most difficult in dynamic environments where unplanned changes may emerge at unexpected moments. That is, in brief, the context in which PSB presently finds itself and is further exacerbated by: rapid technological changes, wavering political and declining financial support, concern about institutional mission, increasing media competition, and redefining the relation and meaning of audience and broadcaster.[2] These and other features vary from one context to another and from different historical legacies of PSB. If anything, the central message of *Histories of Public Service Broadcasters on the Web* is that conditions differ, much is in flux, and the rates of change vary.

In Chicago, for example, it is difficult to imagine the small–scale PSB initiative *Vocalo* surviving another season, largely because the radical innovations in redefining the meaning of local radio extend beyond that community's understanding of what radio listening means. Doomsday, however, is far from the experience of other PSBs presented in the book, and the British Broadcasting System may be the prize winner as all–around success story, with its award–winning web site and accolades for innovations in journalism. Most of the PSBs profiled in this book find a place between these extremes and are caught in the challenging struggle to create new programming forms and procedures in largely uncharted waters.

Further Research

The scholarship presented in *Histories of Public Service Broadcasters on the Web* provides a rich basis for understanding the diversity of approaches by PSBs to the possibilities in a web environment. As with any basis, however, further exploration is needed, if only because of the dynamic nature of both entities, the PSBs and the web. Several questions, general in character, might serve to initiate an ongoing research agenda for this area of scholarship:

- How are core principles of public service broadcasting reformulated as the environment shifts from a conventional media framework to one increasingly web–based?
- During that shift, what tensions emerge and what strategies for resolution are considered by the different actors involved (e.g., by regulatory bodies, management, programming staff, audience members)?
- How are traditional conceptualizations of broadcaster and audience transformed in the interactive multimedia environment made avail-

able on the web where notions such as citizen journalist and user-generated content are prominently propagated?

Four basic research design principles merit consideration in development of an ongoing agenda: comparative, longitudinal, multiple method, and diversity in disciplinary approaches. It is beyond the remit of this foreword to elaborate in detail about these principles, but perhaps it is sufficient to stress that understanding of a phenomenon as central to society as public service broadcasting deserves all the sophistication contemporary scholarship can muster. The cultural historical approach as reflected in the contributions to this volume has provided the basis from which a multi-pronged exploration of public service broadcasting might develop that considers the web not only as new environment for PSB, but as a resource for undertaking research. Such awareness is one of the rationales behind exploration of how scholars in the humanities can make use of myriad web potentials for collecting, archiving, analyzing and disseminating research. This approach is frequently identified through terms such as digital humanities, e-scholarship, and e-research (e.g., Schreibman, Siemens & Unswort, 2004; Borgman, 2007; Jankowski, 2009). A broad array of new methods and tools is being developed to facilitate humanities scholarship in a web environment (e.g., van Zundert, Antonijevic, Beaulieu, Dalen-Oskam, van Zeldenrust & Andrews, 2011). The legacy of *Histories of Public Service Broadcasters on the Web* may well become orientation for the next wave of studies addressing the interplay of PSB and the web, and doing so through harnessing the potentials for scholarship within that very networked environment being studied.

Notes

1. There are exceptions to this national myopic vision where systematic cross-national comparative study of public service broadcasting is undertaken, e.g., Lee & Yu (2006), Nakamura & Bourdeau de Fontenay (2006), and McKinsey & Co. (2004).
2. These and other characteristics of PSB in a digital environment are elaborated in a wide range of studies, including Armstrong & Weeds (2005), Barksdale & Hunt (2005), Collins, Finn, McFadyen & Hoskins (2001), and Hargreaves Heap (2005).

References

Armstrong, M. & Weeds, H. (2005, July 26). *Public service broadcasting in the digital world.* University of Essex, Colchester, UK. February 15, 2011 Retrieved from: http://129.3.20.41/eps/io/papers/0507/0507010.pdf

Barksdale, J. & Hunt, R. (2005). *Digital future initiative: Challenges and opportunities for public service media in the digital age: A report of the Digital Future Initiative Panel.*

Retrieved February 15, 2011, from http://www.newamerica.net/files/nafmigration/archive/Doc_File_2766_1.pdf

BBC (2004). *Building public value: Renewing the BBC for a digital world.* Retrieved February 15, 2011, from http://downloads.bbc.co.uk/aboutthebbc/policies/pdf/bpv.pdf

Borgman, C. (2007). *Scholarship in the digital age: Information, infrastructure and the Internet.* Cambridge, Mass.: MIT Press.

Collins, R., Finn, A., McFadyen, S. & Hoskins, C. (2001). Public service broadcasting beyond 2000: Is there a future for public service broadcasting? *Canadian Journal of Communication, 26*(1). Retrieved February 15, 2011, from http://www.cjc-online.ca/index.php/journal/article/viewArticle/1192/1128

Hargreaves Heap, S. P. (2005). Television in a digital age: what role for public service broadcasting? *Economic Policy, 20*(41), 112–157.

Hills, J. & Michalis, M. (2000). The internet: A challenge to public service broadcasting? *Gazette, 62*(6), 477–493.

Hooper, R. (2002, January 29). A sound view of public service broadcasting. Speech by Chair of the Radio Authority, Broadcast Conference: The future of public service broadcasting. Retrieved February 15, 2011, from http://www.ofcom.org.uk/static/archive/rau/newsroom/speeches/archive/A%20Sound%20View%20Of%20Public%20Service%20Broadcasting%20-%2029.1.htm

House of Commons (2004). House of Commons, Culture, Media and Sport Committee, A public BBC. Retrieved February 15, 2011, from http://www.publications.parliament.uk/pa/cm200405/cmselect/cmcumeds/82/82i.pdf

Jankowski, N. W. (Ed.) (2009). *e-Research: Transformation in scholarly practice.* New York: Routledge.

Lee, V. & Yu, M. (2006). Public service broadcasting in selected places. Research and Library Services Division, Hong Kong. Retrieved February 15, 2011, from http://www.legco.gov.hk/yr06–07/english/sec/library/0607rp01-e.pdf

McKinsey & Co. (2004). Review of public service broadcasting around the world. Study for Ofcom's review of public service broadcasting (PSB). Retrieved February 15, 2011, from http://www.mckinsey.com/practices/mediaentertainment/home/content/pdfs/PSB_Review.pdf

Nakamura, K. & Bourdeau de Fontenay, A. (2006). A critical analysis of public service broadcasting in a digital environment: Its changing role in Japan from the international comparative viewpoint. Retrieved February 15, 2011, from http://web.si.umich.edu/tprc/papers/2006/540/PSBJapan.pdf

Price, M. E. & Raboy, M. (Eds.) (2001). *Public service broadcasting in transition: A documentary reader.* Düsseldorf, Germany: European Institute for the Media.

Schreibman, S., Siemens, R. & Unsworth, J. (Eds.) (2004). *A companion to digital humanities.* Oxford: Blackwell. Retrieved February 15, 2011, from http://www.digitalhumanities.org/companion/

van Zundert, J., Antonijevic, S., Beaulieu, A., Dalen–Oskam, K., van Zeldenrust, D. & Andrews, T. (2012, in press). Cultures of formalization: Towards an encounter between humanities and computing. In D. M. Berry (Ed.), *Understanding digital humanities: The computational turn and new technology.* London: Palgrave Macmillan.

Introduction: Histories of Public Service Broadcasters on the Web

Thematic Concerns

Maureen Burns & Niels Brügger

An Invitation to Discussion

Histories of Public Service Broadcasters on the Web challenges members of its readership to rethink their existing ideas of public service broadcasting and of the World Wide Web. We offer this collection of histories as an open invitation to further discussion: for instance, we leave the definition of 'public service broadcasting' open. There have been many previous attempts to define 'public service broadcasting' (Broadcasting Research Unit, 1985; McKinsey & Company, 1999, p. 36), and, as Maureen Burns has argued elsewhere, such attempts at definition may limit the possibilities for rethinking public service broadcasters (PSBs) in an online environment (Burns, 2008, pp. 51–64). In the current volume we are more concerned with recognising difference and providing space for discussions than with affirming similarity. Similarly, the book lays no claim to representativeness nor comprehensiveness of nations, regions or regulatory frameworks. Instead we offer a number of probes into ways that organisations which understood themselves as PSBs actually developed web services.

Public Service Broadcasters and the Web

In the following chapters we analyse dynamics between the World Wide Web and PSBs in various parts of the world. Instead of regarding World Wide Web services as mere 'add–ons' to pre–existing television and radio services, *Histories of Public Service Broadcasters on the Web* details actual instances where the technologies, practices and ethics of the World Wide Web melded and/or collided with the technologies, practices and ethics of public service broadcasting. In many cases such collisions altered the very organizations in which they occurred: in all cases the intersections were richly productive.

Histories of Public Service Broadcasters on the Web explores the ways that new questions were raised when public service broadcasting confronted the World Wide Web in particular, or the global digital media environment more generally. PSBs had to reimagine what it meant to be a PSB in a global digital environment. They confronted such questions as: How does one operate as a national organisation in a global environment? How does one justify the public costs of public service broadcasting when there is a proliferation of information and entertainment media available on the web? and: How does a broadcaster enter a pre–existing internet environment comprised of a variety of actors and with almost no regulation?

Although there were elements of public service ethics, ideals and principles that were a perfect fit for World Wide Web services, there were also ways that expectations of the internet were challenged by the intersections of the World Wide Web and PSBs. Notions of audience participation and engagement—long a goal of the public service broadcasting tradition—were similarly valued in World Wide Web environments. But intersections with PSBs raised some questions: Is the web really best described as a many–to–many medium in most instances? How can one create a many–to–many relationship in a public service environment? How does one give a voice to the users, and not only the broadcaster?

In the following chapters these questions are examined from a historical perspective. Both public service broadcasting and the internet had separate, diverse and long histories before they intersected—and they continue to develop separately afterwards. But what interests us in this volume is when and how the existing—but separate—histories of public service broadcasting and the internet interacted, from their first meetings onwards.

Despite much of the hype, the move from a broadcast world to a World Wide Web world was not as simple as the shift from a one–to–many communication environment to a many–to–many communication environment. Nor was the shift linear (from broadcasting to the World Wide Web). The diverse histories detailed in the following attest to the fact that this is a complex and dynamic field.

The interactions differed depending on a number of factors including the national setting: there were different histories of PSBs, different histories of the internet and different histories of their interactions in each country.

In the responses to our call for chapters we identified five recurring themes that crossed national boundaries, and it was these themes that we have used to structure the separate histories in this book. This structure enables us to openly explore the richness and variability of media systems, financing models, and theoretical perspectives without being limited by typologies.

Five Recurrent Themes

Differences in funding models and media contexts are so fundamental to PSBs that it is not (or is no longer) useful to refer to a norm, or even norms, to which specific broadcasters conform or from which they diverge. This is another reason that we group the following histories thematically rather than by nation or funding model. In this, the first foray into a field we foreground the *variability* and *complexity* of media contexts, regulatory frameworks, and finance models. *Histories of Public Service Broadcasters on the Web* is neither a summary of policy positions nor a direct intervention in present policy debates. We leave it to future scholars to schematise the many regulatory and policy approaches that are mentioned in this collection, and instead we offer separate histories, organized into five themes. Each chapter will focus on a particular theme, on the understanding that there are often overlaps between themes—ethical matters might arise in many chapters, as might the intersections between commercial and public service goals, for example.

What's New about Online Journalism?

Part One: 'What's New about Online News?' relates actual stories of online news practices at PSBs. Because PSBs often have less commercial pressure than other news services, there is also more opportunity to innovate and take risks. Some of those risks are successful and some not, but from each we might learn more about what is new about online news, and which previous practices can be successfully adapted and applied in a new environment.

In their chapter "When Public Service Is the Name of the Game: The Evolution of British and Spanish Public Service Broadcasters in Online Journalism" An Nguyen and Alberto García compare the online migration of PSBs with that of commercial news media to argue that the former's public service remit itself—based on a relative freedom from commercial concerns—was a crucial contributor to their remarkable and distinctive online news successes. The authors explore the key moments, decisions and strategies of two of the biggest European PSBs—the British Broadcasting Corporation (BBC) and Radio Television Española (RTVE)—in the history of their online news operation. The BBC and RTVE have two very different funding models and had two notions of what a PSB should be, and they therefore experienced quite opposite trajectories in the online news environment. Both, however, enjoyed quick successes after their launch, thanks to their underlying public service principles.

Einar Thorsen's chapter, "The Second Digital Wave: BBC News Online, Embedded Video and the iPlayer," focuses on some of the defining moments in the BBC's use of online video. The BBC had experimented with online audio and video since the mid-nineties, and was therefore well equipped for its second digital wave in 2006. Some early audience–produced online video helped to create both a drive for user generated content, and a change in the acceptance of its accepted form and aesthetics. These experiments received little public attention—perhaps because they resulted from individual innovation rather than specific corporate strategy. This chapter recognizes these early experiments, and considers how the Corporation's continued push into online video may influence distribution of public service broadcasting in the future.

Nikki Usher, Patricia Riley and Vikki Porter's "NPR Online: Public Service Communication at the Center of National Public Radio" examines the evolution of public service broadcasting online in the U.S. through an analysis of National Public Radio. The authors describe NPR's internal history of change, and then explore the news organization's efforts at creating the digital strategy that made NPR a pioneering news organization in the U.S. The chapter uses the idea of a "digital change capacity," according to which organizations may be change–ready through the combination of leadership, strategic communication, systems thinking, and an accountable culture.

Commercial vs Public

Part Two: 'Commercial vs Public' details histories of the tensions that exist across various registers between commercial and public pressures at different PSBs. This part of the book reiterates some of the commercial/public intersections that have been tried at various PSBs around the world, some of which have been successful and some which have not.

Maureen Burns' chapter, "Protecting the Brand: A History of ABC Online News–as–Commodity" is a history of the ways in which ABC news online has, since its inception, been a part of commercial strategies at the ABC. In the early nineties in Australia the new medium of the World Wide Web was hailed for its potential commercial possibilities as much as for its potential to engage with audiences in new ways. The web was also seen as one way to address a perception that the ABC was too centralised in Sydney and Melbourne. The launch of an online commercial news service in Brisbane was not successful in its own right, but led to the highly successful ABC Online news, the content of which later came to be sold via the ABC's commercial division. Given this history, Maureen Burns asks: Is it time to reconsider whether the commercial/public service distinction remains a valuable way to think about PSBs?

Kenneth Murphy's "RTE Online: Public Objectives and Commercial Imperatives" offers an overview of the political, economic and institutional factors that shaped the development of RTE, i.e., in the period 1996–2007. It argues that underfunding, policy vacuums and commercialisation strategies all shaped the development of RTE's online content and services. These contexts have affected the design and content of RTE's website—privileging remediation and redistribution of broadcast content as a necessary strategic dynamic. It also argues that during this period, policy towards the public broadcaster placed pressure on RTE to support national solidarity in its output as a quid pro quo for its institutional survival. This narrowing of autonomy from the corporatist state affected RTE's ability to reflect pluralistic and critical aspects of the culture. This in turn was reflected in RTE's online output.

Hallvard Moe's chapter, "Between Public Service and Commercial Venture: The Norwegian Broadcasting Corporation on the Web 1994–2000," deals with tensions between public and commercial funding in the early development of web activities at the Norwegian Broadcasting Corporation (NRK). When the NRK moved into the online world from the mid–1990s, it argued for the public service value of internet activities. However, late in 2000, the NRK introduced commercial banner advertisements on its publicly funded website. Although this change at NRK was atypical of PSBs internationally, the practice was to continue for a decade. The chapter scrutinizes the process behind the decision to use banner advertising.

A Perfect Match?

Part Three is 'A Perfect Match? Ideals, Policies and Practices of Public Service Broadcasters on the Web.' Many of the ethics, principles and practices of public service broadcasting were ideal for the World Wide Web environment. Issues of access and the need to address mass and niche audiences had long exercised PSBs. But the advent of the web also meant that PSBs had to rethink their remits. There were also consequences for how one could think about the World Wide Web. In this section the authors examine histories of the intersections between ethics and practices of public service broadcasting and the practices of the World Wide Web.

Niels Brügger's chapter is titled "The Idea of Public Service in the Early History of DR Online." One of the most interesting issues of the history of PSBs online is the intersection between the self–understanding of the PSB and the many new possibilities offered by the web. Did the broadcaster interpret its role and mission on the web in light of its broadcast history, based on old media such as radio and television, or in light of the history of the web and the affordances made possible by this new medium? This is the question that this chapter sets out to explore through a close analysis of the case of the national Danish PSB Danmarks Radio (DR). The chapter's focus is on the foundational period from 1994 to 1996, when the website was conceptualized and established. It concludes that when DR met the web the new medium was by and large understood in line with what DR had been doing as a broadcaster for years, and less in light of the history of the internet.

In "' . . . [and] They Formed Themselves into a Single Unit': The Development of the Israeli Broadcasting Authority Website," interviews conducted with employees at the Israel Broadcasting Authority (IBA), and analyses of IBA's website over its history allow Amit Schejter and Merav Katz-Kimchi to describe how IBA's culture of "tinkering" led to an irresolute process in which IBA's fractured nature, technological inferiority and succumbing to government pressures retarded the creation of a unified website despite the good-willed intentions of the professional brass. The authors conclude that, although web implementation had important public service functions, its main role at the IBA was that of uniting the organization.

In "Southern European Public Service Broadcasters Expanding Online: A Policy Study of RAI and RTVE's Online Activities," Benedetta Brevini compares the online expansion of RAI and RTVE, and explores RAI's and RTVE's historical and political legacies. Brevini analyses RAI's and RTVE's regulatory and funding frameworks, and concludes that the intense politicization of broadcasting in both countries led to substantial differences between their responses to the internet world.

Local, National, International, Global?

Part Four: 'Local, National, International, Global?' analyses the histories of the ways that national remits of PSBs were and continue to be challenged by the global medium of the World Wide Web. In this section authors describe the ways that intersections between PSBs and the web altered perceptions of audience from the merely national.

Meghan Grosse and David W. Park are the authors of "Public Media and the Web in the U.S.: The Case of Vocalo." The Vocalo venture from Chicago Public Radio was proposed as a way to crowd-source local radio programming, using experimental methods of generating content, and diverging from familiar U.S. public broadcasting norms. The authors examine the difficulties that Vocalo experienced, and come to four conclusions. Firstly, that the creators of

Vocalo characterize the entry into new media as a return to originating impulses; secondly that the hopes invested in Vocalo are similar to hopes generated by other once–new media; thirdly that structural arrangements continue to matter to broadcasting, no matter the new technology; and finally that user–generated content may address what audience members wish to say, but may not address what audience members wish to hear.

In her chapter "Regional Radio and Online Media Production: An Australian Broadcasting Corporation Case Study" Anne Dunn uses the Local Radio network of the Australian Broadcasting Corporation (ABC) as a case study to describe and analyse how local PSB radio has introduced and is using production for the World Wide Web. Drawing on empirical research, the chapter argues that broadcasters' professional identity, production roles, and relationships with their audiences have all been profoundly affected by new ways of working. The chapter concludes that the challenges of online media also offer the potential for the PSB to create, engage with and serve new kinds of communities.

Brian O'Neill and Michael J. Murphy's chapter "Canadian Content, Public Broadcasting and the Internet: CBC's Online Strategy 1995–2000" notes that the Canadian Broadcasting Corporation, like many public broadcasters around the world, identified the importance and the advantage of being a pioneer on the web. The CBC's strategy between 1995 and 2000 attempted to leverage new media in the service of a cultural policy to protect and promote Canadian content. The policy, though later abandoned as a result of funding crises, gave the Canadian national broadcaster a head start, enhancing its image nationally and internationally as a public service media content provider.

Talking Back to Aunty

Part Five: 'Talking Back to Aunty: Interactivity and Public Service Broadcasting Sites' reminds the reader that interactivity has a history that is longer than that of the World Wide Web, and the section also details some of the innovative ways that PSBs around the world have incorporated their users as content producers.

In "Vox Populi, Vox Dei: ABC Online and the Risks of Dialogic Interaction" Fiona Martin argues that for the large part of a century public service broadcasting disseminated information and expertise, caution and encouragement. Broadcasters, their guests and interviewees re–presented society to itself, carefully gatekeeping their interaction with audiences. This chapter introduces their perspectives on the difficulties of translating that paternal relationship online; establishing 'a conversation' with more autonomous users and communities. Martin analyses the evolution of ABC Online's attempts to encourage user participation, creativity, discussion and critique—arguing that mutually negotiated models for interaction can be less risky approaches to online encounters than highly regulated models.

Anja Bechmann's chapter: "User Participation at the Danish Broadcasting Corporation 1998–2010: Changing Patterns" analyzes the ways in which the Danish Broadcasting Corporation historically sought to incorporate the web's potential for audience participation. The chapter shows that despite inspiration from web 2.0 initiatives and regulatory changes towards non–broadcast content the history of the web cannot be described simply as one of increasing user participation. At one point DR actually reduced its reliance on user created material due to 'quality' considerations. The chapter illustrates that the patterns of public service content are distributed across different web–based platforms and that dialogue flows between users instead of being only between broadcaster and user.

In "From Broadcast to Networked Journalism: The Case of Al–Jazeera English," Shawn Powers details how the youngest of the networks surveyed here, Al–Jazeera English (AJE), embraced the digital environment in part because of the difficulties it experienced in both gathering and disseminating its news products via traditional means. Launched as recently as 2006, AJE utilized cutting edge communication technologies and platforms in order to report in conflict situations, at times introducing online platforms that other mainstream news organizations would embrace years later. While certainly a non–traditional model for public service broadcasting, AJE's online history indicates some of the promising ways in which the World Wide Web can enhance and embolden an organization's public reach, significance and scope.

Acknowledgments

If it were not for the internet this edited volume may never have been published. Obviously, without the internet there would have been no object to study. In addition, the internet also enabled the two editors, previously strangers, to begin contact and to concoct the idea of editing a book together about the history of PSBs online. Niels Brügger was preparing an introduction to another book, and had found a relevant journal article by Maureen Burns, published in an Australian journal which was not available in Denmark. He emailed to ask for a copy of the article, and after a couple of emails back and forth Maureen proposed: "I wonder if we could put together a book on PSBs going online around the world? Would that be cool, or what?" And the rest is history—and this history would probably never have been written in a pre–internet era. We can therefore thank the internet that the idea of this book ever emerged.

We would also like to thank our universities for having accepted that email alone would not be enough, and that face-to-face meetings were also needed: the Department of Information and Media Studies and the Centre for Internet Research at Aarhus University housed Maureen while she was in Aarhus in April 2010, and she remains very grateful for the hospitality and inspiration of that stay. The Centre for Critical and Cultural Studies and the School of English, Media Studies and Art History at the University of Queensland housed Niels while he was in Brisbane in May 2011.

In addition, all the authors deserve to be thanked for having entered this new and unknown territory with us and for having been so patient with the editors' endless stream of emails.

The quality of the chapters is, of course, the achievement of the authors, but on the way to the final version each chapter has been blind reviewed by a number of internationally acclaimed scholars whom we would also like to thank: Marko Ala–Fossi, James Bennett, Andrew Crisell, Niels Ole Finnemann, Ben Goldsmith, Gay Hawkins, Peter Humphreys, Liz Jacka, Jason Jacobs, Per Jauert, Greg Lowe, Graham Murdock, Tom O'Regan, Patrick Parsons, Christina Spurgeon, Jeanette Steemers, Trine Syvertsen, Henrik Søndergaard, Barbara Thomass, and Esben Ytreberg.

We also owe many thanks to Senior Acquisitions Editor Mary Savigar, and Design & Production Supervisor Sophie Appel at Peter Lang Publishing, New York for having handled the manuscript with care, interest, and accuracy.

We are very grateful to the Department of Information and Media Studies, Aarhus University for its financial support of the typesetting, and to Anders Foss for his meticulous work with the reference system of the manuscript.

In particular Maureen would like to acknowledge her ongoing debts to Liz Jacka, Gay Hawkins, and Graeme Turner for their mentorship and intellectual generosity over many years. And last, but not least, we would like to thank Nicholas W. Jankowski, who generously agreed to write the foreword.

References

Broadcasting Research Unit. (1985). *The Public Service Idea in British Broadcasting.* London: BRU.

Burns, M. (2008). *ABC Online: Becoming the ABC.* Saarbrucken, Germany: VDM Verlag.

McKinsey & Company. (1999). *Public Service Broadcasting around the World.* London: McKinsey & Company.

PART ONE

What's New about Online News?

1 *When Public Service Is the Name of the Game*

The Evolution of British and Spanish Public Service Broadcasters in Online Journalism

An Nguyen & Alberto García

Introduction

Web-based news has been around for more than two decades, purported to serve democracy in a better, more efficient and effective way thanks to a rich range of socio-technical advantages. But up until a few years ago, it was still not much more than what was seen in other media: many of its much-touted exclusive features—such as immediacy, multimedia, interactive participation—remained scarce or underdeveloped on even the biggest newspapers and broadcasters' news sites (Nguyen, 2008, 2010). As an American news executive observed when discussing how to harness broadband technologies in 2006:

> Rather than getting starry-eyed about fat-pipe applications, I'd rather see us focus on doing a better job of the basics. The amount of local breaking news on many newspaper sites is abysmal. Their weather maps lack depth and dynamism. Their sports are boring. And their functionality—from search to calendar to recruitment databases—is barely passable. We should be ashamed of how poor our sites compare to Yahoo! and Monster in basic areas. (As cited in Finberg, 2006)

This failure to exploit online news has been traced to "the fear of marginalization" (Hermida & Thurman, 2008, p. 347) or the long-established fear-driven innovation culture of the news media. In the 1990s, as the web penetrated daily life with an impact measured by Negroponte at "10.5 on the Richter scale of social change" (as cited in Dizard, 2000, p. 5), it was quick to become a nerve-wracking medium to journalists and news executives. Threatened by the possibility of being driven out of the market by the "all too powerful" web, they hastily established online presences to ring-fence markets and ensure they had a future in the internet era. But because they were established as low-cost place holders to protect traditional market positions, most early news sites were allocated inadequate resources to harness the potential of the medium, thus offering little more than content repurposed from traditional products. In addition, being too obsessed by the potential disruptive power of the new medium and left with little time to pause and think, the traditional news media adopted online strategies that were "checkered with visionary action, misguided concepts, and curt dismissal" (Stovall, 2004, p. 23). As scant attention was paid to the web's possibilities, online news was shoe-horned into the same old static, one-way, text-and-picture model that is largely at odds with its uniqueness.

Here and there in this not so brilliant picture, however, were a number of illuminating points, namely the online news services of public service broadcasters (PSBs). Although PSBs constitute a tiny group of news providers, many of them have long gone far beyond the basics online, with some—such as the BBC in the UK, DR in Denmark or the ABC in Australia—being listed among the most innovative online news services in their national and/or international contexts. BBC News Online, for instance, has been ranked among the world's top news sites and been an oft-mentioned model in research and text books on online journalism around the world. The prominence of PSBs in the online world is in stark contrast to the fact that most of them have had to develop their new media ventures, in Fiona Martin's words, "on the smell of an oily rag" due to the lack of extra funding (as cited in Jacka, 2006, p. 348).

This invites an intriguing question: How could PSBs be so superior to their commercial rivals in the online news world? This chapter sets out to argue that the public-service remit itself, based on a relative freedom from commercial concerns, has been a positive contributor to the success of PSBs in the online news world. In order to do so, we explore the key moments, decisions and strategies of two of the biggest European PSBs—the British Broadcasting Corporation (BBC) and Radio Television Española (RTVE)—in the history of their online news operation. These PSBs are based on two very different funding and regulation models, with two notions of what a PSB should be, and therefore experienced quite opposite trajectories in the online news environment. Both, however, enjoyed quick successes after their launch, due to their underlying public service principles. The implications for the future of online news will be briefly discussed in the context of recent commercial media's attacks on what they call the unfair competitive advantage of PSBs in the online world.

Public Service in the Evolution of BBC News Online

"And now for the news—at last" is the headline with which the *Times* greeted the launch of BBC News Online on November 4, 1997. "Finally, it's the BBC's turn," wrote the *Times*. "Yesterday Auntie launched its own news web site, months—if not years—after its commercial rivals in Britain and abroad." At a time when the number of traditional news organisations with a web presence went steeply up from virtually zero in 1993 to more than 12,000 in 1998, such a late arrival of the BBC in online territory was quite difficult for many to understand. The £3–million site itself seemed to have been an artefact designed in a hurry, being given 16 weeks that represented, in the words of its first editor, a sudden shift from a "stop–stop–stop" to a "go–go–go" mood (Smartt, 2007). As Brandon Butterworth, the man who registered the bbc.co.uk domain name in 1991 and looked after the site's technical infrastruture, recalled: "With an October deadline, there was no point continuing with meetings. A committee wasn't going to make it. A ninja squad was needed. I got a small bucket of cash and got told to do whatever was needed."

These facts provoke questions: Why did a leading news organisation that has historically functioned to inform democracy and citizenship and has acted as a technological pioneer migrate to the web so late and in such a rush? Was it a failure of a "dear old Auntie, always regarded as a little dotty" (Withworth, 1997), in building a strategic, provident vision in the early days of the web?

A strategic delay

Indeed, it was not a late hasty rush into an unknown territory at all. Ten years after the launch, Mike Smartt (2007) commented that the no–hurry embracement of online news by the BBC was "probably a good thing when there are big sums of public money at stake." Our research suggests that it was a strategic delay, representing a correct online approach that distinguished the BBC as a PSB from the commercial media from the outset. At the very least, its freedom from commercial pressures helped the corporation not to fall into the trap of the "This will kill that" climate that swept commercial news media into the massive but uncertain and half–hearted online migration of the 1990s. Instead, it calmly but rigorously experimented with the various possibilities associated with the new medium: by the time of the above launch, there had been on bbc.co.uk a 1995 budget news site, a 1996 budget news site, a 1997 election and general politics site, and, most importantly, a hugely successful tribute site on the tragic death of Princess Diana in autumn 1997 that finally "convinced everyone that the internet would be big and that the BBC would be there—properly" (Butterworth, 2007). Everything was done cautiously until the last minute, with "the start being more like a swimmer carefully inching into icy waters than an ocean liner proudly splashing in a spray of champagne" (BBC News Online, 2007). These years allowed the BBC to have more time to assess different options for harnessing the potential of online news and to arrive at many proper decisions that were to have a lasting impact on BBC News Online and the standards it set for news sites around the world.

The most fundamental of these came from the top: the decision not to commercialise BBC news on the web. The medium entered daily life when the BBC was under mounting pressures to exploit new media for commercial purposes (Thorsen, 2010). The pre–launch years of BBC News Online saw numerous debates on whether and how to commercialise the BBC, including its news, online. In those years, according to Smartt (2007), "MSNBC might have been MSBBC" if a potential deal with Microsoft had not been turned down after the software giant expressed its wish to have a voice in editorial matters. According to Thorsen (2010), this led news to become part of another commercial operation called beeb.com, a joint venture between the BBC and a computer company. "At the eleventh hour" in December 1996, however, the then–Director General of the BBC, John Birt, "withdrew news and sport from the equation, deciding instead to make them public service offerings" (Connor, 2007). Whether it was "a madcap moment . . . that saw Birt act on impulse" (Connor, 2007), it was to make history. As Bob Eggington, BBC News Online's project director, acknowledged: "He's not my cup of tea, but had he not brought his determination and authority to the internet, it just wouldn't happen" (as cited in Connor, 2007).

Birt's bold move was probably rooted, at least in part, in his fear that a digital divide was widening in an environment where people increasingly had to pay for their media. This is echoed in the various speeches that he made to justify the public service of BBC Online. "We may see," he warned in a New Stateman lecture, "the emergence of an information–rich and an information–poor—an underprivileged knowledge underclass, denied access to the quality of information, insight and entertainment enjoyed by the richer members of the community" (BBC News Online, 1999). This, for Birt, could only be addressed if a universally accessible public service exists with proper funding to cater for everyone's information needs. This was formalised in the BBC's submission to the license fee review panel in 1999, when its online operation continued to be under external pressures to go commercial (Thorsen,

Allan & Carter, 2010). Of the six stated core objectives, the provision of news and information came first, with two of the other five concerning fostering citizenship via building coummunities surrounding BBC content.

Along with these developments was a strong determination to proactively explore and exploit the potential of online news. Whereas its commercial rivals positioned the internet as an intruder into the news landscape, the BBC saw a horizon of new opportunities, embracing it as a "third broadcast medium alongside radio and TV" (Smartt as cited in Thompson, 1997). As Edward Briffa, then the Controller of BBC Online and Interactive, declared:

> The BBC reinvented itself once, when television was invented. And now we feel we have got to do it again. It's not that radio and television are going to diminish, but it is that people's time is going to be taken up, in increasing amounts, with this third opportunity. (As cited in Thorsen et al., 2010)

Thus, in stark contrast to the defensive ring–fencing strategies on commercial news sites, BBC News Online set forth as an aggressive opportunity seeker, with an overt ambition to expand its influence online. "We have one aim: to be better, broader and richer than everyone else," said Tony Hall, the chief executive of BBC News in *Inside Multimedia* (1997).

The innovative news site and its meteoric rise

These developments at the top generated a generous space for the much needed enthusiasm and freedom to think outside the box among the early BBC News Online team. With more time than their commercial colleagues to prepare for an online migration, the team found news to be "one of those things ideally suited to the new medium" (Eggington as cited in Venes, 1999), wholeheartedly recognising and endorsing its unique capacity for multimedia, immediacy and depth. Not less importantly, they understood that this unique capacity could only materialise when fresh and, if necessary, expensive approaches were taken. Thus, instead of following the cheap and safe route of repurposing news content from traditional outlets like most in the commercial world, the BBC was committed to pouring resources into developing an innovative news site. While taking advantage of the BBC's vast amount of content and its natural edge in breaking news, for instance, it refused "to regurgitate anything that wasn't highly suitable for the medium" (Eggington as cited in Venes, 1999). In areas that are not its traditional strengths such as text news, it did not hesitate to recruit journalists from outside. Or at the time others were asking journalists "to write code as well as stories," the BBC found it to be a "madness" and "a single wayward backlash," developing a content management system that made journalists using HTML "a sackable offence" (Smartt, 2007).

Open to new possibilities, BBC News Online was able to go beyond traditional news qualities, finding that the web was not just about multimedia, depth and immediacy but also about interactivity and its associated capacity for public participation in news and current affairs. The "we publish, you accept" mindset that did not start to leave the mind of those running commercial online news until the mid–2000s (Nguyen, 2008) was questioned by BBC News Online right from its early experiments (Butterworth, 2007). For instance, the sheer volume of public responses to its trial site on Diana's death in 1997, according to Eggington, "was a huge revelation to me that people wanted to participate and what they wanted to read was what they, not the BBC, had written" (as cited in Thorsen, 2010, p. 217). Thus, one of the only five sections of the launch site was the opportunity for readers to make their voice heard, a forerunner to its Have Your Say later (BBC News Online, 2007). [The other four were UK & World News, Business, Science & Technology, and Sports.] In this context, it is perhaps not surprising that BBC was the first news organisation in the world to establish a separate editorial department, called the UGC Hub, to handle user–generated content, in 2005.

With all this, BBC News Online did not wait long to become "better, broader and richer than everyone else" as Hall declared above. Immediately after the launch, the news site was praised for its innovativeness by supporters and critics alike. Drawing one million hits on the first day, BBC News Online quickly established itself as a leading news site in the UK, with its page views reaching 5.3 million in January 1998 and 24 million one year later (Reevel, 1999). It won a significant number of prestigious awards in its first year and prompted a scramble to offer more substantive online news services among major national and international outlets—from portals such as AOL, Yahoo!, Excite and MSN to traditional providers like CNN, ABC, ITN and Sky (Venes, 1998). BBC News Online, and the whole bbc.co.uk that was launched a month after it (December 1997), enjoyed such a quick success that as early as January 1998, John Birt was confident enough to declare: "If there is a better web site than the BBC's on the internet, I have yet to find it. It is informative, imaginative and beautifully designed—and already Europe's largest" (BBC News Online, 1998). Reflecting on this success in 1999, Eggington pointed to the fundamental element of the creative liberty underlining its public funding model:

> We're funded largely out of the license fee, which makes a tremendous difference as you don't have to worry about your revenues. The BBC brand is also a huge advantage, and we don't have to use any of our real estate to give up to ads onscreen. (As cited in Venes, 1999)

In reality, this freedom from commercial concerns has been acknolwedged as a key contributor to the innovative online news services of not only the BBC but also other PSBs around the world. In Australia, for example, the ABC's Managing Director recently echoed Eggington when telling an audience of journalism educators that "it's easier to innovate at the ABC compared to Fairfax. We don't have to ask 'will we, and when will we, make money?'" (Scott, 2010).

It should be noted, however, such freedom was necessary but insufficient for BBC News (or ABC News and the like) to succeed online. In the case of the BBC News Online, there was a strong commitment to public service, as we have seen. And not less importantly, there is a regulatory system that, although increasingly hostile to the BBC, is still favourable to the exercise of such commitment. This point will become clearer by comparison in the next section, where we examine how the BBC's Spanish counterpart, RTVE, has struggled, survived and thrived in the online news world as its regulatory system went through a recent fundamental shift from being unsupportive to supportive of PSBs.

Public Service and the Unusually Late Emergence of RTVE News on the Web

At the time of writing, the website of Radio Televisión Española (RTVE) is a leader on the Spanish web. It was one of the six most visited sites in Spain by the end of 2009, with unique users amounting to 7.7 million in April 2010. As of June 2010, according to OJD (the "Spanish Nielsen"), it attracted a total of 213,834,484 pageviews, a number far ahead those of its major competitors, antena3.com (167,836,262) and telecinco.es (126,673,974). By comparison, in June 2008, telecinco.es collected 83,200,388 pageviews per month, antena3.com 23,809,873, and rtve.es only 17,188,252. While specific news traffic figures are not available for this chapter, critics have attributed much of the site's position to its innovative offerings in news and current affairs. As García and García (2010) commented:

> Rtve.es offers the best online selection of news and information: the enormous volume of its digital archives, the magnitude of its human resources, the possibility of seeing live news broadcasts 24 hours a day, as well as the large number of exclusive news stories drawn from the web, make it the standard bearer for the Spanish television network's transition to online services. (p. 260)

Looking it at its shape and success today, however, few would imagine that only a few years ago, it was no more than an also–ran news site in Spain. Unlike most major news organisations around the world, RTVE was unusually late in embracing online news opportunities. Up until 2006, the online news strategy at RTVE had been to have no strategy at all (Llorens, 2008), with the site offering no more than a shortened four–minute version of its television bulletin and a collection of items from its teletext service (Salaverría, 2007, p. 356). All this came to an end in May 2008, when the site went through a drastic revamp and then quickly gained the status of a leading online news site in Spain. This was thanks to a number of political and structural changes that saw a perception of RTVE's nature as a PSB being renewed and prevailing. Our interest here is, again, how this renewed public–service ethos came about and contributed to the quick evolution of rtve.es from a mere corporate site to a leading news site in Spain.

From political dependence and financial difficulties to a strong public service ethos

RTVE declined rapidly in the first fifteen years of the web. With an administration instability associated with constant changes of directors and a primary reliance on advertising, RTVE faced an era of increasing media competition with the worsening of two already perennial problems: an ideological dependence on whichever political party was in power; and a progressive debt that reached an alarming 7.5 billion in 2006 (Arriaza, 2008). Added to this was an indifference to online opportunities among RTVE's top managers, who seemed to be more interested in news as a political weapon than a public service (Llorens, 2008). In their eyes, online news was an investment for a too distant future, offering neither short term profit nor immediate political influence. As Bustamante (2002) wrote, "RTVE is so seized with its political, administrative and financial crisis in the analogical world that it is hardly capable to face, in a planned and coherent way, the digital challenge."

Changes, however, started to take place after Zapatero's Socialist government was elected in 2004. As the Amsterdam Protocol on the System of Public Broadcasting had created a stronger perception of public service and led to a fundamental transformation of the television landscape in every European state (Azurmendi, 2007), RTVE's mounting problems forced the new government to commit to a series of profound reforms. Inspired by a Green Paper ("Review of the BBC's Royal charter: a strong BBC, independent of Government") and a White Paper ("A public service for all: the BBC in the digital age") by the British government, it appointed a "Committee of Sages" to re–think the structure, mission and the public entity of RTVE. The resulting 2005 report provided the justification for undertaking dramatic changes so that the network could be more competitive, more efficient and of better service to the public. With news at the centre of its recommendations, the report specified seven public service principles for RTVE: (a) communicative functions for citizens, not consumers; (b) social, not economic, profitability; (c) independence from government; (d) a new mixed funding mechanism (so that RTVE is no longer primarily relied on advertising revenues as it had done throughout its history); (e) democracy, peace and plurality; (f) quality and innovation; and (g) contribution to the information society as a leader on the internet.

This served as a launching pad for the revamp of RTVE Online in 2008 and its quick advancement in the Spanish online news realm. The new public–service ethos paved the way for a constant interest in and an obligation to being innovative (Fernández, 2010). On the first anniversary of the revamped site, RTVE's president claimed that "rtve.es wants to be the avant–garde of innovation in interactive media" (as cited in Menéndez & Plaza, 2009). Another, probably more important, outcome of the new remit was the ability to stay away from commercial pressures, with the revamped site being less obsessed with revenues and more concerned with serving the public. Rosalía Lloret, the Director of Interactive Media for RTVE until April 2010, explained the fundamental change at the site as follows: "We used to have a corporate web, directed outward from the Corporation to the user; now we are doing things the other way round: we are focusing on the user" (Varela, 2008). This allows rtve.es to be able to commit fully to building a universally accessible news outlet of public benefits rather than of commercial profits. As Lloret explained:

> All of our (online news) initiatives are guided by the intention of offering the maximum accessibility . . . for every Spanish citizen, the real shareholders of RTVE, so that they have a chance to access every piece of our content—even if they are late at home or if they are abroad—and to comment on that content and participate in the debate over it. (As cited in Nielsen Online España, 2009)

The strategic vision and leadership of Luis Fernández between November 2006 and November 2009 was fundamental to the process of materialising that citizenship–oriented philosophy. A man who, in the words of Eduardo Matilla at Multimedia Corp, "wrestled a civil and political consensus about the need for a certain ideological neutrality" (as cited in Hopewell & Pablos, 2009), Fernández shared many values held by John Birt and others at the BBC, particularly the belief that "it is a public and essential service to offer an open, free and on–demand access" (as cited in RTVE, 2009). In order to achieve it in the online world, he made a strong commitment to expending resources on developing its online news operation. While cutting RTVE's staff by a third early in his presidency, for instance, Fernández increased the online team from just 12 people in 2005 to a team of 35 at the time of its relaunch, 27 of whom were journalists (Marcos, 2009). And since news was at the centre of his public service vision, the number of people serving its online news site almost doubled from 27 to 50 within one year of the relaunch.

The resulting innovative news site

As a result of all this, rtve.es offers a rich range of expensive news services, including many that will probably not make money but are important for public connection to the news. The news site diferentiates itself from its commercial rivals in three main ways:

First, with millions of hours of programming in storage, rtve.es is the first Spanish news site that builds an archive to offer an increasingly abundant amount of audio–visual local and international news; it is an added value for the viewer and allows him/her to catch up missed programmes or retrieve old news whenever he/she wants. As of 2009, according to Marcos (2009), news services on rtve.es offered "more images than the rest of Spanish television networks" and took advantage of having a local/regional station in almost every major city to both produce original content and to repurpose network content.

Second, to put the internet's immediacy to use, rtve.es embeds a live stream of its 24–hour channel in the sidebar of the News homepage. In addition, updated textual and audio–visual blogs are run by a solid network of news correspondents around Spain.

Third, rtve.es is now the most advanced site in Spain in terms of multimedia storytelling and is showing the most serious commitment to presenting the news in a web–specific manner. With "one foot in television and the other in radio" (Marcos, 2009), they have experimented with enriching some of their news with podcasts from their radio channels and, as mentioned above, utilised their news archive to make the news more thorough and complete.

Thus, although much more—such as the opportunities for public participation—remains to be done on rtve.es, its two years of innovation have led it, as mentioned, from being an also–ran to being recognised as the best news site in Spain.

Public Service under Attack: Implications for the Future of Online News

Through the two different cases of the BBC and RTVE, this chapter has demonstrated that a relative freedom from commercial interests and an obligation to serving the public have been a, if not *the*, fundamental driver of PSBs' generally more innovative and substantive adoption of online news technologies. Both, despite being late in their respective online news landscapes for peculiar reasons, established their leading positions within a short time thanks to their primary commitment, from the top to the grassroots level, to citizenship and innovation, not economic profits.

Ironically, the public service remit and the associated creative liberty that constitute these successes have been a reason for the commercial media to threaten the rationale for the existence of strongly funded PSBs in the new media landscape. While admitting the innovativeness of online news services by PSBs, the commercial media have been dismissing them as little more than an inevitable outcome of an unfair competitive advantage that needs to be removed. In 1998, in response to the quick rise to prominence of BBC News Online, Garron Baines, the New Media Director of ITN (the BBC's key domestic rival), said:

> The BBC has £24 million of public money supported by the government to develop a site. I have the support of shareholders and directors of ITN but that support is contingent on me making a profit for them on cross promotion. (As cited in Venes, 1999)

Meanwhile, Hugo Drayton, the Marketing Manager of the *Electronic Telegraph*, put it more bluntly:

> I'm pretty pissed off with them, to be honest. If you chuck millions of pounds of tax payers' money at something, of course, it will work. There is a distinct disadvantage to us, because with so much tax money and huge amounts of staffing, they can have a far superior service by having access to the best journalists in the country—they are able to deluge on volume. (As cited in Venes, 1998)

Today, as the commercial media continue to face tremendous financial problems and are yet to find a good way to make money from their online operations, similar attacks on PSBs are being intensified. In Spain, the recent reform and quick rise to prominence of RTVE, both online and offline, reheated a decade–long campaign by its commercial rivals, led by the Association of Spanish Private Television (UTECA), to call for a stop to what they call an unfair system of mixed funding (i.e., a combination of public funds and advertising revenues). The campaign came to fruition in May 2009, when the government, without consulting Fernandez, announced that RTVE would remove all advertising from its broadcasting programs and website from 2010 to become fully publicly funded. The decision was believed to lead Fernandez, who led RTVE to achieve full independence from political meddling, to resign and left the PSB at risk of falling back into the pre–reform control of the government (Hopewell & Pablos, 2009). Meanwhile, in the UK, News Corporation and others have campaigned for a significant reduction in the license fee so that the BBC does not become "too big." The "chilling" prospect, of the BBC becoming too big, said James Murdoch in 2009, would allow a distortion of the online news market and harm to the independence and diversity of journalism. According to Murdoch, a dominant BBC would inhibit commercial news providers from investing in and charging for online news (BBC News Online, 2009). It remains to be seen where this campaign will lead us but, as of writing, the new Murdoch–backed Conservative government, in its austerity plan, has frozen the TV license fee while diverting part of BBC's budget to operations that used to be beyond its financial responsibility (most notably the World Service that was formerly funded by the government). This "austerity measure" was announced just several months after the BBC had dropped a number of its services, including some online non–news operations, to save costs.

Given what has been discussed in this chapter, these recent developments might not provide good news for the future of online news. It is clear that PSBs have set high professional standards and forced their commercial rivals to innovate and to strive for excellence in online journalism. Without a continued strong presence of PSBs in the online world, there will be little to ensure that, as technologies continue to evolve fast in the years ahead, the public will be offered online news services that are pertinent to the internet's expanding socio–technical potential.

Acknowledgments

The authors are grateful to the Spanish Ministry of Science and Innovation for its financial support through the research project "Evolución de los cibermedios españoles en el marco de la convergencia. Multiplataforma e integración periodística" (CS02009–13713-C05–03).

References

Allan, S., & Thorsen, E. (2010). Journalism, Public Service and BBC News Online. In G. Meikle & G. Redden (Eds.), *News Online: Transformation and Continuity.* Basingstoke, UK: Palgrave Macmillan.

Arriaza, K. (2008). Origen y culminación de la reestructuración del ente público RTVE en la nueva corporación RTVE [Electronic version]. *Enlaces: revista del CES Felipe II*, 8. Retrieved March 15, 2010, from http://tinyurl.com/365xk3g

Azurmendi, A. (2007). *La reforma de la televisión pública española.* Valencia, Spain: Tirant Lo Blanch.

BBC News Online (1998). BBC digital plans will guard against "two–class" society. Retrieved May 30, 2010, from http://tinyurl.com/2vxknoh

BBC News Online (1999). Birt warns of digital threat. Retrieved May 30, 2010, from http://tinyurl.com/3amfu5x

BBC News Online (2007). Ten years of the BBC News website. Retrieved May 30, 2010, from http://tinyurl.com/3c6avb

BBC News Online (2010). Murdoch attack on "dominant" BBC. Retrieved May 30, 2010, from http://tinyurl.com/m8z3h7

Bustamante, E. (2002). Hacia un nuevo sistema televisivo: errores y frenos en el camino digital [Electronic version]. *Telos*, 53. Retrieved April 5, 2010, from http://tinyurl.com/36swqml

Bustamante, E. (2005). Radiotelevisión Española: oportunidad para un auténtico servicio público. *Chasqui*, *92*, 30–37.

Butterworth, B. (2007). Brandon's history of the BBC on the Internet. Retrieved April 15, 2010, from http://tinyurl.com/23yatx

Connor, A. (2007). Revolution, not evolution. Retrieved March 28, 2010, from http://tinyurl.com/33qy7kp

Dizard, W. (2000). *Old Media, New Media: Mass Communications in the Information Age.* New York: Longman.

El País (1997, October 1). "La competencia desleal de TVE no tiene límites," según Tele5 [Electronic version]. *El País.* Retrieved July 3, 2010, from http://tinyurl.com/32nrhw2

Fernández, L. (2008, March 27). TVE ofrecerá gratis en internet programas y fondos de su archivo histórico audiovisual [Electronic version]. *El País.* Retrieved June 23, 2010, from http://tinyurl.com/yvvbto

Fernández, R. (2010, May 31). Ricardo Villa: "Internet no tiene aún un lenguaje audiovisual propio" [Electronic version]. *Público*.es. Retrieved June 23, 2010, from http://tinyurl.com/2uj9kqx

Finberg, H. (2006). Broadband power drives news use. Retrieved September 11, 2006, from http://tinyurl.com/344zf54

García Avilés, J. A., & García, A. (2010). Informativos 2.0., una transición inacabada. Las webs de noticias de las televisiones generalistas. In B. León (Coord.), *Informativos para la televisión del espectáculo* (pp. 252–262). Sevilla/Zamora, Spain: Comunicación Social.

Hermida, A., & Thurman, N. (2008). A clash of cultures. The integration of user–generated content within professional journalistic frameworks at British newspapers websites. *Journalism Practice*, *2*(3), 343–356.

Hopewell, J., & Pablos, E. (2009, November 23). Spanish TV transition. *Variety*, p. 14.

Jacka, E. (2006). The future of public broadcasting. In S. Cunningham & G. Turner (Eds.), *The Media and Communications in Australia* (pp. 344–356). Sydney: Allen & Unwin.

Llorens, C. (2008). Las políticas de Internet de RTVE y BBC: la redefinición e implementación del servicio público en los nuevos medios [Electronic version]. *Eptic. Revista de Economía Política de las Tecnologías de la Información y Comunicación*, *10*(2). Retrieved May 21, 2010, from http://tinyurl.com/34wjug2

Manfredi, J. L. (2006). El reto digital de las televisions públicas en Europa. Las estrategias de la BBC y de RTVE [Electronic version]. *Telos*, 68. Retrieved April 9, 2010, from http://tinyurl.com/3yftx20

Marcos, C. (2009). RTVE.es News Content Director. Personal Interview, 28 May.

Menéndez, M., & Plaza, A. M. (2009, May 29). Luis Fernández: "RTVE quiere estar a la vanguardia de la innovación de los medios interactivos." *RTVE.es.* Retrieved June 30, 2010, from http://tinyurl.com/34ce9q6

Nguyen, A. (2008). Facing the "fabulous monster": The traditional media's fear-driven innovation culture in the development of online news. *Journalism Studies*, *9*(1), 91–104.

Nguyen, A. (2010). Harnessing the potential of online news: Suggestions from a study on the relationship between online news advantages and its post-adoption consequences. *Journalism: Theory, Practice & Criticism*, *11*(2), 223–241.

Nielsen Online España (2009, February). Entrevista con RTVE, a Rosalía Lloret. *Newsletter Febrero '09*. Retrieved May 15, 2010, from http://tinyurl.com/cntwl3

Reevel, P. (1999, March 4). What's on the PC tonight then? Will the race to interactive TV make broadcasters' websites obsolete? *New Media Age*, p. 16.

Salaverría, R. (2007). Ciberperiodismo: Diez años de prensa digital en España. In J.J. Fernández Sanz (coord.), *Prensa especializada actual: doce calas* (pp. 355–383). Madrid: McGraw–Hill/Interamericana de España, S.A.U.

Scott, M. (2010). Public broadcasting in a time of innovation. Opening speech at Journalism Education Association of Australia's Annual Conference. Universtity of Technology Sydney, 24–26 November.

Smartt, M. (2007). The days before launch. Retrieved March 28, 2010, from http://tinyurl.com/2aj2fy4.

Stovall, J. (2004). *Web Journalism: Practice and Promise of a New Medium*. Boston: Pearson.

Thompson, R. (1997, November 21). Not the Nine O'Clock News as we know it. *PR Week*. Retrieved May 15, 2010, from LexisNexis.

Thorsen, E. (2010). BBC News Online: A brief history of past and present. In N. Brügger (Ed.), *Web History* (pp. 213–232). New York: Peter Lang.

Thorsen, E., Allan, S., & Carter, C. (2010). Citizenship and public service: The case of BBC News Online. In G. Monaghan & S. Tunney (Eds.), *Web Journalism: A New Form of Citizenship?* Eastbourne, UK: Sussex Academic Press.

Varela, J. (2008, May 13). Rosalía Lloret: "RTVE.es tundra publicidad como cualquier web commercial." *Soitu.es*. Retrieved June 23, 2010, from http://tinyurl.com/3qlrn4

Venes, R. (1998, December 10). This is the web. *New Media Age*. Retrieved May 15, 2010, from LexisNexis.

Venes, R. (1999, May 27). And finally . . . here is the news. *New Media Age*. Retrieved May 15, 2010, from LexisNexis.

Whitworth, D. (1997, November 7). Auntie's new babies. *The Times*. Retrieved May 30, 2010, from LexisNexis.

2 *The Second Digital Wave*

BBC News Online, Embedded Video and the iPlayer

Einar Thorsen

"Yes, we have one of the best websites in the world but it's rooted in the first digital wave," proclaimed the BBC Director General, Mark Thompson, during his Royal Television Society Fleming Memorial Lecture in 2006. Traditional media had coped quite well, in his view, with the challenges posed by this first wave by launching new (digital) linear channels, text-based websites, and some experimentation with mobile devices. He also maintained that the BBC had played a significant part in the success of this first wave, through pioneering high quality on the web, and playing a leading role in digital broadcast services and infrastructure.

"Anyone who thinks that that's the size of it—and there's plenty of them across British broadcasting—has got a big shock coming," Thompson warned. Rapid developments in technology and audience adaptation were according to him heralding "a distinct second digital wave" with dramatic consequences.

I believe that this second digital wave will turn out to be far more disruptive than the first, that it will be fundamentally disruptive, and that the foundations on which much of traditional media is built may be swept away entirely. (Thompson, 2006)

In order to prepare the BBC's websites for "the second digital wave," Thompson declared that the Corporation needed "to re-invent it, fill it with dynamic audio-visual content, personalise it, open it up to user-generated content" (Thompson, 2006). Moreover, the relationship with the audiences also needed renewing—"they won't just be audiences anymore, but participants and partners" (Thompson, 2006).

In his eagerness to herald the future of public service broadcasting, Thompson failed to give due recognition to the Corporation's own history of online video and audience interaction. The BBC was in fact well positioned to take on these challenges with a rich history of online audio and video experimentation, dating back more than a decade before Thompson's speech in 2006. Some of this early online video even stemmed from audiences, helping precipitate not only a drive for such content, but also a change in its perceived acceptable form and aesthetics. The lack of public attention for these early experiments may be in part since they were not the result of specific corporate strategy, but rather the product of a broadcast culture where individuals had the freedom to innovate (see Thorsen, 2010).

The emphasis on text is also reflected in most scholarly literature concerning web history and online public service broadcasting. Such accounts deal superficially with important examples of early online video and technological challenges that hindered its widespread adaptation. In so doing, this version of web history undervalues many important developments that have helped shape the forms and practices of what now constitutes online public service media. The future of online public service media may yet turn out to be one centred more exclusively on its traditional roots of audio–visual content, as suggested by Thompson above, and as such its history warrants close attention. In taking a historical approach, this chapter will therefore focus on some of the defining moments in the BBC's use of online video to date, mapping both the Corporation's early experimentation and how online video evolved since the 2006 strategic realignment. The chapter will demonstrate how traditional broadcast conventions have shaped BBC's inflection of public service media online, but also yielded a tension between using the web to formulate new content and audience engagement versus using the web as an alternative distribution channel for existing content. Both news footage and nonlinear viewing of television programmes are the subject of discussion, with particular focus on where these intersect with audience interaction or engagement. The chapter will conclude by considering how the Corporation's continued push into online video may influence distribution of public service broadcasting in the future.

Early Online Audio and Video from the BBC

Experimentation with online content began several years prior to BBC Online's official launch in late 1997 (see Thorsen, 2010). In the period ranging from 1994–1997, several proof-of-concept websites were created based on content solicited from around the BBC. The internet was seen as a great opportunity for producers to deliver new services—including on–demand audio and video, as well as unedited material that would otherwise not have made it to broadcast. The BBC eventually ditched formal collaborations with commercial organisations and focussed on producing all content in–house, though this posed some unique challenges for a traditional broadcast organisation. "What we didn't have was an abundance of text skills," the first project director of BBC News Online, Bob Eggington (2007) recalled. "Broadcast scripts were not suitable for repurposing as text news stories. It became clear everything had to be written specifically for the web." Reflecting on the *Budget '95* website, Mike Smartt, BBC News Interactive's editor–in–chief for the first eight years, similarly acknowledged that even major news organisations were novices at this new form of journalism:

> The craft is still being learnt of gathering material generated on a major story for dispersal elsewhere—text from the PA's service to other news organisations, pictures and sound from BBC radio and television programmes—and then quickly adapting it for the Net. (Smartt, 1995)

The BBC's first public video stream was on June 30, 1997, with a "one–hour RealVideo special" of the handover of Hong Kong powers from Britain to China. This was published on *Politics 97*, a BBC News micro–site created as a general political news offering on the back of *Election 97*'s success. Video streaming was technologically more complex than audio and required much greater bandwidth from consumers' internet connections than other content. The RealVideo feed was therefore available in two different formats, one for 28.8k modems and one for ISDN connections. Whilst the latter was positioned as the "high–quality" option, it was in reality only a stamp–sized, pixelated moving image—far removed from the traditional broadcast experience audiences would have been accustomed to.

The defining moment in BBC's move online came in the aftermath of Diana Spencer (Princess of Wales) and Dodi Al–Fayed's deaths in a car crash on August 31, 1997. "There was nobody around to update the homepage," one of the principal engineers behind BBC's websites, Brandon Butterworth, recalled, "so I worked with a friend at World Service, who was in on the Sunday updating their site, until News arrived" (Butterworth, 2007). Overnight they had put together a tribute site and published a video stream. The sub–site was expanded throughout the week and peaked with the funeral ceremony on the Saturday, which included a video stream that was fed to internet service providers in Europe and AOL in the US. The site also prominently featured RealAudio and RealVideo streams of tributes from Diana's brother, Earl Spencer, her friend Elton John and the then Prime Minister, Tony Blair.

Prior to this, most of the Corporation's online activities had been ad–hoc, unofficial, and conducted by people alongside their normal jobs. However, the response to its online Diana coverage ultimately convinced the BBC to make the necessary investments in an official web presence. BBC News Online eventually went live in an official capacity on November 4, 1997, with the main BBC Online website going live on December 15, 1997. Originally the BBC was granted a one–year trial by the Department for Culture, Media and Sport (DCMS), which was ratified a year later (Barrett, 2007).

Original plans for the BBC News website had been to present a rich audio–visual experience, reflecting the Corporation's desire to repurpose broadcast content and build on its existing brand and expertise. However, the site ended up being less ambitious than "the great ideas" the design team had originally intended. The site even had to be redesigned three weeks prior to launch since it would have taken "several hours to render on people's screens down ponderous dial–up connections" (Smartt, 2007). It did, nevertheless, carry a RealVideo stream of the BBC Nine O'Clock News and a RealAudio news bulletin updated every hour.

"It's very exciting indeed," proclaimed BBC News Online editor, Mike Smartt. "This medium is now our third broadcast service alongside radio and TV, and we believe it could take over as the main way people receive BBC journalism in the UK and around the world" (Smartt as cited in Thompson, 1997). This view was shared by the independent panel on the future funding of the BBC in 1999, which rejected external pressures to turn BBC Online (including news and sport) into a commercial operation, as they expected it:

> to become a core part of the BBC's public service in the next few years. We also expect that closer convergence will take place between websites and broadcast services, so that the BBC's domestic audience will increasingly access BBC output via the website. (Davies et al., 1999, p. 65)

Unless the BBC were to drop audio–visual content, the statement is a clear indication that the Corporation's websites were expected to carry a greater amount of what was perceived as traditionally broadcast output in the future. This chapter will now turn to examine some examples of how this prophecy of convergence manifested itself in BBC's online portfolio.

Audience Videos Telling the Story

Relatively poor image quality and intermittent caching of streaming video in the early years inevitably contributed to a conceptualisation of the BBC's web presence as a predominantly text–based medium. However, concerns about aesthetics and broadcast conventions diminished when footage from eyewitnesses to various crisis events helped define the news narrative.

The Sumatra–Andaman Earthquake that lead to the Indian Ocean Tsunami on December 26, 2004, is generally considered to be one of the most powerful ever recorded and—having killed at least 283,000 people—was one of the deadliest of all time. Very few Western news organizations had reporters nearby that could respond quickly to the disaster. Instead it was ordinary citizens recording the events as they witnessed them unfolding who provided the vast majority of the extraordinary imagery used in the mainstream media (see Allan, 2006, 2009; Gordon, 2007; Liu, Palen, Sutton, Hughes, & Vieweg, 2009; Schechter, 2005). Audio–visual material from citizens was used to illustrate BBC News online and in broadcast, whilst emails sent to the news website were read out on BBC News 24.

Only months later, on July 7, 2005, there was a coordinated terror attack on London with three bombs exploding within a minute of one another and a fourth blowing up a double–decker bus less than an hour later. The principal source of news for many people already at work was the internet, with iconic images and eyewitness reports again provided by ordinary citizens caught up in the events (see Allan, 2006; Allan & Thorsen, 2010). Having learnt from the Indian Ocean Tsunami some eight months previous, the BBC quickly began soliciting eyewitness accounts and photographs from ordinary citizens. Richard Sambrook, Director of Global News, recalled an incredible response of "more than 1,000 photographs, 20 pieces of amateur video, 4,000 text messages, and 20,000 e–mails" (Sambrook, 2005). In his view, "audiences had become involved in telling this story as they never had before."

> The quantity and quality of the public's contributions moved them beyond novelty, tokenism or the exceptional . . . Our reporting on this story was a genuine collaboration, enabled by consumer technology—the camera phone in particular—and supported by trust between broadcaster and audience. (Sambrook, 2005)

This remarkable admission demonstrates not just citizen journalism coming of age, but also an acceptance by traditional news organisations that audience material is integral to online news reporting—not least in times of crisis. In the years that followed, several high–profile events were driven by images or video footage captured by eyewitnesses—including explosions at the Buncefield (UK) oil depot in December 2005; the execution of Saddam Hussein in December 2006; the attempted suicide attack at Glasgow airport in June 2007; the Burma uprising in September–October 2007, also known as the "Saffron Revolution;" the Mumbai attacks in November 2008; and the Iranian election protests in 2009–2010 (for a discussion of BBC News Online's reporting of these events, see Allan & Thorsen, 2010). Whilst broadcast also capitalised on these unique sources of citizen journalism, online news was able to publish a much greater range of material. The low–fidelity of video from citizen journalists was also less of an issue for news websites and online audiences already accustomed to restrictions in image quality imposed by technological limitations.

Reinventing the Online Video User Experience

Another problem with much of the early audio–visual content on the BBC websites was that it played in a separate pop–up window or an external application in Real or Windows Media formats. This separated the different forms of media, creating in effect multiple distinct forms of media, as opposed to a tightly integrated multimedia product. Moreover, since text linked to audio–visual content, and rarely the other way round, audio and video had an additional navigational barrier to consumption. According to Pete Clifton, head of BBC News Interactive at the time, online video ought to be embedded into news articles, where it should complement as opposed to replicate the text. "It's something we don't really do very well," he confessed. "We need to get to a point where we can present the story as an overall proposition in one place. The text and the video work much better like that" (as cited in Thurman & Lupton, 2008, p. 445).

The Corporation's solution to bridging this gap between content types was the Embedded Media Player (EMP) officially launched on March 13, 2008 after successful trials in early 2007 (O'Donovan, 2008). This new media player enabled producers and journalists to insert a Flash video into any of the BBC's web pages, streaming audio–visual content live or on–demand. Embedding, according to Steve Herrmann, editor of BBC News interactive at the time, would "compel journalists to think much more about how video integrates with their story" (as cited in Thurman & Lupton, 2008, p. 447).

The Embedded Media Player rapidly increased audiences for online audio and video on the BBC News website. Within a month of launch the daily unique users of audio and video had risen from 528,000 to 726,000, with average daily plays of content increasing from 636,000 to 978,000 (BBC, 2008a). The conversion rate of people reading a text story page and then choosing to access audio or video went from an average 2.5% to 20% in the same period. For Pete Clifton the success of the new presentation format embodied the core values of the Corporation. "Our mission is to make our content easier to find, play and share," he argued, "and the embedded player hits all those aims perfectly." In his view it finally did "justice to all our fantastic video and audio clips" (BBC, 2008a).

Several high-profile events followed in 2008 that allowed the BBC to showcase its new Embedded Media Player. In particular the European Football Championship (Euro 2008) and the Beijing Olympics provided a rich source of video footage that could be embedded into news and sports websites. The dedicated sub-websites created for these tournaments became themselves spectacles of innovation in specialist journalism. The experimentation with presenting video alongside other rich content continued during the 2008 US Presidential elections. Results day, November 5, was the main showcase, where the Corporation embedded a live video stream above a live-blog and an automatically updating results map to the right of the page. Audio-visual content also proved popular with audiences, with one in five of the 9.2 million unique visitors to the site that day accessing audio or video (Barack Obama's victory speech being the most popular) (Herrmann, 2010d). The grandeur of the occasion clearly lent itself to being presented in video, though the richness of the storytelling enabled through a convergence of formats began to demonstrate the type of multimedia journalism Clifton had envisaged.

Democratic Spectacles and Video Walls

During a speech given in Westminster on January 15, 2008, the BBC Director General, Mark Thompson, announced an ambition to transform the way the Corporation could "connect British democracy—and all its many democratic institutions—to the public." This reflected a core BBC mission, he maintained, "not just to report journalistically on Parliament and the wider democratic process, but to be the public gallery from which citizens could see and hear proceedings for themselves" (Thompson, 2008).

Claiming that the Corporation already connected the British public with democratic society across its many services, Thompson stressed that his transformative vision was to "bring this gallery to life, to make it real, to make it potentially relevant for every citizen" through no less than "the most engaging, the most creative multimedia portal for democracy in the world" (Thompson, 2008).

The portal was eventually unveiled as *Democracy Live* on November 2, 2009, after 18 months of development. The sub-site brought together for the first time on BBC Online live and on-demand video footage of all the proceedings from UK national political institutions and the European Parliament. These were displayed on an eight-screen video wall on the *Democracy Live* home page, creating a rich visualisation of political institutions and committee proceedings. "Democracy Live is an important addition to the way the BBC brings politics to our audiences across the UK," head of BBC Political Programmes, Sue Inglish, declared upon launch, "allowing people to see first hand the work of their elected representatives and ensuring we have a healthy and informed democracy" (BBC, 2009). Moreover, she argued that "this is precisely the sort of different content the BBC should be providing in fulfilling our public service remit and representing all of the democratic institutions in the UK" (BBC, 2009).

Whilst the Embedded Media Player had made Thompson's grand vision for the site possible, the key innovation with *Democracy Live* was how it had reinvented non–linear navigation of such video content. "The real magic lies in the site's search function," maintained Mark Coyle, launch editor of the site, "which is unlike anything the BBC has done before" (Coyle, 2009). Powered by a speech–to–text system built by Blinkx and Autonomy, the website was able to automatically generate transcripts of spoken words in the video feeds with more than 80% accuracy. Citizens would then be able to search for specific word(s) and the results returned links to the relevant points in the video where they were spoken. This dramatically enhanced the usability of on–demand video and ensured the site was awarded the prestigious Media Guardian Innovation Award for best use of web platforms in March 2010.

Video was also central to the Corporation's website for the May 2010 UK general election. "Our focus will be on up–to–the–minute live reporting and video of all the key moments," Steve Herrmann, editor of BBC News Online, commented upon launch of the *Election 2010* microsite, "as well as in–depth information, analysis and context to help make sense of it all" (Herrmann, 2010a). The major new feature to achieve this was the BBC's new "Live Page" that contained "running text updates, video and audio"—effectively a meta–narrative of the day's events, incorporating not only news reports, but also linking to content on external blogs and tweets, as well as highlighting BBC output.

One of the Live Page features that set the BBC apart from its live blogging competitors was the inclusion of multiple concurrent live video streams. Whilst some other websites occasionally included a single video stream, the Corporation was able to accommodate three separate streams at any one time. Updated throughout the day these included press conferences and important events, as well as scheduled political programmes and the BBC News channel.

The BBC's *Election 2010* website also contained another major video feature on its home page, entitled "If I Were Prime Minister." This video wall showcased ordinary citizens stating the one thing they would do if they were prime minister. At the end of the campaign, 139 video clips had been published through a combination of journalists actively seeking vox pops, and people submitting their own responses via the website.

Video was clearly utilized on a much greater scale than in previous elections (UK or otherwise), which was made possible largely due to the Embedded Media Player (EMP). This increase in video content also translated into record viewing figures. The live stream of the BBC's prime–ministerial debate on April 29 had over 350,000 plays (television audience by comparison was an average 8.4 million), surpassing the debates hosted by ITV and Sky, also streamed online by the BBC (Herrmann, 2010b). For the first time BBC's live broadcast was simultaneously streamed on the Corporation's website and Facebook, whilst several UK newspaper sites, Yahoo, Fox News and the New York times also embedded the feed. After the debate, the BBC published an online searchable video and transcript along the same principles as *Democracy Live.* On results day, May 7, the BBC estimated more than 9 million requests to play online video throughout the day, with the *Election 2010* site receiving a record 11.4 million unique visitors and over 100 million pageviews in total (Herrmann, 2010c). The figures demonstrated an incredible appetite among audiences for online video, but also the Corporation's ability to fully utilise its wide range of audio–visual material that would previously have been heavily edited or not made it to broadcast at all.

BBC iPlayer: Responding to "The Second Digital Wave"

During his speech in 2006 about the "second digital wave," Mark Thompson announced that one of the key responses to this "fundamental disruption" would be called the BBC iPlayer and deliver on–demand video to the British public. Originally unveiled as the MyBBCPlayer during Thompson's speech at the Edinburgh International Television Festival on August 27, 2005, the concept had been in development since 2003 when it started life as the iMP (Integrated Media Player). The purpose of the BBC iPlayer was to provide online access to the Corporation's broadcast programming via a single point of reference. This differed from the purpose of the Embedded Media Player discussed above, which was a technology designed to simplify inclusion of video content, usually only short packages or raw footage, into BBC Online and its sub–sites.

The iPlayer project was approved by the BBC Trust January 31, 2007, following its first ever Public Value Test (see Collins, 2007) and a market impact assessment from Ofcom. "Our view is that the BBC's new on–demand services are likely to deliver significant public value, and should be allowed to proceed," announced Diane Coyle, chair of the public value test steering group, but stressed it would be "subject to certain conditions in order to reduce the potential negative market impact" (as cited in Deans, 2007). Specifically the ability to download whole series was seen as problematic since this might limit commercial exploitation of secondary rights (e.g., DVD sales). Following necessary modifications to the proposals, including limiting the availability of content to seven days after original broadcast, the iPlayer was first made available as an "open beta" download Peer-to-Peer player in July 2007. The functionality to stream content was first added in early December (for a more technical discussion, see Lanxon, 2009). Watching on-demand did not necessitate a television licence, but one was required for watching any live streaming content on the BBC's websites, including the iPlayer (not available abroad).

Despite early technical glitches and controversy surrounding choice of proprietary technology (Windows Media Player) and associated Digital Rights Management (DRM) issues, Mark Thompson hailed the launch of the BBC iPlayer beta as the most important milestone for the Corporation since the arrival of colour television (Sweney, 2007). The official version was eventually unveiled on December 25, 2007, and was an instant success. Within a fortnight some 3.5 million programmes had been streamed or downloaded—the most popular being the Dr. Who Christmas Special—but nearly half of the programmes were from outside the traditional top 50 most popular shows (BBC, 2008b).

Not everyone shared the Corporation's delight at the popularity of the new on-demand programming service, however. Internet service providers in particular felt aggrieved, and threatened in April 2008 to charge customers extra due to costs they incurred to accommodate the popularity of the BBC's new service. The claims were dismissed outright by Ashley Highfield, then head of BBC's Future Media and Technology, who argued instead that the "success of the iPlayer should be of benefit to the whole UK broadband industry, increasing those who want to take up broadband" (as cited in Wakefield, 2008).

Despite resistance from competitors and ISPs, the BBC iPlayer grew rapidly throughout its first year, culminating in a record 41 million requests for television programmes in December 2008 with the total for the year being 271 million (Khan, 2009). "The BBC wasn't the first mainstream media company to offer a video-on-demand service," admitted director of BBC Future Media and Technology, Erik Huggers recently, "but I do think we were the first to get it right" (Huggers, 2010). He argued the iPlayer's early success was down to simplicity of access (i.e., streaming), quality of content, clarity of message, and platform neutrality.

There was room for improvement though, and the first major evolution of the iPlayer came in July 2008. The Corporation combined TV and radio into a single player, integrated live streaming, and added charts of most popular programs and contextual recommendations based on individual audio or video clips. In addition to this feature upgrade, presentation of content was moved to the Embedded Media Player (EMP), which the iPlayer technical team had helped develop earlier that year. Unifying audio–visual playback using the EMP was intended to facilitate simultaneous feature upgrades and a familiar user experience across the BBC websites. The Corporation also sought to increase its reach by gradually porting the iPlayer to work on a wider range of platforms and devices, including games consoles.

These changes contributed to new record numbers at the end of 2009, with the iPlayer receiving more than 100 million requests in a single month for the first time in December that year. One in eight of all television requests were from either a Nintendo Wii or a Sony PS3 console, demonstrating the increased reach provided by the platform diversification policy (BBC, 2010). Moreover, when the BBC Trust published its review of the BBC's on–demand services in May 2010, it claimed that one third of all UK adults said they had used the iPlayer and concluded that it represented "good value for money" (BBC Trust, 2010).

Audiences as Tastemakers

The challenges for the first revision of the iPlayer in 2008 were of a predominantly technical nature—dealing with growth, image quality, and platform neutrality. However, Mark Thompson's 2006 vision had been greater than simply providing a successful on–demand service. The third iteration of the BBC iPlayer, launched as a beta on May 26, 2010, therefore focussed on redesigning the service around the next fundamental challenge of non–linear viewing: shepherding audiences to their desired content.

According to Anthony Rose, controller of BBC's Online Media Group and Vision, the scheduler was the leading "tastemaker" of linear television. That is, by scheduling programmes at certain times of the day, "the scheduler is both creating and satisfying the desire to view that programme" (Rose, 2010). The previous version of the iPlayer satisfied in his words "the time–shifted desires of the scheduler: the BBC schedulers create the desire to watch a programme; iPlayer lets you see it at a time that's convenient to you" (Rose, 2010). In order to be prepared for a future where the linear broadcast no longer has the same influence, the BBC needed to identify who or what could take the scheduler's role as tastemaker.

In order to meet this challenge the BBC deployed a combination of personalisation, socialisation, and customisation. It added a personal recommendation engine based on previously viewed content and enabled users to flag individual programmes or series as personal favourites. By integrating the

BBC's own login system (BBC iD) with Twitter and Facebook, it created a "social recommendation ecosystem" that can be scaled to cover other networks in the future. Whilst this enables people to send and receive recommendations for content, the BBC also added the ability to chat with friends in real–time whilst watching a chosen programme. At present this requires connecting with a Microsoft Windows Messenger Live account, though again it has the potential for being expanded to other networks in future.

Whilst personalisation of the iPlayer epitomises the transformation of the BBC's role in "the second digital wave," it also signals a significant institutional shift for the Corporation. "We needed to make iPlayer something more than TV catch–up alone," explained Anthony Rose, "we wanted it to become a driver of demand" (Rose, 2010). Links to external catch–up services are also planned, thus allowing demand—stimulated by the BBC's ecosystem of recommendations—to be driven to third party partners (currently ITV, Channel 4 and Five along with Clic and SeeSaw). This has drawn criticism from BSkyB, which accused the Corporation of reinventing the iPlayer "as an online aggregator of third–party content without appropriate regulatory review" (as cited in Sweney, 2010). Whatever the outcome of that particular debate, the latest version of the iPlayer has again stressed the Corporation's strategic emphasis on audio–visual content when inflecting public service broadcasting in an online environment.

Conclusion

As this chapter has sought to demonstrate, the BBC's commitment to online video began during the "first digital wave," anchored in a broadcast tradition that influenced the Corporation's very first experimental entries into the online domain. The quality and the purpose of this content, however, have been unclear. Pete Clifton agreed in 2007 that historically the BBC has "put huge amounts of video on the site, and it's just really been what's been on the Ten O'clock News." In his view the video too often did not perform a very useful function, since "there are too many people here who are still very focused around the traditional outlets" (as cited in Thurman & Lupton, 2008, p. 445).

The "second digital wave" was proclaimed by Mark Thompson to justify the start of a transformative shift within the BBC towards new forms of online audio and video. The strategy has arguably yielded some success, with the most prominent being catch–up television via the BBC iPlayer. However, as this chapter has demonstrated, online video is much more than the iPlayer and permeates all of the Corporation's websites. The web has provided a platform for distribution of niche and unedited material that would otherwise not have made it to broadcast. Thus not only facilitating greater access to the content funded by licence fee payers, but also challenging traditional broadcast aesthetics and narrative structures.

News in particular has been strongly influenced by a change in conventions around quality, stemming in part from citizen journalism and the BBC's willingness to embrace what it traditionally termed user–generated content. Technological advances have been important too, with the Embedded Media Player renewing the relevance of video on BBC News Online by allowing integration of video with text content on the web. This is a significant step towards achieving multimedia storytelling, though such is the pace of change that this will undoubtedly be a never–ending process.

However, the most disruptive change of the "second digital wave" is likely to be the redefinition of how demand for online video is stimulated. This may either be through new opportunities to navigate video, such as the search functionality introduced as part of the *Democracy Live* website, or through creating new drivers of demand, such as the iPlayer's new "social recommendation ecosystem." Together with a re–appraisal of how public service broadcasting is distributed, these developments have the potential to transform what for the BBC constitutes public service media. For better or worse, it appears the Corporation is preparing the possibility of a future of public service broadcasting where online is not simply "the third broadcast medium," but *the only* medium.

References

Allan, S. (2006). *Online News: Journalism and the Internet.* Maidenhead, UK: Open University Press.

Allan, S. (2009). Histories of Citizen Journalism. In S. Allan & E. Thorsen (Eds.), *Citizen Journalism: Global Perspectives* (pp. 17–32). New York: Peter Lang.

Allan, S., & Thorsen, E. (2010). Journalism and Public Service: The Case of BBC News Online. In G. Meikle & G. Redden (Eds.), *News Online: Transformation and Continuity* (pp. 20–37). Basingstoke, UK: Palgrave Macmillan.

Barrett, C. (2007). Revolution Not Evolution: The Birth of bbc.co.uk. *BBC Internet Blog* [Article originally appeared in Ariel, reproduced in the blog by Alan Connor].

BBC. (2008a). BBC News: Embedded player sends audiences rocketing. *BBC Press Office.*

BBC. (2008b). More than 3.5 million programmes accessed via BBC iPlayer in first fortnight. *BBC Press Office.*

BBC. (2009). BBC launches Democracy Live. *BBC Press Office.*

BBC. (2010). BBC iPlayer breaks new record of 100 million requests. *BBC Press Office.*

BBC Trust. (2010). Trust finds iPlayer fulfils audience expectations. *BBC Trust.*

Butterworth, B. (2007). Brandon's History of Online BBC. *BBC Internet Blog.*

Collins, R. (2007). The BBC and "public value." *Medien und Kommunikationswissenschaft, 2*(55), 164–184.

Coyle, M. (2009). Democracy Live. *About the BBC Blog.*
Davies, G., Black, H., Budd, A., Evans, R., Gordon, J., Lipsey, D., Neuberger, J., & Newton, T. (1999). The Future Funding of the BBC: Report of the Independent Review Panel: Department for Culture, Media and Sport.
Deans, J. (2007, January 31). BBC iPlayer gets go–ahead, *Guardian Unlimited.*
Eggington, B. (2007, November 13). In the front line, online, *Press Gazette.*
Gordon, J. (2007). The Mobile Phone and the Public Sphere. *Convergence: The International Journal of Research into New Media Technologies, 13*(3), 307–319.
Herrmann, S. (2010a). BBC News online coverage of Election 2010. *BBC Editors Blog.*
Herrmann, S. (2010b). BBC News online coverage of prime–ministerial debate (2). *BBC Editors Blog.*
Herrmann, S. (2010c). A new record. *BBC Editors Blog.*
Herrmann, S. (2010d). US election success. *BBC Editors Blog.*
Huggers, E. (2010). The evolution of BBC iPlayer. *About the BBC Blog.*
Khan, U. (2009, January 7). Popularity of BBC iPlayer leads to renewed concerns internet could grind to a halt, *Telegraph.co.uk.*
Lanxon, N. (2009). iPlayer uncovered: What powers the BBC's epic creation? *CNET UK.*
Liu, S. B., Palen, L., Sutton, J., Hughes, A. L., & Vieweg, S. (2009). Citizen Photojournalism during Crisis Events In S. Allan & E. Thorsen (Eds.), *Citizen Journalism: Global Perspectives* (pp. 43–64). New York: Peter Lang.
O'Donovan, J. (2008). News & Sport Embedded Media. *BBC Internet Blog.*
Rose, A. (2010). Introducing the all new BBC iPlayer (This time it's personal). *BBC Internet Blog.*
Sambrook, R. (2005). Citizen Journalism and the BBC. *Nieman Reports, 59*(4), 13–16.
Schechter, D. (2005). Helicopter Journalism: What's Missing in the Tsunami Coverage. *Mediachannel.org.*
Smartt, M. (1995, December 4). Why Ken Drank Alone on the Net, *The Independent.*
Smartt, M. (2007). The Days before Launch. *BBC Internet Blog.*
Sweney, M. (2007, June 27). BBC seeks more content for iPlayer, *Media Guardian.*
Sweney, M. (2010, May 26). BBC iPlayer upgrade attacked by BSkyB. *Guardian.co.uk.*
Thompson, M. (2006). *Creative Future—The BBC programmes and content in an on–demand world.* Paper presented at the Royal Television Society Fleming Memorial Lecture, London.
Thompson, M. (2008). *The Trouble With Trust: Building Confidence in Institutions.* Paper presented at the Speech given at QEII Centre, London.
Thompson, R. (1997, November 21). Not the Nine O'Clock News as we know it, *PR Week.*
Thorsen, E. (2010). BBC News Online: A Brief History of Past and Present. In N. Brügger (Ed.), *Web History.* New York: Peter Lang.
Thurman, N., & Lupton, B. (2008). Convergence Calls: Multimedia Storytelling at British News Websites. *Convergence: The International Journal of Research into New Media Technologies, 14*(4), 439–455.
Wakefield, J. (2008, April 9). BBC and ISPs clash over iPlayer. *BBC News Online.*

3 *NPR Online*

Public Service Communication at the Center of National Public Radio

Nikki Usher, Patricia Riley & Vikki Porter

American broadcast and print news organizations are struggling with a decline in viewers, listeners and readers as well as the aftermath of a deep global recession. Many news organizations are attempting to reinvent their cultures and practices to compete in a transmedia digital world where information is plentiful and often free. This chapter examines one news network organization in the U.S., National Public Radio (NPR), as it navigates in a complex and growing digital space.

NPR, a system of noncommercial radio stations, was incorporated in Washington, D.C. on March 3, 1970 following the passage of the Public Broadcasting Act in 1967. It offers both news and cultural programming. Based in Washington, D.C., NPR's programs are aired by more than 800 member stations across the U.S. It produces eleven news shows, two entertainment shows, nine music shows, and four special series—including some offered only online. Many of its flagship shows are also broadcast in Europe over NPR FM Berlin, which first aired on April 1, 2006.

NPR has significant penetration in day–to–day life in the U.S. For example, its weekday news show "Morning Edition" airs during the morning commute to work reaching an average of 7.6 million people. This audience is larger than either of the two leading morning television shows in the U.S.—ABC's "Good Morning America" or the "Today" show on NBC (Hamilton, 2009). NPR's audience grew during the downturn in the news industry and the recession of 2008 (Farhi, 2009), grew again in 2009 and has held steady in 2010 (NPR, 2010). NPR has approximately 30 million listeners a week in the U.S. (Kamenetz, 2009) and 38 bureaus around the world.

Research Project

Our research goals are first, to document the sometimes tense and contested evolution of NPR's online strategy, and second, to examine the activities and processes NPR has utilized to develop an online strategy for its network of stations. The data were gathered during three years (2008–2010) of field site visits, interviews, document collection, observations during strategy workshops and assessed using the Constant Comparative Method (CCM) (Boeije, 2002).[1]

NPR's online strategy implementation is analyzed through a concept we call "digital change capacity" (Usher & Riley, 2009). In its more general form, the construct of change capacity is a holistic organizational attribute that includes: competent and involved management and leadership, strategic and systemic communication, and an accountable culture that utilizes systems thinking (Judge & Elenkov, 2004). Holt, Armenakis, Field, and Harris (2007) explain that the context and content of the change are also important when studying the process of organizational change.

The digital transformation of long-standing media and publishing organizations (e.g., broadcast, newspapers and book publishers) is a critical context for the study of organizational change as it is often a story of an industry culture "facing a profound change in its mode of production, but so encumbered by its past as to be unable to seize opportunities offered by technological change" (Epstein, 2011, p. 28).

There have been few studies of digital and online strategic change in newsrooms (e.g., Klinenberg, 2005) and fewer still in public service broadcast organizations. Organizational change tends to be particularly difficult in the news industry (Boczkowski, 2005; Esser, 1998; Lowrey, 1999; Seelig, 2002; Singer, 2003, 2004a, 2004b) so is important to add to the body of knowledge on digital and online strategic change in newsrooms. We begin this chapter with a brief history of NPR as a network.

The U.S. Public Media Structure

Commercial media dominate the news and information landscape in the U.S. on older formats such as radio, television and print, and new for-profit platforms and delivery systems such as satellite and HD radio continue to proliferate. There is, in addition, a longstanding tradition of noncommercial radio in the U.S. Early in the 20th century, many nonprofit radio stations were licensed to colleges and universities (Douglas, 1987) and they created a trade group called the Association of Educational Broadcasting Stations, later renamed the National Association of Educational Broadcasters (NAEB) in 1925. The radio division of the NAEB, National Educational Radio (NER) formed in 1963 and their executive director, Jerrold Sandler, was instrumental in the development of U.S. congressional legislation that begat the public broadcasting system. Importantly, Sandler insisted that the Act include radio. Although only $260,000 of $5 million, or a little over 5% of the initial funding, was designated for radio it was the start of a network (McCauley, 2005).

Following the formation of the private, nonprofit Corporation for Public Broadcasting (CPB) in 1967, the CPB board and its director of radio activities, Albert Hulsen, investigated ways to organize the existing noncommercial stations into a national radio system. They decided NER was not a viable model and created a new private, nonprofit organization, National Public Radio. The planning board for NPR met in 1970 and an educational broadcaster, William Siemering, was lead author of the following mission statement:

> National Public Radio will serve the individual: it will promote personal growth; it will regard the individual differences among men [sic] with respect and joy rather than derision and hate; it will celebrate the human experience as infinitely varied rather than vacuous and banal; it will encourage a sense of active participation, rather than apathetic helplessness. (As cited in McCauley, 2005, p. 23)

What Constitutes Public?—Follow the Money

Paying for these lofty goals has challenged NPR from the start. Its business model assumes some CPB funding but the bulk of its revenue is from member stations and underwriters. In 2010, the CPB received $420 million from congressional appropriations for the Public Broadcasting Company (PBS) and NPR—which is up from $340 million in 2001 (Public Broadcasting Policy Database, 2001; Corporation for Public Broadcasting: Operations Budget, 2010). That is a significant sum, but in contrast to public media support in other countries, NPR and its affiliates receive relatively little of their operating budgets from the federal government, as the U.S. has neither a national tax nor a license fee to fund public broadcasting (Pickard, Stearns, & Aaron, 2009).

Today, NPR generates the majority of its revenue from member station dues and programming fees. Only about 1–2% of its funding comes from the CPB or other national grants (Annual Reports, Audited Financial Statements, and Form 990s, 2010). Donors are also important. For example in 2003, Joan B. Kroc, the widow of McDonald's Corporation former CEO Ray Kroc, bequeathed over $225 million to NPR, bolstering its endowment significantly.

NPR produces most of the news content used by public radio stations in the U.S., and those member stations pay for the right to broadcast these programs. In metropolitan areas or university towns, stations may produce a significant portion of their own content but many stations have limited capacity for local newsgathering or content creation and rely heavily on the CPB for funds (although they also receive listener contributions, grants, and money from other donors). In 2010, for example, the CPB distributed $65,415,000 in direct grants to local public radio stations, bypassing the NPR organization itself (Corporation for Public Broadcasting: Operations Budget, 2010).

NPR Online: Change Comes to an Analog Culture

NPR's life on the web emerged from innovative ways to service and engage its community of listeners. In 1993, Rich Dean, then an associate producer and director of the radio program *Weekend All Things Considered*, learned about internet sites and networks like America Online, Compuserve, and Prodigy. He discovered that listeners were talking about NPR content in forums on these sites and decided that NPR should be part of these growing online communities: "The mission was driving everything . . . providing as much public service as possible through the web site" (Dean, 2010, personal communication).

This did not mean that NPR was a quick adopter of online activity. In the early 90s, the organization had a decidedly "analog culture"—for example, reporters and producers still used typewriters, and its core products, radio shows, were recorded on analog tape which could not be streamed over the internet. Dean realised the web was the future when he was producing a weekly cooking show segment. Rather than respond to every listener's request forrecipes, he built a website and posted the recipes. This first NPR site was created in Dean's apartment and went live in December 1993 as the *Weekend All Things Considered* site, followed by the *Weekend Edition Sunday* site a few months later. Convinced that the internet would be a critical means of reaching NPR's audience in the future, Dean persuaded the executives that he should develop and run the organization's website. His new title was "Producer, New Media Services," and in 1994, NPR.org was launched.

Dean recalls that there was tremendous internal resistance: Hosts and reporters did not want to make their email addresses public for fear that they would be overwhelmed by audience email; and they were scared to have their pictures up on the web even though their pictures were regularly provided to media outlets through the public information office (Dean, 2010, personal communication). The site itself was quite bare—it offered the basic outline (called a rundown) of what had happened on the shows. Thus if a listener wanted to know the name of a book that had been discussed on a certain show;

he or she could look it up. But internally, these documents were not considered ready for public consumption. There were spelling errors and typos, and even though the rundowns were sent daily to member stations across the country, there were concerns about their appropriateness for the public.

This early period, according to former Senior Vice President for Digital Media, Maria Thomas, had little input from the newsroom and, she claims, "Was just a bunch of engineers geeking around. There was very little involvement or interest from the editorial side" (Thomas, 2010, personal communication).

In 1995, NPR benefitted from an important technological advancement: Real Audio came to NPR with technology that would allow audience members to listen to streaming audio using a dial–up modem. But according to those who remember it, the audio sounded absolutely terrible and actually presented the organization with a serious dilemma because it cut against NPR's self–described identity as producers of superb audio. Current staff at NPR believe that the organization's mission statement guided their decision–making during this period—the audience's ability to access content when they want it was perceived to be more important than audio quality.

Streaming audio of less than stellar quality and posting the rundowns online are both examples of mission–driven actions overriding cultural and technical norms. Stories of mission driven decision–making were repeated often during our study.

Rules of Engagement: The Evolving Online Strategy in a Network Environment

The relationship between member stations and NPR headquarters has often been strained due to the inevitable competition over funding (McCauley, 2005). As NPR's leaders allocated resources so they could create a state–of–the–art website, they faced concerns from the network that NPR might create a situation where listeners could bypass local radio stations and simply go to NPR.org for their content. And if anyone in Washington's NPR offices did not understand the concerns of the stations, NPR's board, composed of individuals representing the member stations, would remind those in the Washington headquarters that the radio stations are their primary funders.

As NPR.org became more robust, NPR member stations' concerns about losing their listeners grew. Nonetheless, NPR began archiving content for shows and suddenly an NPR library was available to people all over the world—for free—true to its public media vision. The NPR.org website, following the lead of *Wired* magazine, displayed banner ads from their corporate sponsors and generated revenue for the Washington offices (Dean, 2010, personal communication).

Other internal struggles included the desire of some staff and executives to put more text and visual material on the web in order to look more like CNN and other news sites since "those who come to us for news online don't understand how much smaller we are than other news organizations. The internet makes us all look the same and raises their expectations" (Thomas, 2008, personal communication). NPR at that point did not regularly produce photos or video content so the organization found it difficult to compete online with news organizations like *The Washington Post* or CBS. The web staff initially thought the solution was to have transcripts instantly available, but like the rundowns, broadcast transcripts are full of typographical and spelling errors. In addition, NPR could lose revenue since it was in the business of selling its cleaned-up transcripts. The decision of management, ultimately, was to have the transcripts department post them all online—warts and all—for free (Free Transcripts now Available on NPR.org, 2009). Again NPR privileged the public's right to the information in developing its digital strategy, increasing the value of NPR as a public good in digital space.

By 1998, Thomas said the site had developed the "look and feel" that would last until 2009 (Thomas, 2010). There were links to the archives and information about ways to contact NPR. The site featured five main navigation tabs: News Now, Programs, Inside NPR, Member Stations, Your Turn and Search. In the "News Now" tab, there was a link that offered readers/listeners a chance to discuss the news: "Your (Their) Turn." This section represented early efforts to involve website users in the discussion of news content. The "Member Stations" section simultaneously highlighted local station content and forged a link between the national organization and its stations—a decision that highlighted NPR's efforts to lessen the tension with its stations over NPR's growing online presence.

Beyond Radio: NPR.org in the New Millennium

NPR began an important initiative that signaled a change in strategy in 2000—it created original content for NPR.org with the launch of *All Songs Considered.* The show featured stories about the carefully selected songs that were used as bumper music (the little blips of music that signaled turns between each story) on *All Things Considered.* This program later webcast and podcast live concert music and was the genesis of NPR Music—a music discovery website that expanded its arts and culture offerings. As M.J. Bear, then vice president of NPR Online, stated, "The internet allows radio to become a truly interactive medium." She continued, *All Songs Considered* was "a pioneering hybrid of NPR News and NPR Online. It represents NPR's first major thrust into internet-only programming and delivers the same high quality our radio listeners have come to expect" (Alvear, 2000). Also launched during 2000 was a modest NPR.org gift shop, positioned as a way to raise money by enhancing the connection between NPR and its listeners and "spreading the brand" since "Our audiences are so incredibly loyal," said former Senior VP for Programming Jay Kernis, the original producer of *Morning Edition* (Kernis, 2007). NPR's website took on a new architecture and "feel" in 2001 and 2002. According to Daniel Jacobson, director of application development, new editors were incorporated into the web team to create stories that were not just for radio—they were web stories with images, text and related links. "There was much more of an experience around the story, versus, 'here's an audio link and this is what you are going to get,'" Jacobson said (Jacobsen, 2010, personal communication). Previously the NPR web team, which was not integrated with the rest of NPR's news or cultural program production, primarily migrated content from the shows to the website.

In 2002, Thomas was asked to create a better infrastructure for NPR.org, which meant rethinking the underlying architecture of the site and its use by the audience. Thomas' epiphany came when she and her staff realized they needed to change the core organizing principle of the site. An audience research study indicated that people cared less about the program that aired the story they were trying to locate on the website than the story itself. "The fact that we [now] care more about the story than about the program was a big thing to say," noted Thomas, since NPR's programs are recognizable entities akin to shows on television. They proceeded to reorganize the site around the ways people remember things: Time, Topic, and People (Thomas, 2010, personal communication). Listening to the audience meant the online team had to disassemble the structure of the shows and highlight its story elements much the way iTunes breaks apart music albums to sell individual songs.

The next big moment in NPR's digital transformation came in 2004, when it became a national leader in podcasting. NPR was already producing mp3s for every story, as Jacobson attests, so it was not difficult for NPR to respond to audience requests. NPR launched its podcasting service on August 31, after it received numerous email requests and saw a spike in online searches for podcasts (Glaser, 2005).

NPR developed its podcasting service in conjunction with its member stations. The website team did not want to podcast *All Things Considered*, for example, right after it aired or its member stations could potentially lose listeners. "In navigating this evolving relationship, NPR works with an advisory group of member stations, whose interests it protects in myriad ways in the digital space" (Dorroh, 2008). As well as offering content from NPR's shows, their podcasts increasingly included original content like news recaps of political events.

Taken together, these examples indicate that NPR was enlarging its digital commons in part by placing its audience and the network at the center of its decision making.

"NPR–ness": Identities Converge as Platforms Diverge

The new strategy was for NPR.org to no longer be seen as just an archive for radio shows past but as a platform for the delivery of news and cultural content. As part of this strategy, the first NPR blog, *Mixed Signals*, was created during 2005–2006. It was designed to "look at stories of note and issues that never make it to air" (NPR Launches a Daily Blog, 2006) and was a significant departure from the carefully edited tone of the newsroom. Eight months later, the blog was abandoned as "too scattershot" but "NPR has decided that yes, this blogging thing might have some legs" (Sutherland, 2006).

A broader vision for both the digital and the radio realms of NPR was being discussed during this period. Then CEO Ken Stern asked Jay Kernis, former Senior VP for Programming, to work on a set of strategic questions: Could radio be used to drive people to the web? And if so, what would it take to do that? Or was the web its own medium, and if you were never an NPR listener, what value would the website have? And how should NPR ensure that member stations did not get left behind?

In 2006, Kernis created what he called the "Ness" document following a large meeting with member stations, NPR radio and web staff. NPR–ness, they decided, includes Public radio's core values; Integrity; Context that helps the audience make sense of the world; Compelling storytelling; Serendipitous discovery; and Personal connection. The meeting and the "Ness" document helped to ensure that digital and editorial content were imbued with a shared identity and a renewed vision of public radio that enhances the lives of its audience (Kernis, 2007).

Newsroom 2.0

There was a good deal of executive turnover in 2007–2008 with the departure of CEO Ken Stern and the exit of Thomas, Kernis and a 7% reduction in staff due to a decrease in corporate sponsorships and foundation giving during the recession. Yet the implementation of the online strategy progressed and became clearer through an infusion of other resources.

Stern's initial digital strategy was called, "Newsroom 2.0," and it called for NPR to not only be in audio but "in text, and video, and photography, and graphics, and whatever else comes along" (Kernis, 2007, p. 3). Prior to his departure, Kernis outlined a convergence strategy that was anchored by a "single/editorial production line—one digital newsroom, where editors, reporters and producers can access a single system to coordinate, approve and edit content for multiple platforms" (2007, p. 6). As part of its quest to remove the walls between digital production and radio production, NPR received a grant from the Knight Foundation for $1.5 million in 2007 to transform itself into a multimedia company. The Knight Digital Media Center—a joint program between the University of Southern California and the University of California, Berkeley, offered strategy workshops that taught leadership skills and organizational change management techniques to 40 senior NPR managers and developed an onsite training program for 600 NPR staff in new audio production and content management systems. The Center also taught 400 NPR employees to be multimedia content providers (Fest, 2007). This training program has had its bumps and re-starts (Usher & Riley, 2010). But NPR has undergone a significant culture change as reporters and producers discovered new ways of storytelling using multimedia content and platforms according to Ellen Weiss, former Senior Vice President for News. They also discovered that not all reporters and producers were meant to be multimedia storytellers—training was very time consuming and, for example, not all radio reporters had the eye for photography.

Following the first iteration of the training program, NPR's multi-media goals became more modest and the training program was revamped (Dorroh, 2008). But the process of trying something new and then assessing it and redesigning the process slowly became more comfortable for the organization. Weiss said the purpose of the Knight Foundation grant was to help NPR change: "To move people out of their comfort zones, out of a system that grew up when there was one program and it is suddenly not just multiple programs, but an entity that is never going off the air" (Weiss, 2010, personal communication).

As part of this strategy, Thomas launched NPR mobile in 2007, long before most phones were capable of receiving digital streaming content. NPR was thus established as a leader in this innovation. That same year, they launched *NPR Music*, featuring more than a dozen member stations with exceptional music content on NPR.org. *NPR Music* leverages the resources of the network by giving visitors access to music not offered by their local stations.

NPR's current CEO, Vivian Schiller arrived in 2009 from *The New York Times* where she was the Senior Vice President and General Manager of NYTimes.com. She has added a new emphasis to the digital strategy—a focus on partnerships. One of her goals is for NPR to fully embrace its member stations. For the past two years of this study, significant time and resources were devoted to supporting stations in "their own online strategy development journey" (Weiss, 2009, personal communication). NPR's leadership team found this strategy to be challenging and has struggled with its implementation. The most recent Knight Foundation workshops brought together NPR executives and digital experts with leaders of network stations to focus on digital strategy. These sessions also allowed the station leaders to focus on ways NPR could improve collaboration and the transparency of decision making.

Rapid Prototyping and Collaboration

During Weiss' tenure, experimentation at NPR flourished. Podcasts that are not broadcast on the radio are huge hits—NPR's *Planet Money* is the best example. Created in the wake of the 2008 financial crisis, it utilizes reporters from NPR and Public Radio International (PRI), a partnership Schiller formed (Drew, 2010).

There have also been innovations that failed, such as the web-focused *Bryant Park* Project that was geared toward developing a younger audience. Failures are important learning experiences, Weiss argued, "Because *Bryant Park* gave us the flexibility needed to create *Planet Money*" (Weiss, 2010, personal communication). Weiss' objective was to encourage innovation through experimentation, and this requires the ability to repurpose resources and lessons learned from one experiment to the next. This is challenging for a culture that developed its identity through shows that have strong brand recognition, and stakeholders inside and outside the organization often have strong personal attachment to the shows.

Weiss held countless town halls, Q & A sessions and regular "communication meetings" with NPR employees. She explained the strategy at multiple workshops with executives and producers from member stations. She relentlessly communicated that the growing stream of innovations in communication technology required NPR to experiment and that failure had to be recognized as an important part of the process. "Letting go," she would say, is a critical part of their new culture in order to create the "next big thing" (Weiss, 2010, multiple observations and personal communication). We found this rapid prototyping process along with strategic partnering to be key components of NPR's growing digital change capacity.

Weiss helped hire other web-savvy executives, notably Dick Myer and Kinsey Wilson, to share her vision for digital news: "I don't want digital news to be derivative of radio news—that is not how the web should be produced" (Weiss, 2010, personal communication). Dick Meyer, hired from CBSNews.com, agrees that NPR's web innovations should focus on listening to the audience but also claims that it is important to search for new connections: "We want to be wherever the public radio listener is—our goal is to serve the needs of the audience wherever they want to find us. And we will try to find them" (Meyer, 2009, personal communication).

The Digital Core Competencies

A major redesign of NPR.org was undertaken during 2008–2009 for two reasons. First, the staff learned that "a quarter of the visits to NPY.org come from search engines. Although Google and Yahoo! don't search audio, NPR feeds the search engines its scripts" (Dorroh, 2008). Still users complained that NPR's content could be very hard to find. Second, NPR wanted to dramatically increase its website traffic. (Interestingly, NPR's published goals for the redesign focused primarily on making the site easier for the staff to use but that was not mentioned in any of our interviews.) The website changes were heavily guided by data from their listener advisory group, NPR Listens, which was formed in 2007. The panel is an example of a key communication skill that enhances their capacity for change—strategic listening.

The core areas in NPR.org's new digital strategy are: mobile, verticals, NPR music and social media, according to Kinsey Wilson, Senior Vice President and General Manager for Digital Media. To help their stations across the country expand their own unique news operations, NPR developed Project Argo. This system feeds content into NPR.org's "verticals" and simultaneously gives member stations exposure to a wider range of viewers, readers and listeners.

NPR management sees social media as an important new skill area in its quest to increase audience engagement. Social media allow the website and public radio audience to share news and information with each other—and inform NPR how to better do its job. NPR currently has over 2 million followers on its various Twitter accounts, over one and a half million "likes" on Facebook but the Unfund NPR Facebook page has also grown to over 23,000.

Social media director Andy Carvin noted that NPR used multiple approaches such as Flickr, YouTube, and associations with CBS and American University to cover the inauguration of President Obama. Andy noted that, "Part of what I do at NPR is to really help our journalists think about how online communities can be used to improve the quality and diversity of our journalism," (as cited in Lascia, 2009).

NPR's staff recently created Open API, an application programming interface software that provides member stations or members of the public easy access to NPR materials. The vast majority of API requests are still from NPR itself, but users and member stations are finding ways to harness material for their own purposes. One measure of the API is how many stories are delivered by NPR over the course of a month—in March 2010, for example, it delivered over one billion stories (Jacobson, 2010). Thus the Open API is another example of the way NPR is growing both its digital capacity and as a digital commons.

Conclusion: Putting Communication and the Public at the Center of Decision Making

It is common today for leaders of organizational change efforts to ask what new skills they and their managers will need in order to "lead in a network" (Cross, Cowen, Ventucci, & Thomas, in press). NPR executives discovered that leading in a network means opening up multiple lines of communication, creating collaborative strategies and projects, and working out differences in as transparent a way as possible so that NPR and their member stations can mature as a network. The leaders had to develop communication "campaigns" to ensure everyone understood the current goals as well as multiple listening strategies. Their focus on engagement and partnerships put the stations and the audience at the center of their decision–making: a key element of digital change capacity that we refer to as "communication at the center." Their concerns about their online strategy led them through a critical conversation that improved their online strategy and matured the network. Future research projects will focus on specific communication and decision making practices that enhance strategy development.

NPR's website is constantly undergoing revisions and depending on the assessment standard, it is either wildly successful or sorely in need of growth. It was in last place in a list of top 30 global news websites, and is ranked as the #125th top website with approximately 8.5 million visitors a month (whois.npr.org, 2009; Saba, 2009). And while most of its visitors are from the U.S. (closely followed in second place by Denmark) it is increasing its global reach with visitors from from other nations (Alexa, 2011). This is both a very positive sign for the relatively small, non–profit news organization, and also a challenge to grow its brand. In 2010, NPR.org was awarded a Peabody Award for "its exceptionally rich offerings," and being "a model for other organizations" (Memmot, 2010).[2] This does not mean the organization is without its detractors as it is often critiqued for accepting corporate sponsorships (which make up a third of its budget) and for having a liberal bias (May, 2010).

U.S. public broadcasting organizations were initially constructed on the margins of the American media landscape (Avery & Stavitsky, 2003) and many would argue that they continue to be dwarfed by commercial entities and stunted by the relative dearth of public funding. Because of NPR's local, national, and international news gathering capacity, its successful digital innovations and its funding structure, it has recently been suggested as a model for other news organizations (e.g., Downie & Schudson, 2009). Its online strategy and NPR's ability to implement it has thus far been an important element in their quest to position the network as a significant public good.

Notes

1. This research is supported by grants from the McCormick Foundation and the Annenberg Foundation. Full disclosure, two of the authors are speakers during a new technology program attended by NPR executives at USC.
2. "First presented in 1941, the George Foster Peabody Awards recognize distinguished achievement and meritorious service by broadcasters, cable and webcasters, producing organizations, and individuals" (Peabody Awards, 2011).

References

Alexa (2011). *NPR.org*. Retrieved March 1, 2011, from http://www.alexa.com/siteinfo/npr.org#

All Things Considered: About the program (2010). *NPR.org*. Retrieved from http://www.npr.org/templates/story/story.php?storyId=1001

Alvear, J. (2000, April 24). NPR launches internet–only music program. *StreamingMedia.com*. Retrieved from http://www.streamingmedia.com/Articles/News/Featured-News/NPR-Launches-Internet-Only-Music-Program%0D%0A-62401.aspx

AOL Radio @ Network and NPR team up to offer award–winning radio programming to AOL members. (2003, March 10). *Business Wire*.

Annual reports, audited financial statements, and form 990s (2010). *NPR.org*.

Avery, K. & Stavitsky, R. (2003). The FCC and the Public Interest: A selective critique of U.S. telecommunications and policy making. In M. McCauley (Ed.), *Public Broadcasting and the Public Interest* (pp. 52–60). Armonk, NY: M.E. Sharpe.

Boczkowski, P. J. (2005). *Digitizing the News: Innovation in Online Newspapers*. Boston: MIT Press.

Complete List of Recipients of the 69th Annual Peabody Awards. (2010, March 31). *Peabody Awards*. Retrieved from http://www.peabody.uga.edu/news/event.php?id=66

Boieje, H. (2002). A purposeful approach to the constant comparative method in the analysis of qualitative interviews. *Quality & Quantity*, *36*, 391–409.

Corporation for Public Broadcasting: Operations Budget (2010). Fiscal Year 2010 Operating Budget. *Corporation for Public Broadcasting*. Retrieved from http://cpb.org/aboutcpb/financials/budget

Cross, R., Cowen, A., Vertucci, L., & Thomas, R. (in press). Leading in a connected world: How effective leaders drive results through networks. *Organizational Dynamics*.

Dorroh, J. (2008, October/November). The transformation of NPR. *American Journalism Review*. Retrieved May 30, 2010, from http://www.ajr.org/article.asp?id=4606saz)

Downie, L. & Schudson, M. (2009, October 19). The reconstruction of American journalism. *Columbia Journalism Review*. Retrieved from http://www.cjr.org/reconstruction/the_reconstruction_of_american.php

Douglas, S. J. (1987). *Inventing American Broadcasting*, 1899–1922. Baltimore: Johns Hopkins University Press.

Drew, J. (2010, March/April). NPR amps up. *Columbia Journalism Review*. Retrieved from http://www.cjr.org/feature/npr_amps_up.php?page=all

Eagleton, T. (2000). *The Idea of Culture*. Oxford. Blackwell.

Epstein, J. (2011, February 10). Books: Onward to the digital revolution. *The New York Review*, 28–29.

Esser, F. (1998). Editorial structures and work principles in British and German newsrooms. *European Journal of Communication*, *13*, 375–405.

Farhi, P. (2009, March 24). Consider this: NPR achieves record ratings. *Washington Post*. p. C01.

Fest, M. (2007, September 17). Knight Foundation investments intend to speed the news industry's digital transformation. *John S. and James L. Knight Foundation*.

Free Transcripts Now Available on NPR.org. (2009, August 19). *NPR.org*. Retrieved from http://www.npr.org/blogs/ombudsman/2009/08/free_transcripts_now_available.html

Glaser, M. (2005, November 29). Will NPR's podcasts birth a new business model for public radio? *Online Journalism Review*. Retrieved from http://www.ojr.org/ojr/stories/051129glaser

Hamilton, A. (2009, March 24). NPR Morning Edition audience way larger than GMA and Today. *Live Internet Television*. Retrieved from http://blog.ivi.tv/2009/03/morning-edition-radio-audience-much-larger-than-gma-and-today

Holt, D. T., Armenakis, A. A., Field, H. S., & Harris, S. G. (2007). Readiness for organizational change: The systematic development of a scale. *The Journal of Applied Behavioral Science*, *43*, 232–255.

Jacobson, D. (2010, April 19). API usage and metrics: NPR. *NPR.org*. Retrieved from http://www.npr.org/blogs/inside/2010/04/12/125882632/api-usage-and-metrics

Judge, W. Q. & Elenkov, D. (2005). Organizational capacity for change and environmental performance: an empirical assessment of Bulgarian firms. *Journal of Business Research*, *58*, 893–901.

Kamenetz, A. (2009, March 18). Will NPR save the news? *Fast Company*. Retrieved April 14, 2009, from http://www.fastcompany.com/magazine/134/finely-tuned.html

Kernis, J. (2007). Association of Schools of Journalism and Mass Communication Speech. St. Louis, MO.

Klinenberg, E. (2005). Convergence: News production in a digital age. *Annals of the American Academy of Political & Social Science*, *597*, 8–64.

Lascia, J. D. (2009, April 11). NPR's experiments with social media. *SocialMedia.biz*. Retrieved from http://www.socialmedia.biz/2009/04/11/nprs-experiments-with-social-media

Lowrey, W. (1999). Routine news: The power of the organization in visual journalism. *Visual Communication Quarterly, 6*, 10–15.

May, C. (2010, October 21). NPR has a history of being accused of liberal bias. *Daily Caller*. http://dailycaller.com/2010/10/21/npr-has-history-of-being-accused-of-liberal-bias

McCauley, M. P. (2005). *NPR: Trials and triumphs of National Public Radio*. New York: Columbia University Press.

Memmot, M. (2010, March 31). Peabody honors NPR, others for work done in 2009. *NPR.org. The Two–Way*. Retrieved from http://www.npr.org/blogs/thetwo-way/2010/03/peabody_awards_honor_npr_other.html

NPR Launches a Daily Blog. (2006, March 8). *NPR.org*. Retrieved from http://www.npr.org/templates/story/story.php?storyId=5251865

NPR (2010, October 10). Retrieved from http://www.npr.org/templates/archives/archive.php?thingId=125885971

Ombudsman (2009). Birthdays at NPR. *NPR.org*. Retrieved May 30, 2010, from http://www.npr.org/blogs/ombudsman/2009/11/birthdays_at_npr.html

Peabody Awards (2011). Retrieved February 17, 2011, from http://www.peabody.uga.edu/overview_history/index.php

Pickard, V., Sterns J., & Aaron, C. (2009). *Saving the News: Toward a National Journalism Strategy*. New York: Free Press.

Public Broadcasting Policy Database (2001). Amounts authorized and appropriated for CPB, 1969–2001. Retrieved from http://www.current.org/pbpb/statistics/cpbapprops.html

Saba, J. (2009, February 20). Top 30 global news sites. *Editor and Publisher*. Retrieved April 14, 2009, from http://www.editorandpublisher.com/eandp/search/article_display.jsp?vnu_content_id=1003943439

Seelig, M. (2002). The impact of new technologies on journalistic routines. *Web Journal of Mass Communication Research, 6*(1).

Singer, J. B. (2003). Who are these guys?: The online challenge to the notion of journalistic professionalism. *Journalism, 4*(2), 139–163.

Singer, J. B. (2004a). More than ink–stained wretches: The resocializaization of print journalists in converged newsrooms. *Journalism & Mass Communication Quarterly, 81*(4), 838–856.

Singer, J. B. (2004b). Strange bedfellows? The diffusion of convergence in four news organizations. *Journalism Studies, 5*(1), 3–18.

Sutherland, J. J. (2006, January 18). We've run our course, but stay tuned. . . . NPR.org. Retrieved from http://www.npr.org/templates/story/story.php?storyId=6290118

Usher, N. & Riley, P. (2009, April). Reshaping the public radio newsroom for the digital future. Paper presented at the International Symposium for Online Journalism, Austin, Texas.

Whois.npr.org (1993). *Whois.org*, retrieved from whois.org 2009.

PART TWO

Commercial vs Public

4 *Protecting the Brand*

A History of ABC Online News-as-Commodity

Maureen Burns

This chapter analyses intersections between ABC (Australian Broadcasting Corporation) Online News and ABC commercial ventures. Such intersections have their history in the Australian dual broadcasting system, in efforts by the ABC to supplement government funding at a time of extreme political hostility, and in episodic attempts at decentralization by the ABC. The chapter explores the development of an understanding of the ABC as a brand, and news as a commodity, and asks whether changing relations between public service broadcasting and commercial ventures in the online news environment alter the position of the ABC in the social imaginary.

Australia has one of the most concentrated media markets in the world (Tiffen & Gittens, 2004, p. 182), and although the Australian dual free–to–air broadcast system is often regarded as having "the best of both worlds" (the worlds being the UK–style public broadcasting system and the US–style commercial networks), Jones and Pusey have recently taken issue with that evaluation, arguing that there is a "disconnection" of Australian media policy discourses from the normative democratic framework of informed citizenship. Their research further suggests that those who use public service broadcasters (PSBs) have better knowledge of the political process than those who rely on the commercials (Jones & Pusey, 2010, pp. 451, 454).

Jones and Pusey conclude that commercial and public service broadcasters in Australia "inhabit almost different social worlds" (Jones & Pusey, 2010, p. 461). Their research focuses on television news—the source on which most people surveyed rely for television news and current affairs. Only 6 per cent of those who responded to the Australian Survey of Social Attitudes (2007) identified internet sites as the source upon which they most relied for news and information (as quoted in Jones & Pusey, 2010, p. 461). Notably the survey did not discriminate between commercial and non-commercial online news sites, and indeed, it would be difficult to ask survey respondents to do so. In the case of internet news, the public service "producer" of online news (say, the ABC) need not be its "distributor" (which might be, say, Yahoo! or msn). The dual system of commercial and public service broadcasting is therefore far less apparent online, changing the position of the ABC in the social imaginary. The history of ABC Online news demonstrates fluid and multiple intersections between the market economy, the public sphere, and the self-governing people (Taylor, 2002, p. 92).

The ABC and Commerce

There are two PSBs in Australia. Here I focus on the larger public service broadcaster, the ABC, which was established in 1932, began its official online site in 1995, and which is almost fully funded by Government appropriation, with a small proportion of its budget provided by commercial activities. Commerce at the ABC includes shops that sell items such as program-related DVDs, CDs, books and toys; and the sale of programs (to other broadcasters). Commerce also includes content licensing. Over the years there have been structural shifts and name changes for the commercial area from the Business Development Unit, to Enterprises, to Content Management, to Commercial Division, but these are largely unimportant to the history of content licensing, which has continued under one organisational grouping or another.

Content Licensing and News

According to the ABC website, content licensing:

> delivers customised content to clients—including operators of internet, mobile and emerging platforms such as video-on-demand and commuter services—who seek to build audiences in both traditional and emerging media. With access to the ABC's three output areas—Radio, Television and News—Content Licensing provides clients with access to the ABC's high quality content, highly sought after brands and diverse range of genres. (ABC, 2010a)

Content licensing accounts for a tiny proportion of the ABC's commercial revenue, which is in turn a small proportion of the ABC's overall budget. News—one of the most successful commodities licensed—is packaged as follows:

- Business Bulletin;
- News Bulletins;
- News Updates;
- Sports Wrap;
- Headlines;
- News;
- Premium News;
- Regional News;
- Rural News;
- Sports News and Results;
- Weather News; and
- News Transcripts (ABC, 2010a)

or can be customised. The metadata attached to ABC Online news allows clients to choose news feeds on particular topics—all news stories on mining, for example, or all stories on education—for a negotiated fee. Content Licensing operates as a business–to–business enterprise, and to be aware of its existence from the ABC Online home page, a general user must scroll to the very bottom of the page, where Content Licensing appears under a small monochrome "Explore the ABC" headline. After clicking through to content licensing and then to "catalogue," the user can read the following on the news pages:

> ABC News is recognized as Australia's leading source of authoritative information on the events of the day. A rich source of news and current affairs programs are produced with the credibility and independence from commercial interests that only a Public Broadcaster can offer. (ABC, 2010b)

News and current affairs programs are produced with the "credibility and independence from commercial interest that only a public service broadcaster can offer"—and then sold, business to business. Is there anything paradoxical in this arrangement? Should defenders of public service broadcasting ethics be worried about the ABC selling its news? Or, to take a different spin, is there anything to be learnt from the success of ABC Online News and its relationship with the Commercial Division? Is this a lesson in value in the online news environment? Perhaps the best way to address and complicate these questions is to historically contextualise the relationships between news and revenue generation at ABC Online.

History of ABC Online News

Although at first it seems counterintuitive that news should be so commercially exploited at the ABC, there are historical reasons for the connexions between news and commercial ventures. For one thing, when the ABC was searching for alternate ways of earning revenue, news (unlike drama, for example) had been protected from outsourcing, and so there were no complex copyright trails to be followed before it could be sold to commercial operators. Secondly, the quality of the news output of the ABC was (and remains) very high, especially in comparison with Australian commercial broadcasters' breadth and depth of stories. The networked and centralised domestic operations of commercial outlets produced very little rural and regional news, and commercial operators had far fewer overseas reporters than did the ABC. As Stuart Watt, Manager of ABC Online News told me in 2009:

> We can provide an Australian viewpoint on stories that are breaking internationally, because as I'm sure you would have noticed, more and more of that international news is homogenous because all the web agencies are taking their news from AFP or Reuters or something similar. . . . And it's written into the charter, . . . that that's a key reason for our existence, is to take the events that are happening around the world or around the country and present them in an Australian context. . . .
>
> We recognised very early on in our development that regional news was something that the ABC does that no one else can do in quite the same way. . . . we provide three or four stories from each of those regional stations each day. And it's a very important part of . . . what Mark Scott likes to call the "virtual town hall" that he wants ABC Online to be, for all of these places around the country. (Watt, 2009)

For reasons of depth and breadth of content, then, and for an Australian perspective, ABC News was preferable to that produced by other Australian media sources. Thirdly, ABC Online news had first mover advantage, because when web–based news services were being introduced in Australia in the early nineties, the ABC was the only truly multiplatform media operation in Australia, and it adapted quickly to online (Burns, 2000).

At first, ABC staff had to readjust to a text–based medium, utilising production documents such as television and radio scripts, but other advantages of the ABC overcame what proved to be a shortlived concern. Whereas newspapers and television networks, accustomed to a daily deadline, had to change their production methods to meet the 24 hour schedule of the web, the ABC had the experience of hourly radio bulletins to which it was able to add its televisual experience and its local and overseas reporters. It thus entered the web world with several advantages over many other media organisations. As I have argued elsewhere, the staff of ABC Online utilised these advantages to offset their precarious political and economic position in the early–mid nineties (Burns, 2000, 2008a).

Selling the News

The January 1994 implementation of Broadcast News Australia (BNA) in Brisbane (around 1000 km away from ABC headquarters in Sydney) combined a politically motivated intention to decentralize ABC operations with an urgent need to increase revenue at the ABC. The Federal Government was extremely hostile to the ABC, and in the context of severely reduced funds the ABC considered further commercial options (it already ran successful shops, and sold programs to other broadcasters). It initiated commercial projects including a (doomed) Pay TV project (Westfield, 2000) and BNA.

Dissatisfied clients of the news wire service Australian Associated Press (AAP) had convinced the ABC that, if one was available, they would buy an ABC news service in preference to the AAP service. BNA was formed to meet that need, offering news copy and audio services to commercial media, private enterprise, government departments and tertiary institutions. In response AAP improved its service to a level with which the ABC could not compete, and undercut BNA pricing. As a result, most clients remained with AAP, and as at January 1995, BNA had five customers in commercial radio and four customers for its wire service, as well as supplying read–to–air news bulletins to the Australian Radio Network, which marketed and distributed them to other clients. This was not enough to keep BNA afloat, and by April 1995 BNA was dissolved, leaving underemployed news staff in Brisbane. Half were employed on the Newsradio channel (a 24-hour radio news service that ran on the parliamentary channel whenever parliament was not sitting) and half were employed to produce an internal wire service of news stories for use by ABC staff.

Meanwhile, various program websites were being implemented by ABC program makers—mostly in Sydney but also in Adelaide—who used it as an extension of their programs (Burns, 2008a). As was the case with other PSBs, sites were initiated independent from management or policy by television or radio program makers (Burns, 2008a). The sites proved successful, and by mid 1995 the Multimedia Unit was formed in Sydney to co–ordinate the ABC web presence. In early 1996 the Brisbane internal wire news crew, who had been redeployed from BNA, began to co–ordinate political stories for the upcoming Federal Election. According to Stuart Watt:

> During that election campaign, Bob (then manager of the Brisbane internal wire service) pitched . . . that we should post the news stories online to see what hap-

> pened. And of course they went gangbusters. And from that point I think there was a realisation that news was going to be a valuable *commodity* online, and yeah, we started planning from that point for ABC News Online. . . . (Watt, 2009, emphasis added)

The success of the news service online during the dotcom boom encouraged Michael Kroger, an ABC Board member, to propose that ABC Online be sold to raise revenue for the ABC. In early 1999 he told current affairs program *The World Today* that he believed ABC Online could be worth $500 million (Fagan, Lyall, Lehmann, & Dore, 2001), and that 49% could be sold to raise revenue for the ABC. The suggestion was ludicrous, as was pointed out at the time by journalist Stewart Fist (1999), but Kroger's proposal highlighted a risk for ABC Online.

The Multimedia Unit

The ABC Charter was devised long before the advent of the World Wide Web, and so it did not protect ABC Online, even ABC Online news, in the ways that television and radio were protected (Burns, 2008b). To address that risk, and also to manage the commercial exploitation of online content in a manner that accorded with the spirit of the ABC charter, the Manager of the Multimedia Unit, Colin Griffith, created a new unit—the Business Development Unit—to co-ordinate licensing of content in line with ABC Codes of Practice. The Business Development Unit sold "off the shelf" content, in a trial, to buyers such as Yahoo!, Excite, and America Online. The first mention of such sales in the press was in November 1998 (Dasey, 1998).

Exclusivity vs Distribution

Like any change at the ABC, sales of news content did not occur without internal debate. Some argued that, unlike in broadcasting where exclusivity of content was important, online information had to be available everywhere to be successful. One staff member argued that the ABC needed:

> To be able to put our package out in branded syndication . . . so that if you're using Yahoo! Or msn, you're still using ABC. And if you require them to put a link back to the ABC site you're constantly using the net for its own purposes. . . . Putting nodes of your service all over the net—as widely as possible. (Bardwell, 2000)

Other staff members argued that the ethics and principles were the same, no matter what the platform, and that for this reason ABC news should not be licensed. This argument regarded any commercial relationship as dangerous to the ABC's independence. John Millard, an ABC staff member who had uncovered improper commercial dealings on three ABC television programs in the early nineties, said:

> The internet is merely a delivery mechanism. So when it comes to the important matters of independence, advertising, commercial influence or editorial integrity, it is the news service and the editorial content that are corruptible, not the delivery method. So all the proper editorial rules that apply to news on television apply as readily to news on the internet. (Millard, 2000)

What these two quotes demonstrate is the complexity of news–as–commodity; and ABC–as–brand; in an online environment. Of course Millard was correct that appropriate editorial structures and practices must be in place if the credibility of the ABC was to remain intact. But it was not as simple as just "applying" the older rules, because the context demanded that these rules be re–examined. As well as the risk of ABC Online not being protected in the same ways as broadcasting, there was also a risk that in an online world, ABC news may disappear amid a plethora of news services such as the BBC, CNN, and Australian commercial news sites that were yet to be fully imagined or implemented. The ABC would have to renegotiate its identity in an online environment, and news content was pivotal.

News as Commodity

Staff and management experimented with the ratios of and relationships between market and public, (at the same time as other ABC staff were negotiating the boundary between public sphere and government in dealing with a Minister's claims of bias (Jacka, 2005)), trying to forge an ABC identity that ethically addressed shifting economies of brands and communication. Could news be a commodity at the same time that it was a public service intended to construct informed citizens?

The ABC was one of only a few major Australian content sites at the time (others were AAP and Fairfax). As had been predicted by Peter Manning (then General Manager, Radio National) in 1995, some of the "fundamental values" of the ABC became highly saleable in the World Wide Web environment. Manning had listed such values of the ABC as its independence and associated accrued credibility, its aim for quality in the marketplace; its accuracy, relevance and comprehensiveness as a provider of information; its trustworthiness; and its commitment to education and educational values (Manning, 1995, p. 2). It was these saleable features that were utilised in trials of online content sales. The trials of content sales were largely free of public scrutiny until 2000, when details of a deal that was being negotiated with Telstra (a major telecommunications provider that was part government owned and part publicly owned), were leaked to the press.

The Telstra proposal was for a deal with the ABC worth $67.5 million over five years. It included non–exclusive content sales (with a proviso for discussions of advertising revenue after five years); exclusive co–production arrangements; exclusive repurposing of ABC content for Telstra wireless internet services; and shared research and development arrangements. I have argued elsewhere that what was at stake was the integrity—or wholeness and distinctness—of the ABC as an institution. Whereas the non–exclusive sale of content was something that the ABC had been doing for some time, and something that did not blur the boundaries of where the ABC began and ended, the breadth of the Telstra agreement and its exclusive elements were unfamiliar to those from a broadcast world, and caused understandable concern. What was at stake online for the ethical relation between the audience and the ABC was a shift from the ABC being an organisation with a goal of integrity to being one that merged, borderless, into the online landscape. It was not the content sales that were the threat, but the aspects of strategic alliance between Telstra and the ABC (Burns, 2000).

Telstra as Strategic Alliance

In the press there was a focus on the dangers of (non–exclusive) content sales and the possibility of advertising, though at a Senate Committee Hearing there were those who recognized that more was at stake. Quentin Dempster (an ABC broadcaster and at one time the elected staff member on the ABC Board, who had had previous experience with a failed PayTV venture) argued:

> Because it is a strategic alliance. . . . It involves the ABC in a fully commercial business plan with another operator and delivery system. This arrangement will cause us all sorts of trouble with Optus, and with any other player.
>
> . . . that provokes commercial rivalries. Everybody's attitude to the ABC changes because of that. . . . (Dempster, in Parliament of the Commonwealth of Australia, 2000, p. 24)

And the Democrats political party held similar views:

> The Australian Democrats share the mystification of many witnesses as to why such a disparate series of elements have been combined into an agreement whose central component, as the ABC explains, is the sale of online content. The Australian Democrats agree that the very wide scope of this proposed agreement potentially exacerbates an atmosphere in which editorial values could be put under pressure.

> (Democrats, in Parliament of the Commonwealth of Australia, 2000, s. 1.5, 1.103)

According to the official rhetoric of both the ABC and Telstra, negotiations were eventually cancelled for commercial rather than ethical reasons. And, contrary to public concern about advertising as the main issue of commercialisation of ABC Online, The Managing Director of the ABC at that time, Jonathon Shier, argued in 2001: "What I'm more interested in is the e–commerce possibilities, I don't see advertising being a major source of revenue" (as quoted in Kaye, 2001). Shier's plans for e–commerce (including an ABC credit card, and links from ABC sites to internet retail sites) were not implemented after his forced resignation in October 2000. The licensing of news content continued for each new platform as it arose, however. Stuart Watt, who has worked at ABC Online News almost since its inception, said of content licensing:

> Our web content has been licensed to third parties almost since we were first set up. . . . There's a separation, as there ought to be, between the content makers and the people who are doing the commercial deals. And that's handled by ABC Commercial. And . . . it's relatively simple. ABC Commercial sells packages of ABC news material. (Watt, 2009)

ABC as Brand

The licensing of content itself has never been the major problem for those who defend the ABC against commercial influence. The problem has more often been articulated as being the proximity of advertising to ABC news content, and the possible consequent lack of credibility, independence and integrity. Initially advertising was not allowed either on the ABC sites nor beside ABC content on third party sites. More recently, however, advertising was seen alongside ABC content on third party sites, though not on ABC sites. Mark Scott, Managing Director of the ABC since 2006, made this distinction on *Media Watch* (an ABC television program that exposes foibles in the Australian media industry):

> Most of the mobile phone operators carry ABC news content on their sites, along with advertising, and have done so for a number of years under licensing agreements with the ABC. There are no plans for m.abc.net.au sites to carry advertising. (Scott, n.d.)

There is a fine distinction made here between advertising beside ABC content on ABC sites, and ABC content on other sites. This way of protecting the ABC brand is unusual. Celia Lury has distinguished between the dangers of confusion and dilution of brands as the basis of legal challenges. In the commercial world, whereas once the issue was to ensure that a brand was not confused with other brands, a more recent concern is that one's brand will become too diluted by becoming too widely available across the marketplace (Lury, 2005, p. 94). In the case of the ABC, however, the risk of confusion with other brands—and *not* the fear of dilution—remains a major concern. In speaking about mobile platforms and the possibility of linking to non–ABC sites from ABC mobile content, Mark Scott said:

> part of the design challenge is to ensure that it is clear to users that they are leaving the www.abc.net.au site and going to a commercial site. This design work is currently under way. (Scott, n.d.)

The ABC has always operated within a media system that included commercial media; its charter has always acknowledged that it must take account of that commercial element; and the ABC has always had commercial dealings of various kinds. Even since the failed Telstra deal, the ABC has had commercial dealings with any number of suppliers, program makers, and commercial web services, for example. Nor is the idea of linking to other sites a new practice for ABC Online. In the very very early days of ABC Online there was a section called "Explore your Interests" which allowed users to click through to all sorts of non—ABC content, some of it commercial.

Until the nineteen nineties, however, news programming was exempt from commercial dealings, having been identified as core programming and only to be funded through arms' length government appropriation. But the digital environment constructed a different economy for the distribution of news, if only through its instantaneity and fragmentation of audiences. As was noted above, more and more commercial "distributors"—mobile phone services, email providers, and so on—required quality news content to "anchor" their users. And the sale of ABC content—content that would be produced anyway for ABC users—proceeds, its managers claim, without endangering editorial independence, because the news is sold "off–the–shelf" from what is already produced under editorial guidelines, and because the licensees follow ABC rules (they cannot delete anything from the feeds, and they must link back to the ABC site, for example). Corruption of the quality of the news would kill the goose that laid the golden egg.

It is also worth noting that the proportion of ABC revenue earned from licensing of content is minimal, not providing much of an incentive for manipulation of news stories. Geographical separation of news editorial from the content licensing division may provide further protection. Stuart Watt is convinced that there is no pressure from the Commercial Division on the news area, partly because

> the aim was to set it up at arms' length, and that's how it's turned out. Maybe geography's got something to do with that. Maybe the fact that we've been up in Brisbane and there's no commercial arm in Brisbane? (Watt, 2009)

Watt also told me:

> I don't even think about the commercial aspect of it. I never do. It becomes a pain when things break and stuff's not being delivered to clients, but that's just process. (Watt, 2009)

Watt recognises that the commercial history of ABC Online news may have even had a positive impact on the ways that the ABC imagined itself in the web environment, particularly in the newer social networking sites:

> There was a view when we first went down the commercialisation road that you could either put sandbags up around your content and keep it all within your own boundaries, or you could not be precious about that and let it go out to a whole lot of different places, so that a whole lot of different people who might not even know you had a website get the opportunity to see your stories. So from that perspective, it's been a very great benefit. . . . It's very evident to us that whenever our stories get picked up[on social media websites] the hits go up markedly. And it's sort of a syndication by the audience, rather than for any commercial reason. (Watt, 2009)

There is very little disagreement on what constitutes the value of ABC news, but perhaps Miller's more abstract point that "the definition of value varies according to the context of the transaction" is worth noting in the context of changed value in an online rather than broadcast environment (Miller, 2000, p. 78). The qualities listed by Peter Manning in 1995 and reiterated above remain as components of what most commentators consider as the value of ABC news. However the issue online is whether exclusivity or dispersal of ABC News makes it more valuable. What is also at stake, perhaps, is whether this value should be characterised as a "brand"—a word that was once more commonly used by and for those in the market economy than in the public sphere or government. Watt—who is quoted above characterising online news as a commodity—says in this regard:

> Being the ABC, the most important thing is the brand. Well, it's the most important thing I'm sure to any organisation but the brand is so . . . the number one thing we've got going for us is that people trust us. So that is paramount, protecting that. (Watt, 2009)

For Watt, protecting the ABC brand is protecting the trust that people have for the institution. And, as Lury has noted, this was the historical intention of the brand name—to create trust in the consumer as a guarantor of the quality of particular products (Lury, 2005, p. 93). But Lury argues that in a world that "comes into existence as media"

> increasingly the brand name is not the mark of an originary relationship between producer and products but is rather the mark of the organisation of a set of relations between products in time. (Lury, 2005, p. 94)

Rethinking the Social Imaginary

The ABC accepts co-productions, outsources programming, sells toy bananas and classical music CDs, and it licenses content to third parties online. It produces radio, television and online content, and it buys such content from other sources. It can most certainly be understood better as a set of relations between products in time rather than as an origin or author, or even (only) a provider of services.

There are undoubtedly further debates to be had about the position of the ABC in the social imaginary. If, as Taylor asserts, the social imaginary is not a set of ideas but "rather, it is what enables, through making sense of, the practices of a society," the history of the intersections of ABC online news and commercial ventures might allow us to reconsider how we locate public service broadcasting news on the web more generally. Should we understand PSBs on the web as occupying a space in the social imaginary somewhere between the public sphere and government, between the market economy and the public sphere, or as a fluid and shifting presence across all three?

Given that online, and perhaps more broadly, publics are formed in much more complex ways than the distinctions market economy/government/public sphere will allow, it is time to reconsider the social imaginary.

References

ABC. (2010a). About Content Licensing. Retrieved May 15, 2010, from http://www.abccontentsales.com.au/contentlicensing

ABC. (2010b). News Bulletins. Retrieved May 25, 2010, from http://www.abc.net.au/abccontentsales/s1102529.htm

Burns, M. (2000). ABC Online: A Prehistory. *Media International Australia Incorporating Culture and Policy*, *97*, 92–104.

Burns, M. (2008a). Public Service Broadcasting Meets the Internet at the Australian Broadcasting Corporation (1995–2000). *Continuum*, *22*(6), 867–881.

Burns, M. (2008b). Remembering Public Service Broadcasting: Liberty and Security in ABC Online Interactive Sites. *Television and New Media*, *9*, 392–406.

Dasey, D. (1998, November 15). ABC's News for No Net Profit. *Sun Herald*, p. 9.
Fagan, D., Lyall, K., Lehmann, J., & Dore, C. (2001, February 20). Deal that Slipped the Net. *The Australian*, p. 13.
Fist, S. (1999, February 23). Cashing Up on Credibility. *The Australian*, p. 60.
Jacka, E. (2005). The Elephant Trap: Bias, Balance and Government–ABC Relations during the Second Gulf War. *Southern Review, 37*(3), 8–28.
Jones, P. K. & Pusey, M. (2010). "Political Communication and 'Media System'": The Australian Canary. *Media Culture & Society, 32*(3), 451–471.
Kaye, B. (2001, February 15). Will This Cyberspace Be Kept Ad-free? *ComputerWorld.*
Lury, C. (2005). Contemplating a Self-Portrait as a Pharmacist: A Trade Mark Style of Doing Art and Science. *Theory, Culture and Society, 22*(1), 93–100.
Manning, P. (1995, September 20). ABC Staff Memo.
Millard, J. (2000, February 8). The ABC's Reputation Put at Risk. *The Sydney Morning Herald*, p. 15.
Miller, D. (2000). The Birth of Value. In P. Jackson, M. Lowe, D. Miller, & F. Mort (Eds.), *Commercial Cultures: Economies Practices, Spaces* (pp. 77–84). Oxford.: Berg.
Parliament of the Commonwealth of Australia (2000). Senate Environment, Communications, Information Technology and the Arts References Committee Inquiry into ABC On-line (Interim Report).
Scott. M. (n.d.). Media Watch transcript. Retrieved May 3, 2010, from http://www.abc.net.au/mediawatch/transcripts/0831_carroll.pdf
Tiffen, R. & Gittins, R. (2004). *How Australia Compares.* Cambridge, UK: Cambridge University Press.
Taylor, C. (2002). Modern Social Imaginaries. *Public Culture, 14*(1), 91–124.
Westfield, M. (2000). *The Gatekeepers: The Global Media Battle to Control Australia's Pay TV.* Sydney: Pluto Press in Association with Comerford and Miller.

Interviews

Bardwell, H. (2000, June 14). Interview with Maureen Burns.
Watt, S. (2009). Interview with Maureen Burns.

5 *RTE Online*

Public Objectives and Commercial Imperatives

Kenneth Murphy

Introduction

In 1996 RTE, Ireland's public service radio and television broadcaster, began publishing its web site, RTE.ie. RTE.ie was, by 2010, the most viewed Irish–produced web site in the Irish Republic, and also featured in global rankings (Alexa.com). RTE's online presence has undergone two significant periods of development. From 1996 to 1998 the site existed mainly as a promotional and informational resource for RTE and RTE's programmes. From 1998 to 2007 it developed its web presence as an online news and multimedia resource and an additional arm of programme distribution. RTE is currently in the process of attempting to balance its adaptation to user generated content, social networks and mobile communications whilst evaluating strategic options for future dissemination of broadcast content in an evolving digital context.

The present chapter will provide an overview of the two earlier periods in the development of RTE.ie. It will give an account of the political, economic and institutional factors that have helped shape the form and content of its online service in the period from 1996–2007. It will argue that the institutional under–resourcing of the online division, the initial lack of public policy support for RTE as an online multimedia entity, the regulatory emphasis on increasing RTE's indigenous television and radio broadcast output and pressure to commercialise have shaped RTE's online development. These contexts have affected the design and content of RTE's website privileging both remediation and redistribution of broadcast content as a necessary strategic dynamic. The chapter will thus evaluate how the contexts of RTE.ie's development have helped shape its communicative profile and how its online services mediate the wider tension between RTE's public service objectives and its commercial imperatives.

RTE in the Irish Mediascape

Ireland's media landscape is shaped by multiple factors key amongst which is the relative small size of the Irish state (current population 4.2 million), its existence within the highly competitive Anglo-American media sphere and Ireland's particular twentieth-century journey from peripheral postcolonialism to incorporation into the global neoliberal economic system. RTE has been the pivotal political, social and cultural institution within the media landscape of the small state. It has attracted more public and commercial funding than any cultural institution within the state and has the most pervasive output and reach of any singular media or cultural institution within the state (Corcoran, 2004).

Funded by a combination of license fee and commercial revenue RTE has, for the majority of its existence, had to juggle public service and commercial imperatives relative to its low income base, relatively high operational costs and hyper competitive contexts. Whereas the institution retained monopoly status in broadcasting until commercial radio and television broadcasting were introduced in 1988, RTE has always had to compete with the broadcasting services available from the UK (first off air, then via cable, then via satellite) and, because of its dependence on commercial revenue, with the indigenous media industries.

RTE as Public Broadcaster

The key public policy objective (Nissen, 2006) which has ensured political support for RTE's institutional development and survival is its role in contributing to the social, political and cultural cohesion of the nation-state. This represents a central historical and politico–ideological fault line in relation to the struggle over the public purposes of RTE as a public broadcaster (Horgan, 2001). The contract with the nation-state, combined with the license fee/advertising revenue that enables it, has allowed RTE to pursue a largely democratic agenda of universal availability and accessibility in relation to its services ensuring its pivotal position within the political and cultural public sphere. However, the national contract and commercial imperative also generate systemic tension in relation to the public objectives of generating a distinctive public sphere in support of democratic engagement and recognising and representing varied political, social and cultural publics. This is a generic tension experienced by semi–commercial public broadcasters elsewhere (Steemers, 2001). The current chapter will explore the degree to which RTE's historical development of its online multimedia web presence mediates this tension and to what extent public purposes and/or commercialism have been extended via technological developments. First however, the chapter will consider the political, economic, and institutional dynamics that have shaped RTE's online media development.

The Political, Economic and Institutional Evolution of RTE.ie

Historically the political and institutional consideration of new media technology in Ireland has been shaped by its proximity to the UK. Such was the case for both Radio and Television, and it was developments in the UK that prompted RTE's consideration of an online strategy in the early 1990s. In 1994 the UK Department of National Heritage published a white paper on the "Future of the BBC." It emphasised the centrality of the BBC to the broadcasting sector but also the necessity for the institution to adjust to changed technological circumstances (Department of National Heritage, 1994). According to Corcoran (2004), these developments served to sharpen RTE's own consideration of the diffusion of the internet.

In 1994 RTE entered discussions with ICL, a subsidiary of Fujitsu, to discuss the development of a multimedia web site. These considerations were to become sidelined against the background of more pressing policy issues and resource requirements for the broadcaster. Instead, an employee based in RTE's teletext department was required to establish and maintain a web site for RTE. At this point, various RTE producers had developed complementary websites that were accessible as standalone promotional tools for existing radio and television programs. The launch of RTE.ie in 1996 gave the broadcaster a singular portal for these disparate sites. RTE.ie became a meta site for the earlier web pages and also established itself as an online news provider and publicity channel for the institution and its programs.

RTE.ie was initially staffed by a single webmaster. It took its news from the available tele–text site and gradually began offering streamed programs for post broadcast listening. According to Kerr, an important strategic dimension of its early development was the provision of access to news and broadcast based content that was of appeal to the Irish Diaspora (Kerr, 2000). This strategy was partly encouraged by the fact that 70–80% of its 125,000 hits a day originated from outside Ireland. The strategy was also informed by the slow diffusion of internet access in Ireland. By 1996, only 5% of households in Ireland had access (Morash, 2009).

Government policy towards digital broadcasting was first mooted when a left of centre coalition government began to grapple with the potential implications of technological change through first a 1995 Green Paper and later a 1997 White Paper on broadcasting (Department of Arts, Culture and Gaeltacht, 1994, 1997). These policy papers did not directly deal with the internet and the web and, like the broadcasting community itself, were fixed on traditional television production and reception technologies as the site for the potential digital transformation of broadcasting. However, the deterritorialised flows of media via digital telecommunications were the palpable context discernible in both documents.

In 1997 the government was replaced by a right of centre coalition, and the absence in government and state policy towards RTE's adaptation to the internet and the burgeoning web continued. The new coalition government's policy was more distinctively neo–liberal. The emerging phenomenon of technological convergence was interpreted as enabling commodified multimedia markets for internationally traded business and financial software services resting on privatised network development. The digital multimedia future was to be market led (Department of Public Enterprise, 1997).

RTE's limited allocation of institutional resources to the development of its online operations reflected the policy vacuum. The "Interactive" division was a secondary operational division with miniscule budget and staffing. At an institutional level RTE was struggling with a combination of rising costs, increased competition for audiences, advertising and content and systemic underfunding from the license fee. RTE management's perception of the importance of the internet was rapidly changing as both national and international demand drove its diffusion but the sheer weight of its multiple but underfunded public policy duties prevented significant investment.

In the late 1990s the wider European Union policy debates on convergence became an important reference point for RTE's understanding of both the internet and multimedia in the overall process of digitalisation and convergence. The European Union level discussion and consultation on policy towards convergence provided an insight into the emerging technological, regulatory and market logics underpinning the development of digital media. In its response to the European level consultation the Green paper on Convergence, RTE set out its position as follows:

> RTE's response to this Green Paper rests on three essential grounds. The first is that claims of community and citizenship must take precedence over those of mar-

kets and consumerism. The second is that a fundamental distinction exists between convergence of technology and convergence of values, with the corollary that the former does not necessarily entail the latter. The third is that considerations of the public interest in broadcasting require it to be recognised in and advanced by regulatory instruments. (RTE, 1997)

The RTE submission argued that convergence in distribution systems meant that regulatory change at the level of technological distribution could potentially become standardised across the EU. It argued that the cultural form of broadcasting still entailed "medium specific" regulation within particular political, economic and normative dynamics. RTE's strategy was significantly shaped by the evolving position being taken by the European Broadcasting Union (European Broadcasting Union, 1998). RTE's policy statements were also informed by a broader effort to compete with the market–led policy agenda circulating in the national public sphere. However, there was an evident gap between RTE's rhetorical commitment to the public purposes of digital technologies and its institutional ability to invest in their development.

Organisational Development

In 1998 RTE.ie appointed a journalist to staff the RTE News Online section of the website. This innovation put RTE ahead of domestic competition from the print based Irish Times Group and Independent News and Media in terms of the provision of constant news updates written primarily for the web. The change of emphasis indicated a switch in strategic direction; as the internet diffused in Ireland more focus was placed on the domestic users of RTE.ie. More of RTE's broadcast content was given an online dimension and much closer co–operation was encouraged between broadcasting departments and RTE.ie (RTE, 1998). In 1999 the staff was increased to three people including a technical operator alongside the journalist and designer (Kerr, 2000).

These staffing developments within the online department balanced out content production, design and technology staff. Debates within the EU and the EBU had contributed to RTE's understanding of the internet as an additional distribution platform and the convergence of user technologies as the emerging contexts for audience interaction with its content. Multimedia now referred to the variable repackaging of RTE's content distributed across multiple media technologies. At a strategic level broadcast content formed the core of RTE's online content with a gradual development of cross platform and cross media distribution of those broadcast forms. In a 1998 strategic report generated by an internal review group RTE outlined its then strategic concerns in relation to development of online services:

> It is the policy of RTE to originate digital services of indigenous programming on radio, television and in the new interactive and on-line media, and to distribute these services as a public good for the people of Ireland. (RTE, 1998)

This internally circulated document illustrated RTE's recognition that its web operations could potentially extend its public services to its domestic audiences. However, these strategic intentions were not necessarily matched by institutional support.

As a secondary division, RTE Interactive was subsumed within RTE Commercial Enterprises in 1999. The restructuring brought additional resources to the online division. The head of News online now had access to all of the content developed by the broadcast newsroom. Those working within the broadcast newsrooms were expected to file their content for online delivery as well as their dedicated platforms of radio and television (Trench & Quinn, 2003). The repurposing of broadcast content available online was significantly increased. This involved additional capital investment and an ongoing investment in staff.

RTE's online development continued to go unrecognised in government policy. The 2001 Broadcasting Act, which legislated for the structural development of Digital Terrestrial Television, did not include any consideration of RTE's online services. Policy was focussed on the development of digital television via competition between the traditional television delivery platforms as opposed to the distribution of broadcast media across divergent platforms. Within its own terms of reference the 2001 Broadcasting Act excluded internet delivery from the definition of RTE's broadcasting services and omitted it from RTE's objectives. Implicitly, under European State Aid policy, the Act prohibited any cross subsidisation of the online service via the license fee.

Restructuring Public Service Communication

Following the 2001 Broadcasting Act, the government embarked on a wide-ranging review of public broadcasting. The ostensible rationale for the forum on broadcasting was the fact that RTE was operating at a loss and had requested but not received a significant increase in the license fee. However, the wider causes related to the Europe-wide need to reposition public service broadcasting within an increasingly market based broadcasting environment. RTE's financial difficulties were caused by internal factors such as its operating structure, but also by competition for revenue, audiences and content coming from the commercial media sector. The review involved a publicly open Forum on Broadcasting convened in 2001 and a less public, in depth, departmental review. At the departmental level a consultant's review of RTE estimated that RTE's online operations were running at a loss of 1.5 million per year ("Logical Strategy," 2002). The report presented RTE with the option of making its online operation more commercially aggressive or closing it down. RTE in turn defended the strategic purposes of its online development:

> Digital technology will change the way of operating with new production models being developed; RTE will review the services it provides for its audiences and identify new areas for development mindful of Government objectives of facilitating cultural expression and building social solidarity. (RTE, 2002)

One of the key outcomes of the government review was organisational restructuring and the development of integrated business divisions (IBDs) within RTE. The IBDs had the objective of focussing RTE's resources on cost control and increased home produced content in the Radio and Television schedules. The organisational restructuring was promised in return for a license fee increase that would be index linked to inflation, subject to yearly review. The restructuring had the effect of placing RTE on a firmer financial footing but of positioning RTE's online operations within a commercially driven IBD, RTE Publishing.

Whereas RTE.ie was not at this time funded by the license fee, neither had the institution applied overt commercial principles to the web division, seeing it principally as a strategically important service funded by commercial publishing activities. However with the development of the IBDs, RTE was compelled to fully exploit all commercial activities with the results that the online division was encouraged to be more attuned to market demand. According to its own public relations of 2003, RTE publishing would be "more market focussed, sell existing services more effectively and open up new revenue streams" (RTE 2003). Thus the institutional positioning and the public articulation of the purposes of RTE's website were increasingly in tension with each other. The following year a Price Waterhouse Coopers review of RTE reported that the institution was successfully applying more commercial principles to its online operation (Price Waterhouse Coopers [PWC], 2004). These commercial strategies included drawing increased revenue from banner advertising and sponsorship of site/content, opening more commercial sites (property, motors, travel, food and jobs) to increase the site's overall advertising/sponsorship turnover, syndicating content to third party multinational telecommunication companies pursuing localisation strategies and targeting lucrative market segments.

At a governmental level, RTE's online services were soon to gain recognition as a public duty of the broadcaster. The acknowledgement of RTE's multimedia activities was now contextualised by an admission by state agencies of the need for a public policy attention to "digital content development in Ireland" (Forfas, 2002). The embrace of market forces and export–led foreign direct investment was no longer the dominant policy paradigm in relation to digital development. A Public Broadcasting Charter, generated for RTE in 2004, required RTE to "develop content which can be available to audiences across all delivery platforms" and to "maintain and develop the RTE website to the highest standard" (Department of Marine and Natural Resources, 2004). However, RTE was also compelled to direct the majority of its resources towards increasing indigenous broadcast output.

RTE had thus, via the 2004 Charter, been given tentative support for its online services and RTE was now free to articulate its use of the internet as a strategically important transmission platform, even as it lacked actual legislative support to fund it from the license fee as a public service (RTE, 2005).

The opportunity to give the online dimension a legislative and financial footing soon presented itself. The government had come under further pressure from the European Competition directorate to define public service broadcasting and its modes of funding. The result was the development of a new broadcasting bill in 2006 which sought to put the structures in place to meet the commission's requirements for the rationalisation of public broadcasting within state aid legislation. Within the planned new broadcasting legislation, RTE's online activities were designated as one of the objectives of the public service broadcaster (PSB). RTE's retransmission of free to air content via varied electronic networks was considered in keeping with its public service remit. The changed legislative situation (enacted in 2009) also presented RTE with the necessity of conceiving of its online operations as a public service activity.

RTE.ie: Online Content

When RTE.ie was launched in 1996, the centrepiece of the occasion was a live webcast of the Late Late show. The Late Late Show is a flagship RTE television chat–show that has been on air since 1962, making it the longest running same channel television chat–show in the world. It is a core element of RTE's broadcasting identity as it has often provided the deliberative resources for many a national conversation (Gibbons, 1996). The choice of the Late Late Show was symbolic in so far as it represented RTE's key strategic purpose of utilising the online presence for disseminating RTE's broadcast programming. Strategically, RTE.ie, from its very inception, sought to enable anytime anywhere distribution and enhance remediated public service broadcast content for flexible access.

When RTE.ie was launched its site sections were Television, Radio, News, Sport, About RTE, Products, RTE Overseas, 2FM, Audio, Gaeltext and Library. The first version of the site was text heavy and offered 600 pages of news, sport and information about the institution and its programmes. Select radio programmes from Radio One and Radio Na Gaeltachta could also be downloaded and played back as Real Audio files.

On the occasion of the launch RTE committed to develop the multimedia resources on the site as the requisite broadband capacity became available. In 1998 the RTE News site received more prominence as its staffing increased and the other main sub–sites were rationalised to Television, Radio, Music and About RTE. Access to streamed content, both live and archived, was significantly increased.

In 1999, 2000 and 2001, respectively, Sports, Entertainment and Business sections were added to the online site, adding to the News, Television and Radio sections. The multimedia element still relied mainly on the remediation of content from broadcasting but additional pages and sites built around "events of national importance" were also developing as value added dimensions of the site. These projects ranged from the first European live webcast of a mass service from Glenstal Abbey (1997) to a dedicated site celebrating 75 years of radio in Ireland (2001). The latter made good use of RTE's extensive archive for its multimedia content.

In 2006 RTE.ie added another first for its online site by webcasting a provincial GAA football final continuing RTE's history of supporting and pioneering the distinctly Irish sporting code as part of its remit to support and maintain the culture of Ireland. RTE radio coverage of GAA sporting events had been an important factor in the nationalisation of the association and its sport and the international reach of the website sought to continue this trajectory. Another high-profile commemorative site was developed in 2006, the occasion of the 60th anniversary of the 1916 rising. The site thus reflected existing national cultural events and re–enforced the institution's role in promoting social, cultural and political cohesion.

RTE developed its website in line with both the technological developments and the evolving formal properties of online media. However, the remediation and re–distribution of broadcast content continued to be the key strategic dynamic driving the design and content of the online site. Given the institutional under–resourcing of the online division, the initial lack of policy support for RTE as an online multimedia entity and the regulatory emphasis on increasing RTE's indigenous television and radio broadcast output, the strategy had strong material emphases. The content of RTE.ie thus served as an extension of what RTE already did as a PSB. RTE.ie did, however, also enhance the broadcaster's traditional offerings in innovative ways such as the development of site sections for special anniversaries which included on–demand archive content, the addition of blogs in the online coverage of elections, and the generation of online polls related to events of general public interest.

As the internet and the various applications built on top of the internet have developed so too has RTE adapted them to extend its broadcast reach. Part of the strategy of RTE Publishing has been to increase distribution of RTE content across all platforms, including mobile (PDA, SMS and WAP), social networking and UGC sites such as YouTube. From 2005 podcasts were available for key home–produced radio content. In 2007 RTE.ie introduced live streaming of the main television news and current affairs programs. The following year News Now was introduced as an additional online service, offering access to all RTE's live television broadcast news bulletins as a distinct online television channel. These were later joined by a web–only channel which simulcast selected live output from the two main RTE television channels. The following year RTE introduced its catch up service RTE i–player allowing online access to select material produced, commissioned and acquired by the station.

The commercial imperatives of RTE's online division have been made manifest in both its content (websites) and its strategies of distribution (reach). The most notable instances of this in terms of content have been the development of site sections on RTE.ie referred to as "commercially oriented output" such as Property, Motors, Travel, Food and Jobs which were specifically designed to tailor audiences for targeted advertising and sponsorship (PWC, 2004). The sites were launched with commercial partners and drew heavily on links to RTE's more commercial lifestyle television programming. For example the "Property" website launched in 2006 was partnered by a commercial property and homes portal (Daft.ie) and an independent mortgage advisory firm (EZhome). The site also contained many links and banners for both the web sites and content of RTE's television property programmes such as Househunters, Showhouse and Holiday Home Detectives. This uncritical self–commercialisation in the contexts of a property bubble demonstrated the extent to which RTE.ie could digress from the proclaimed public philosophy of its web strategy.

An additional core strategy of RTE publishing has been the attainment of increased "audience reach" for RTE content across the vastly evolving world of digital media distribution and consumption, but primarily through its web site. In its multimedia strategy RTE Publishing have pursued "reach" as opposed to boosting "average revenue per user," the strategy favoured by commercial broadcasters. For RTE, reach is a double–edged sword. By building audiences, potential revenue streams from advertising and sponsorship would follow. However, the advertising dynamic underpinning the distribution of content has also held the potential to skew reach towards particular market segments. For RTE there is a thin line between increasing reach in order to deliver RTE's public service content to non broadcast audiences and following a commercial strategy to reach the lucrative youth market much coveted by advertisers. The Alexa web information site illustrates that in the demographics for RTE's online audiences, relative to the general internet population, the 25–44 old age group are over represented (63% of all users) whereas all other age groups are under–represented (Alexa.com). Likewise individuals with tertiary education are over represented whereas those without are under–represented relative to the general internet population. Whereas online services increase the broadcaster's reach, the market dynamics underpinning the attainment of reach have been highly commercial in character.

RTE can legitimately utilise digital technologies to increase its reach across the general population and those hard–to–reach target groups that may consist of smaller audiences underserved by its generalist offerings (Wiio, 2004). As is the case with the public value tests for the BBC, audience reach will likely become a key measure of RTE's success in ensuring universal availability and equity. However, it has yet to distinguish these strategic purposes of public service media "reach" from commercial "reach."

Conclusion: Public Service Futures

The absence of state support for indigenous multimedia development in the 1990s, a ten-year vacuum in broadcast sector policy towards the internet and the web, and the paucity of institutional investment in online development have all shaped the character and communicative profile of RTE.ie. On one level government policy has pushed RTE's web development towards a commercial imperative and a concern for maximising revenues. On another level, the communicative profile of RTE.ie, for all of the political, economic and institutional reasons recounted above, have developed in a way which can be complementary to the website's public purposes. The remediation of broadcast content for online distribution is conducive to the public objective of sustaining culture and democratic involvement. As suggested by Moe, the dissemination function of public broadcasters is as important to democratic communication as is the oft–fetishised emphasis on networked dialogue. Dissemination of public knowledge remains a key public service commitment to sustaining the public sphere and thus democracy, even in a digital context (Moe, 2008). RTE's emphasis of the dissemination function online is thus compatible with its public objectives. The emphasis on a broadcast dynamic within the appropriation of multimedia communication may be a justifiable "medium specific" argument for the extension of PSBs into public service digital multimedia. A move away from broadcast–based multimedia would undermine the particular medium based rationale for public media presence online.

In Ireland the present policy conjuncture has raised the question as to what RTE online should do differently now that it is covered by the public service remit. At many levels what RTE.ie already does is public service. The broadcast component of communication should always be primary, despite the temptation to move into the domain of commercial networked communication media such as social networking sites. The commercial aspects of RTE Publishing's stewardship of the broadcaster's online strategy, such as commercial content development and the pursuit of lucrative demographics are questionable. Arguably, this issue could easily be addressed by repositioning the online division within one of RTE's media divisions, which tend to be driven by public service cultures of production. However the larger question of how public objectives can be extended online is an institutional, political and regulatory question as opposed to a technological one. This question involves wider consideration of how RTE's primary broadcast output can address the democratic and socio–cultural objectives of public broadcasting through distinctive content and the recognition of varied political, social and cultural publics. Only then can those public objectives be technologically extended.

References

Corcoran, F. (2004). *RTE and the Globalisation of Irish Television.* Bristol, UK: Intellect.

Department of Arts, Culture and Gaeltacht. (1994). *Active or Passive: The Green Paper on Broadcasting in Ireland.* Dublin: DACG.

Department of Arts, Culture and Gaeltacht. (1997). *Clear Focus, the Governments Proposals for Broadcasting Legislation.* Dublin: DACG.

Department of Marine and Natural Resources. (2004). *Public Service Broadcasting Charter.* Dublin: DCMNR.

Department of National Heritage. (1994). *The Future of the BBC: Serving the Nation, Competing World–Wide.* London: DNH.

Department of Public Enterprise. (1997). *Response to the European Commission's Green Paper on the Convergence of the Telecommunications, Media and Information Technology Sectors, and the Implications for Regulation.* Dublin: DPE.

European Broadcasting Union. (1998). *EBU Reply to the Convergence Green Paper.* Geneva: EBU.

Forfas. (2002). *A Strategy for the Digital Content Industry in Ireland.* Dublin: Forfas.

Gibbons, L. (1996). *Transformations in Irish Culture.* Cork, Ireland: Cork University Press.

Horgan, J. (2001). *Irish Media: A Critical History, since 1922.* London: Routledge.

Kerr, A. (2000). Media Diversity and Cultural Identity. *New Media & Society, 2*(3), 286–312.

Logical Strategy and KPMG Corporate Finance. (2002). *Report to the RTE Authority: A Strategic Framework for RTE.* Dublin: KPMG.

Moe, H. (2008). Dissemination and Dialogue in the Public Sphere; a Case for the BBC Online. *Media, Culture & Society, 30*(3), 319–336.

Morash, C. (2010). *History of the Media in Ireland.* Cambridge, UK: Cambridge University Press.

Nissen, C. (2006). *Public Service Media in the Information Society.* Strasbourg, France: Council of Europe.

Price Waterhouse Coopers. (2004). *RTE Licence Fee Adjustment Review for the Department of Communciations, Marine and Natural Resources.* Dublin: PWC.

RTE. (1997). *RTE Response to the Europeans Commission's Green Paper on Convergence.* Dublin: RTE.

RTE. (1998). *Review of RTE's Structures and Operations.* Dublin: RTE.

RTE. (2002). *RTE Submission to the Forum on Broadcasting.* Dublin: RTE.

RTE. (2003). *RTE Announces Executive Director of RTE Publishing* [Press Release]. Dublin: RTE.

RTE. (2005). *Digital Television and Radio Services.* Dublin: RTE.

Steemers, J. (2001). In Search of a Third Way: Balancing Public Purpose and Commerce in German and British Public Broadcasting. *Canadian Journal of Communication, 26*(1), 69–87.

Trench, B., & Quinn, G. (2003). Online News and Changing Models of Journalism. *Irish Communications Review, 9.*

Wiio, J. (2004). *From the Information Society to a Knowledge Value Society: Public Service Digital Television as a Player in the Information Society of the Future.* Paper presented at the Ripe@2004 conference, Copenhagen, Denmark.

6 *Between Public Service and Commercial Venture*

The Norwegian Broadcasting Corporation on the Web 1994–2000

Hallvard Moe

Introduction

This chapter explores the tensions between public and commercial funding in the early development of web activities at the Norwegian Broadcasting Corporation (NRK). Norway is a Scandinavian democratic nation-state with almost 5 million inhabitants. The NRK was established in 1933, and enjoyed a monopoly on radio and later television until the early 1980s, when the NRK met competition from local radio and internationally satellite–distributed television. For the NRK, a line of expansions and favourable re–regulations marked the 1990s. Enjoying strong and steady political support as a non–commercial alternative, the public broadcaster transformed into a state–owned limited company, introduced a third radio channel and a second television channel, and pursued a leading role in the switchover to digital television and radio—all blessed by a broad political consensus. When the NRK moved into the online world from the mid–1990s, it argued for the public service value of internet activities. However, late in 2000, the NRK introduced commercial banner advertisements on its publicly funded website. Although this change at NRK was atypical of public service broadcasters (PSBs) internationally, the practice was to continue for a decade. It became a focal point for commercial competitors' attacks on the NRK, and finally was abandoned in 2010. How did advertisement funding of the web service emerge as a viable alternative for the public institution in the period before the turn of the millennium? And how did the NRK manoeuvre to secure the liberal political framework it needed?

In what follows, I first examine the development of the NRK's web presence up until the introduction of advertisements. I then scrutinize the process behind the decision to explore the specific tensions between public and commercial in this particular case. The discussion is geared at the political and institutional level, and is based on archival research supported by contemporary press clippings.

From Enthusiastic Experimentation to Uniformed Consistency

In November 1994, the NRK reported that the institution had entered the "network age" without even knowing (NRK, 1994, p. 4). Some eager listeners (who happened to be informatics students) of youth radio channel P3's morning show *IRMA 1000* had created a website with information about the program and some images. The group had even digitalized and uploaded program content as sound files. Even though the initiative raised some obvious copyright issues, the NRK did not take action (NRK, 1994, p. 4). At this point, the institution had no internet activities of its own.

By late 1994, Tor Fuglevik, as Head of the Radio Division, asked his employee Rolf Brandrud to write a memo on the potential of the internet. Presented in January 1995, the memo recommended further exploration of the new technologies. Brandrud also suggested a new radio program about new media. Aired for the first time in late February, *Radionettet* was complemented by a website with streaming audio and program information. *Radionettet* was hosted by a University College because the NRK did not have the technical means themselves (Sommerseth, 1999, p. 38 f.). In December 1994, the editorial staff of Saturday prime time television show *Rondo* contacted a commercial internet service provider and set up a website where users could share links, request guests for the show and send questions to the host. The website ran in parallel with the television program (Oslonett, 2001).

These autonomous initiatives illustrate the start of the NRK's ventures on the internet. Throughout 1995, the activities were characterized by creative exploration. Groups of enthusiasts among the staff tried out the novel world of networked computing. Describing the potential value for the NRK, these instigators stressed core public service ideas: The NRK should aim to become the centre of "the big Norwegian Enlightenment database," and it was "in keeping with the best traditions of the NRK to take the lead in developing the new medium" (Brandrud in NRK, 1995, p. 6). It was also claimed that a proactive NRK approach could minimize what became known as the digital divide, and be in line with the institution's enlightenment ideals (Sommerseth, 1999, p. 38).

Together with Tom W. Ottmar, who worked in the NRK communication department, Brandrud wrote a comprehensive report on the NRK's online strategy during 1995 (Brandrud & Ottmar, 1995). The 250–page document laid out current developments and sketched scenarios for the NRK. Brandrud and Ottmar pointed to several ways in which the internet could help renew the NRK's public service mission. The NRK should aim to prevent new class divisions, contribute to make the Norwegian cultural tradition available online, and explore the democratic potential of interactive media (Brandrud & Ottmar, 1995, p. 125). Before Christmas 1995, the NRK Board of Directors discussed the report, and sanctioned a "moderate" strategy, establishing NRK Interaktiv as a group led by Brandrud.

In addition to publishing online information about the NRK, Interaktiv offered to help the broadcaster's editorial staff to establish webpages for their respective programs (NRK, 1996). No funds were allocated to Interaktiv for content production, which meant that editorial staff had to take money away from radio or television to pay for a webpage. To some extent, makers of niche programs seized the opportunity to reach new audiences, whereas major programs, e.g., news, showed less interest in expending funds and energy on the tiny platform of the web (Krumsvik, 2008, p. 92). The resulting NRK web presence was an odd collection of content, dominated by radio programs over television, and by content produced at the Oslo headquarters as opposed to that made in the regions.

Rather than striving for a consistent offering, the aim was still to have fun and experiment (Sommerseth, 1999, p. 45), and the working method was marked by "all–out efforts" by the Interaktiv staff (Nundal, 2001).

Although the initial enthusiasm might have faded in the years that followed, the service remained experimental, not least due to lack of funding. Notwithstanding larger one–off projects made possible by external funding coinciding with major televised events like the Eurovision Song Contest of 1996 (Sommerseth, 1999, p. 45), the service was still described as "random" and marked by lack of money (Brandrud in NRK, 1997a, p. 8). NRK Interaktiv functioned mainly as web hosting for radio and television programs (Brandrud in Rasmussen, 2002, p. 139).

In mid–1997, an internal review called for an overarching strategy for web priorities and funding (NRK, 1997b). This review highlighted key public service ideas as a rationale for internet ventures. Another 1997 NRK–report on the budding digital media, for instance, underlined potentials for two–way communication providing audiences with "a unique possibility for participation in the public sphere" (NRK, 1997c, p. 35). It should be noted that in 1997, only a minority of Norwegians had access to the internet, although access was increasing: In 1997, 13% had internet access at home. One year later, 22% did (SSB/Medienorge).

With NRK Interaktiv having been established as a permanent unit in the autumn of 1997, the content of the NRK web kept developing, despite uncertainties. By early 1999, the NRK website was redesigned with a number of new thematic categories—including news, sports and education. Interaktiv introduced new, shared software tools, and aimed for a unified layout of the web content, a move that triggered in-house journalists to protest against uniformed webpages (NRK, 1999). Still, consistency was becoming the norm. The pioneering phase was over, replaced by a more stable and formalized approach. This development is hardly surprising considering the general growth of the web as a media platform and business domain in the late nineties. The internet now constituted a lasting feature of social life, despite earlier predictions that it was mere hype.

However, the NRK was lagging behind. The public institution had entered the web around the same time as its competitors in the mid-1990s, but in the years that followed, leading news providers like nationwide tabloids VG and Dagbladet had left the NRK stranded. By spring 2000, nrk.no was not even among the top 20 Norwegian websites. Explaining the situation, the NRK pointed to its early choice of strategy, recommended by the European Broadcasting Union: "be present on the internet without spending much money on it" (Nundal, 2001). During the first months of 2000, a more substantial strategy took form. It was grounded in an institution-wide reorganization that turned the small radio development department called NRK Futurum into a full-blown division in charge of all digital media, including web content (Eckblad, 2000a).

In April, Tor Fuglevik, now Head of NRK Futurum, announced the ambitious aim of turning the NRK online news service into the best in Norway before the summer of 2000 (Pettersen, 2000). By June, with nrk.no having climbed only to 16th place among the most visited Norwegian websites, Fuglevik called the results "disgraceful," and stated that the strategy to "be present, but don't spend money" had proved a failure (Dagbladet, 2000). A month later, NRK Futurum was formally launched as a division with four departments, one being NRK Interaktiv, and by early September, nrk.no had been redesigned yet again into a more consistent and, graphically as well as content-wise, more advanced site (Berg, 2000).

The NRK did not, however, just strengthen and coordinate its online strategy. By late autumn of 2000, the PSB also introduced commercial banner ads on its website—the first appearing in the economy section (NRK, 2000). Clearly, core public service values were no longer the only rationale for the web activities—commercial potential was added to the argumentation. Even though the Head of NRK Interaktiv as late as in 1999 had argued that the internet was well suited for public service partly because of the difficulties with charging money for content (Nundal in Sommerseth, 1999, p. 90), the advertising–free, publicly funded NRK had entered the realm of advertising sales. To grasp the tensions between commercial and public in this instance, we need to look into the process behind this seemingly sudden turn.

The Process behind Online Ad Sales

In response to its first serious national competitors in television in the early 1990s, the NRK had launched a forceful argument for a more efficient organization. NRK management also reasoned that the licence fee would eventually be insufficient to fund the NRK response to tougher competition and new technologies. A persistent argument by the NRK for a more flexible framework "paid off" as Parliament changed the organization from a foundation to a state–owned limited company in 1996. This change of status allowed for subsidiaries to exploit commercial potential.

The NRK established the commercial subsidiary NRK Aktivum the following year to take care of all business activities. Already in June 1997, Head of Aktivum Arne Wam presented an ambitious plan for commercial exploitation of the teletext service. The NRK teletext consisted of a few hundred pages with text–based news, weather, sports and related content, produced by the editorial staff and distributed as a "push stream" with the terrestrial television network signals. Ads and shopping services on teletext could generate € 2.5 million in the coming two years, argued Aktivum. Crucially, internet activities had to be developed in parallel: "Within a short period of time, these two functions will have melded together (Wam in Larsen, 1997). Such bold statements attracted the attention of the Norwegian Media Authority as well as the Ministry of Culture. In September of 1997, when Wam hinted that a forthcoming NRK Aktivum business plan would detail a strategy to enter the classified ads market, the Media Authority raised the question of whether teletext should be considered broadcasting or something extra (Eckblad, 1997). The issue came to a head in December. Public institutions used the NRK teletext service as an information channel. These institutions did not pay for the space, but NRK did, however, charge for "technical support." Commercial broadcaster TV2 claimed these charges were equal to advertising income (Løvik, 1997). With that, the issue of NRK's new income streams was put on the political agenda.

Yet, at the same time—in mid–December 1997—Aktivum again voiced its intentions of selling ads via the NRK's internet activities. The statement, widely reported in national newspapers, pointed to a possible new, commercially funded NRK website, to be built on news as well as entertainment content (NTB, 1997). A month later, in January 1998, a NRK strategy document presented five models for commercial exploitation of web activities. In addition to web store sales and subscription models, these included ad sales (Sommerseth, 1999, p. 94). The document also discussed the pros and cons of dividing NRK web activities in two parts—one ad–funded and one publicly funded (Rasmussen, 2002, p. 139).

These ambitious plans required clarification of the regulatory framework. Therefore, in early March 1998, the NRK sent a letter to the Ministry of Culture, asking for further liberalization of the broadcasting law to make room for a wider range of commercial activities. The letter included the NRK Aktivum business plan, and a proposition of how statutes could be revised to allow for ad sales on the teletext as well as the web service (Braanen, 1998).

In August, the Ministry claimed to be nearly ready to conclude its work on NRK guidelines for commercial activities (Granaasen, 1998). By September, Aktivum—still awaiting word from the Ministry—presented another bold initiative: a commercially funded electronic program guide for digital television (Eckblad, 1998a).

A tentative clarification did come by the start of November 1998, when the Media Authority deemed the NRK's practice of charging public institutions money for publishing information on the NRK teletext in violation of the Broadcasting Act. The following week, Head of NRK Aktivum Arne Wam resigned, presenting his decision as a protest against the delayed response from the Ministry and what he labelled a "crazy" ruling by the Media Authority (Berg, 1998). In its formal complaint to the Media Authority, the NRK claimed that the internet would imminently replace teletext (Eckblad, 1998b).

A few weeks later, on December 2nd 1998, the Centre–coalition government in office proposed to remove any restriction on commercial activities, allowing NRK subsidiaries to, for instance, launch pay tv channels (Government, 1998). Importantly, the draft document also allowed ads on the NRK teletext service. The proposal was widely read as a full–blown victory for the NRK because it followed the ideas presented by the institution in March, based on Aktivum's business plan. Yet, even though the NRK repeatedly had linked teletext with the internet, the policy process that followed did not at all address the issue of commercial activities on the web. So while the NRK clearly and consistently included the web in its ambitious plan for commercial ventures ever since the establishment of Aktivum in 1997, the issue put on the political agenda by late 1998 did not cover the internet.

This discrepancy continued into 1999. In April that year, after a public hearing, the Ministry of Culture sent its proposition to Parliament—with no mention of the internet (Government, 1999). In June, a separate White Paper on digital television also steered clear of any substantial discussion of the web. The NRK, on the other hand, repeated its ambition to commercialize both teletext and the web, but awaited formal approval from Parliament (Eckblad, 1999). Around the same time, it became clear that the NRK had abandoned the idea of a separate commercial website (Sommerseth, 1999, p. 94).

In November, the Parliament committee on cultural policy submitted its report, recommending the revisions: The introduction of commercial income streams would strengthen the NRK's position as a leading PSB in the years to come (Parliament, 1999a). After a discussion in Parliament, the Bill was passed before Christmas 1999 with the votes of the coalition parties and Labour. Ads on the teletext service were important, claimed one coalition representative, since the NRK had to "keep at bay the growing, rich variety of commercial channels that force themselves on us from the world outside" (Parliament, 1999b, p. 101). To make this argument viable, the majority stressed that teletext was something different from television broadcasts, not to be regarded as a part of the NRK's public service mission. Importantly, like the original draft document, neither the proposition nor the final decision mentioned the internet. Likewise, neither the formal report nor the debate in Parliament included references to the web (Parliament, 1999a, 1999b). One month before the turn of the millennium, around the height of the dotcom business hype, the politicians, then, did not relate the introduction of ad sales to the NRK web service.

The NRK management, on the other hand, was well aware of the implications. The preparation and handling of the liberalization had taken place side-by-side with an increased attention given to commercial potential. The web was explicitly included. Still, when Parliament approved the liberalizations by the end of 1999—one year after the publication of the draft document, and two years after NRK ad sales had become a political issue—the PSB was not prepared to launch any new services right away. After New Year 2000, the NRK management stated it now had "the freedom to go after commercial possibilities on the web and teletext," and were "working on finding the right balance between our existence as ad-free PSB, and our role as commercial actor" (NRK, 2000b, p. 2). At that time, NRK Aktivum concentrated on teletext, where it already had experience with facilitating external informational material. In February 2000, the NRK launched its first commercial teletext service—an early form of e-shopping (NTB, 2000). NRK Aktivum still presented teletext as a soon-to-be-digitalized medium bound to either converge or compete with the internet (Furnes, 2000).

While the commercial subsidiary seemed to concentrate on teletext, the NRK division in charge of new media—Futurum—kept discussing the introduction of ads on the website. Futurum described commercial income streams as a necessity. While private actors could profit from their expansion on the internet, it was a mere expense for the NRK. Ad funding of the website—an activity not included in the core public service mission—could help secure an ad free environment for the main radio and television channels, according to this argument (Sandberg, 2000).

In late August 2000, the NRK formally decided to introduce ads on its website. The decision did not attract much attention, chiefly because it was overshadowed by reports of the NRK Director General resigning in the wake of an expected 10–12 million deficit (Eckblad, 2000b). Shortly thereafter, the first banner ads appeared on nrk.no. Without any political debate, then, the NRK introduced ads on its publicly funded website—just as the web was getting established as a mainstream media platform. The question is how to understand this peculiar development.

Understanding the Process behind Online Ad Sales

From 1925 until the German occupation in 1940, Norwegian radio listeners were exposed to ads. Originally introduced by the private company that predated NRK, the practice of scheduling blocks of ads was maintained after the establishment of the publicly funded radio monopolist in 1933. Although the NRK expressed concerns about commercial pressure, the main argument against was competition for ad sales with the printed press (Dahl 1999, pp. 61, 123, 326 f.). The German occupants banned commercials and after WWII, radio ads on the NRK were never again put on the political agenda. Advertisers also failed to get an entry into television in the early 1950s (Dahl & Bastiansen, 1999, p. 154). Even when the issue was debated in the late 1960s—with transnational satellite television looming—supporters of an ad-funded NRK were outnumbered (Dahl & Bastiansen, 1999, p. 408 f.). The teletext service also stayed ad-free from its introduction in 1983 until 2000. So while ads were not a completely new issue in the history of the NRK, their introduction on teletext and the web as described here needs to be understood with reference to a specific societal context.

The NRK did not push for commercial funding of its web initiatives from the beginning. When the internet was new, visions of its public service potential were put front and centre. The NRK only expressed ideas about commercial potential as the multimedia platform of the web started to take form and appeal to mass consumers. Long gone were the enthusiastic visions of the web as "a unique possibility for participation in the public sphere," and the NRK as a key node in "the big Norwegian Enlightenment database," which had marked the public broadcaster's arguments during the first years of web experiments. By 2000, as the number of Norwegians with internet access at home for the first time exceeded 50% (SSB/Medienorge), much more pragmatic concerns took centre stage. The introduction of online banner ads, then, was not a random experiment with an emerging medium, but rather the planned result of a strategy where the end—a strengthened public service—was seen to justify the means.

In the early 1990s, when facing serious competition, the NRK took several steps to facilitate the exploitation of its public service activities for commercial purposes. These steps were blessed by a broad political consensus, as all major parties except the liberalist Progress Party expressed support for a strong, national public broadcaster. Much debate in this period took an explicitly pragmatic approach saying that a somewhat more commercially oriented NRK was better than the alternative—no NRK.

The NRK strategy was in line with other European broadcasters, primarily in the UK. In 1994, a Conservative Government White Paper encouraged the BBC's development "into an international multi-media enterprise" (as cited in Steemers, 2005, p. 233). That same year, the BBC presented its dual approach for the digital era: to add new free services to its publicly funded portfolio while a subsidiary, BBC Worldwide, introduced subscription-based thematic channels. The strategy coincided with an internal new public management-inspired reorganisation aimed at gaining additional savings to help fund the digital transition (Born, 2004). On the web, the BBC kept developing two websites—one commercially funded aimed overseas (beeb.com) and one publicly funded aimed at the domestic licence fee-paying users (bbc.co.uk).

Similarly, the gradual liberalization of the Norwegian regulatory framework gave the NRK room to first establish a commercial subsidiary, and then have that subsidiary push the liberalization further through the commercialization of teletext and the web. The NRK's plans for an autonomous commercial website, as presented in early 1998, was clearly inspired by the BBC. Importantly, the BBC operates under more advantageous conditions. Not only is the domestic market thirteen times bigger, the possibilities for export are exceptional given the standing of the English language. This applies to the market for content sales as well as consumer goods. The NRK lacks both a large home market and any major potential for international sales outside the Nordic region. Another important difference between these two institutions lies in the actual web offers and their use: while the BBC, much like the NRK, was off to a slow start online, the British succeeded in the years that followed to build the country's top ranking news website (e.g., Thorsen, 2010). As documented, the NRK still struggled to compete with its online competitors by the time it introduced ads in 2000.

This indicates a distinctive feature of the NRK's strategy. For the BBC, commercial ventures were largely a matter of leveraging commercial potential in international markets to subsidize public services at home (e.g., Birt in BBC, 1998, p. 4). In the Norwegian case, argumentation has instead been about guarding national language and culture. If commercial funding makes the public institution stronger, it must be utilized because such is perceived to be in Norway's best interests (NRK, 2000, p. 7). So while the BBC attacks foreign markets, the NRK defends its homeland.

The process towards ad funding shows the NRK as a strong policy actor. Even though the process was prolonged, the end result was entirely in line with the NRK's stipulations. The lack of substantial public debate and the broad political consensus has created a forthcoming political climate with generous leeway for the public institution (Moe, 2008). As noted, neither the Ministry of Culture nor Parliament explicitly addressed the question of ad–funding web content. Instead, they remained focused on teletext. This should, however, not be seen as a result of deliberate misrepresentation by the NRK: As I have demonstrated, the institution repeatedly and publicly linked potentials for ad sales to its web activities from the 1997 onwards.

Nevertheless, the lack of political attention to NRK web services is puzzling, given the otherwise society–wide massive attention given to everything online during the so–called dotcom–boom climaxing in early 2000. Furthermore, Norwegian authorities were not ignorant to the challenges of digital technologies. A Green Paper on the convergence between telecom, computer industries and the media was commenced in early 1998, and submitted by June 1999—well before Parliament discussed the future of NRK's commercial activities. The neglect of the web in the broader policy discussions may be the result of attention directed elsewhere. Concerning the NRK, other commercial initiatives—like pay television channels—stood out as more controversial. More generally, digital television distribution emerged as a pressing issue: In a June 1999 White Paper the Ministry described digital television distribution as key for Norwegian media policy, including public service broadcasting. In this context, the question of the NRK web service might have been perceived as less prominent.

The history of ads on the NRK web also documents a lengthy process. It took almost a year to develop the draft paper liberalizing the statutes, another year to get it passed by Parliament, and almost yet another year for the NRK to actually utilize its new won freedom. Such a cumbersome course stands in stark contrast to the perceived swiftness of developments in the digital era.

Finally, the process also contains struggles for power within the PSB. In the pioneering years from the mid–1990s, representatives from the radio division stood out as the most enthusiastic. Despite individual exceptions, the television department was more sceptical, warning in late 1995 that the internet should not take funds away from the core activity of television production. When the powerful NRK Futurum was created in early 2000, it also sprung out of the radio division, and was directed by the former Head of radio. On another level, there was obvious antagonism between the bold visions of commercial subsidiary Aktivum and the journalistically grounded ideas expressed by program staff in the parent company. The introduction of banner ads represented a turn in the NRK's approach to new media: the internet was seen as something outside the public service mission, to be developed and used strategically—even commercially—to support the core activities on radio and television. As such, the development of the NRK's online activities up until the end of 2000 is an interesting example of how tensions between public and commercial were played out in a specific context when public service broadcasting met the web.

Concluding Remarks

In early 21st century, the NRK kept building its web presence. And the publicly funded institution continued to sell ads on nrk.no as well as on its teletext service. And, as earlier, neither the wider public nor the politicians paid much attention. As late as 2007, the Norwegian Government confessed that the issue of NRK internet services' place within the public service remit had never been debated by Parliament, and that the development thus far—ad sales included—had been directed by the company's own priorities (Government, 2007, p. 99). At the same time, the Government proposed to ban ads on the teletext service, but still allow them on the web. The somewhat curious line of argument went like this: The internet was at the time defined as within the public service remit (Government, 2007). The NRK earned around € 1 million on ad sales online in 2006. But since it was costly to develop online services, the company should still be allowed to sell ads. Concerning teletext, the argument differed: It was a part of the public service remit. In 2006, the NRK made roughly € 600 000 on teletext ads—which dominated the service and distracted attention from the content itself. If a digital teletext service got developed as a hybrid with text, sound and moving images, it would be a bad idea for the NRK to include ads on it, according to the Ministry. And since the income so far had been minimal, the Ministry proposed a ban on teletext ads. When ads were allowed in 2000, the main rationale was that teletext and the web were something other than public service broadcasting. Seven years later, ads online were still endorsed even though the web was defined as an integral part of the NRK remit.

Not until 2009 did this issue attract much attention. At that time, commercial actors fearing plummeting ad sales in the wake of the so–called global financial crisis attacked the NRK's generous leeway. This attack took place after a longwinded process where the Norwegian government tried to revise NRK regulations to comply with the detailed audit requirements of EU competition law (e.g., Moe, 2009). By early 2010, after the Conservative party had raised the issue of web ads, and NRK employees spoke out in public about the downside of the online ads (e.g., in Jensen, 2009), the NRK itself decided to end its practice and make nrk.no ad–free by the end of the year (NRK, 2010).

As an answer, commercial interests intensified protests against the NRK's general online presence, claiming the public broadcaster was intruding on new markets, and arguing that it drove away commercial newcomers (e.g., Mediebedriftenes landsforening, 2010).

The issue of commercials on the web, then, followed the NRK for more than a decade before it was put to rest—and replaced by new issues in the tension field between public and commercial.

References

BBC. (1998, December 12). *BBC Declares Its Public Purposes for the New Millennium* [Press release].

Berg, H. (1998). "Avsinding vedtak" utløste Wams avgang. Retrieved May 5, 2010, from http://www.digi.no/48938/avsindig-vedtak-utloste-wams-avgang

Berg, H. (2000). Hele NRK involveres i Norges største internettprosjekt. Retrieved May 5, 2010, from http://www.digi.no/62061/hele-nrk-involveres-i-norges-storste-internettprosjekt

Born, G. (2004). *Uncertain Vision—Birt, Dyke and the Reinvention of the BBC.* London: Secker & Warburg.

Braanen, B. (1998, March 5). Førde vil ha frie tøyler. *Dagens Næringsliv*, p. 44.

Brandrud, R., & Ottmar, T. W. (1995). *Internett. NRK Interaktiv—din personlige kanal!* Oslo: NRK.

Dagbladet (2000, June 16). NRK tar selvkritikk, pp. 36.

Dahl, H. F. (1999). *Hallo—Hallo! Kringkastingen i Norge 1920–1940.* Oslo: J. W. Cappelens forlag.

Dahl, H. F., & Bastiansen, H. G. (1999). *Over til Oslo. NRK som monopol 1945–1981.* Oslo: J. W. Cappelens forlag.

Eckblad, B. (1997, September 15). Er rubrikk reklame? *Dagens Næringsliv*, p. 38.

Eckblad, B. (1998a, September 2). NRK vil lage guide med reklamepenger. *Dagens Næringsliv*, p. 40.

Eckblad, B. (1998b, November 26). Benekter reklame. *Dagens Næringsliv*, p. 52.

Eckblad, B. (1999, July 7). Minus i Aktivum. *Dagens Næringsliv*, p. 35.

Eckblad, B. (2000a, February 2). Bjerkaas blir NRK–kringkaster. *Dagens Næringsliv*, p. 44.
Eckblad, B. (2000b, August 22). Ber om å få slutte. *Dagens Næringsliv*, p. 49.
Furnes, H. M. (2000, February 9). Selger reklame på NRKs tekst–tv. *Dagens Næringsliv*, p. 46.
Government (1998). *Videre rammer for NRKs forretningsvirksomhet* [Press release] 114/98.
Government (1999). Om lov om endringar i lov 4. desember 1992 nr. 127 om kringkasting og i lov 15. mai 1987 nr. 21 om film og videogram, *Ot.prp. nr. 55 (1998–99)*.
Government (2007). Kringkasting i en digital fremtid, *St. meld. nr. 30 (2006–2007)*.
Granaasen, I. (1998, August 21). Få løfter til NRK fra Kulturdepartementet. *Aftenposten*, p. 41.
Jensen, M. H. (2009, September 30). Vampyrer og krig på NRK.no. *Journalisten*.
Krumsvik, A. H. (2008). Forholdet mellom kanalstrategi og journalistrollen i NRK og CNN. In R. Ottosen & A. H. Krumsvik (Eds.), *Journalistikk i en digital hverdag* (pp. 87–100). Kristiansand: IJ–forlaget.
Larsen, S. (1997, July 23). NRK med 20 mill. på "ny" tekst–tv. *Dagens Næringsliv*, p. 27.
Løvik, O. A. (1997, December 12). Lovlig eller ulovlig i NRK?: Får på pukkelen for reklamesalget. *Aftenposten*, p. 30.
Mediebedriftenes landsforening (2010). *Helt i sin tid—en mediepolitikk for morgendagen*. Oslo: MBL.
Moe, H. (2008). Commercial Services, Enclosure and Legitimacy. Comparing Contexts and Strategies for Public Service Media Funding and Development. In G. F. Lowe & J. Bardoel (Eds.), *From Public Service Broadcasting to Public Service Media. RIPE@2007* (pp. 51–69). Göteborg, Sweden: Nordicom.
Moe, H. (2009). Between Supranational Competition and National Culture? Emerging EU Policy and Public Broadcasters' Online Services. In I. Bondebjerg & P. Madsen (Eds.), *Media, Democracy and European Culture* (pp. 307–325). Bristol, UK: Intellect.
NRK. (1994). "IRMA 1000" sjanghaiet på internet. *Tidssignalet*, 22.
NRK. (1995). Ambisiøse Internet–planer. *Tidssignalet*, 4.
NRK. (1996). Hvordan kan redaksjonen få egne websider? *Tidssignalet*, 4.
NRK. (1997a). Redaksjonene må samarbeide. *Tidssignalet*, 19.
NRK. (1997b). Strategi for internettjenester. *Tidssignalet*, 14.
NRK. (1997c). *Over den digitale dørstokken*. Oslo: NRK.
NRK. (1999). Nei til uniformering av internet. *Tidssignalet*, 17.
NRK. (2000a). NRK Økonomi—med reklame. *Tidssignalet*, 22.
NRK. (2000b). NRKs nettsatsing. *Tidssignalet*, 5.
NRK. (2010). NRK kutter nettreklame. Retrieved May 5, 2010, from http://www.nrk.no/nyheter/kultur/1.7053523
NTB. (1997, December 14). NRK satser på internett–reklame [News release].
NTB. (2000, February 28). Kommers på NRK Tekst–TV. [News release].
Nundal, A. (2001). Ambisjoner for nrk.no. Retrieved May 5, 2010, from http://nrk.no/informasjon/1393370.html
Oslonett (2001). NRK programmet Rondo på Internett—bakgrunnsinformasjon. Retrieved May 5, 2010, from http://www.oslo.net/historie/rondo-info.html
Parliament (1999a). Innstilling fra familie–, kultur–og administrasjonskomiteen om lov om endringar i lov av 4. desember 1992 nr. 127 om kringkasting og i lov av 15. mai 1987 nr. 21 om film og videogram (Rammene for den forretningsmessige verksemda til

Norsk rikskringkasting AS). *Innst. O. 14 (1999–2000).*
Parliament (1999b). *Forhandlinger i Odelstinget, 6.*
Pettersen, J. (2000, April 1). Fugleviks nye NRK. *VG.*
Rasmussen, T. (2002). *Nettmedier: Journalistikk og medier på Internett.* Bergen, Sweden: Fagbokforlaget.
Sandberg, S. (2000, July 18). NRK selger seg. *Dagens Næringsliv*, p. 34.
Sommerseth, H. (1999). *NRK på Internett—om NRK Interaktivs utvikling, valg og strategier.* Institutt for medier og kommunikasjon. Oslo: Universitetet i Oslo.
Steemers, J. (2005). Balancing Culture and Commerce on the Global Stage—BBC Worldwide. In G. F. Lowe & P. Jauert (Eds.), *Cultural Dilemmas in Public Service Broadcasting* (pp. 231–251). Göteborg, Sweden: Nordicom.
Thorsen, E. (2010). BBC News Online: A Brief History of Past and Present. In N. Brügger (Ed.), *Web History* (pp. 213–233). New York: Peter Lang.

PART THREE

A Perfect Match?

Ideals, Policies and Practices of Public Service Broadcasters on the Web

7 *The Idea of Public Service in the Early History of DR Online*

Neils Brügger

One of the most interesting issues of the history of public service broadcasters (PSBs) online is the intersection between the self-understanding of the PSB and the many new possibilities offered by the web. Did the broadcaster interpret its role and mission on the web in light of its broadcast history, based on old media such as radio and television, or in light of the history of the web and the affordances made possible by this new medium? This is the question that this chapter sets out to explore through a close analysis of the case of the national Danish PSB Danmarks Radio (DR), with emphasis on the role played by the idea of public service.

DR launched its website DR Online in January 1996. The first six months was a trial period, after which DR Online became a permanent activity as part of the newly formed business unit called DR Multimedia. The annual report for 1996 emphasizes that DR Multimedia must "contribute to the development of interactive media [including DR Online] with a view to making them strengthen DR's public service mission" (DR, 1997, p. 20). DR Online is clearly portrayed as an inherent element of DR's public service remit.

But what role did the idea of public service actually play in the creation of DR Online? This chapter concentrates on the foundational period from 1994 to 1996, when the website was conceptualized and established. The focus is on the *idea* of public service, which means that the aim is to investigate the extent to which public service has been used as a strategic concept in order to legitimize and rationalize the creation of a totally new activity within the radio and television organization DR, rather than to investigate whether DR's online–related activities actually conform to the concept of public service.[1]

Source Material and Theoretical Framework

The analysis presented in this chapter will be based primarily on internal documents related to the creation of DR Online. However, this short chapter only permits an analysis of the most important documents, mainly those which have been either pivotal for decision–making or regulative for future activities.[2]

The following analysis is based on a theoretical framework which makes it possible to map and investigate the various entities influencing the creation and development of a mediated artifact such as a website. These entities—or driving forces—may be human (individuals, groups, work routines) or non–human, such as material objects (technological artifacts, the physical environment, resources) or concepts (e.g., the idea of public service). The driving forces behind the history of a public service broadcaster's website may include such forces as the board, the management, sub–divisions, individual employees, physical localities, media–related legislation, the media market, the broadcaster's other broadcast activities (radio, television, mobile media), program policies, the technical and organizational structure of the internet/web, and feedback from users. All these factors may be understood to have an impact on the creation and development of the website, and they may be related to each other, thus forming a network of forces with varying degrees of influence on the process.[3]

An analysis based on the theoretical framework outlined above thus aims to map the network of possible and actual driving forces influencing the creation and development of websites and other mediated artifacts. Space does not permit a thorough analysis of all the factors which have influenced the creation of DR Online. Therefore, focus is exclusively on the role of one central force: the idea of "public service."[4]

DR and the Internet, 1994–96

DR was founded in 1925 as an independent, license–financed public institution. For over 60 years, DR had a monopoly on broadcasting nationwide radio and television in Denmark; but in 1985 local radio stations were allowed, and in October 1988 the rival television broadcaster TV2 was established. DR is headed by a board of 11 members which establishes the guidelines for DR's activities and appoints the members of the management, at the time consisting of the Director General, the Director of Television, and the Director of Radio.

It is difficult to establish what the internet actually looked like in Denmark in 1994–1996, since the history of the Danish part of the internet remains to be written, and reliable data on how many Danes were online are lacking. However, based on the available sources, the following three points probably give an accurate picture of the situation at the beginning of this period. First, the internet was a niche medium: the number of internet users was relatively small, around 50,000–70,000 out of a population of 5 million, and most of them were probably either university academics or students, computer aficionados or employees of the public sector or the media industry. Second, in terms of hardware and software, the internet was highly diverse: modems were frequently used, but high-speed access existed; Bulletin Board Systems, Newsgroups, and Internet Relay Chat were at the top of the agenda, but www was starting to take off. Third, all of this was changing rapidly in the period from 1994 to 1996: the number of internet users was growing (on some accounts, to 100,000–200,000 users in mid–1996), the internet was gradually becoming part of ordinary people's lives, and www was beginning to outmatch the other ways of going online, in part thanks to the spread of the graphic browsers, especially Netscape.

The Concept of Public Service

When setting out to question the role of the idea of public service, it is crucial to know what we are looking for. In other words, what is understood by public service? The following three points have to be taken into consideration to answer this question.

First, we can base our analysis either on public service as it is understood within DR or on sources external to DR, such as the discourse of media legislators, the media industry, and academia. However, with the latter approach, we risk choosing a public service concept which is irrelevant or peripheral to DR. To avoid this, the discussion will be based on the actually existing idea of public service within DR.

Second, we must consider the forms in which the concept has been expressed—whether in writing and speech or as tacit knowledge in actions—and which of these forms can be used as sources. Since speech has not been conserved in most cases, and since the tacit knowledge of the past is difficult to document today, the analysis will focus on archival documents from the past.

Third, we have to keep in mind that not all documents about public service explicitly make use of the word "public service." To address this problem, I begin by identifying the semantic elements related to public service in one of DR's key documents which actually contains the word "public service"; subsequently, these components serve as guidelines for identifying the idea of public service in other texts.

The Concept of Public Service in DR, 1994–1996

One of the key documents for understanding public service within DR in the beginning of the '90s is the report *Danmarks Radio 1995–2005: A Report on DR's Mission Statement, Program Policy, and Development* (November 1994, 133 pages).[5]

Danmarks Radio 1995–2005, the most ambitious strategic paper within DR to date at the time of its publication, was the result of an extensive analysis initiated by the newly appointed Director General just after his appointment in June 1994. The capstone of the report is the mission statement:

> With a view to strengthening the citizens' ability to act in a democratic society, Danmarks Radio must as a broadcasting company increase the number of alternatives compared to market-driven radio and television offerings with particular emphasis on Danish culture, by being dependent on the wishes and needs of the entire population, but independent of economic and political private interests. (DR, 1994, p. 6)

According to the mission statement, because DR is "dependent on the wishes and needs of the entire population," DR must therefore "be deeply anchored in society and in a lively dialogue with listeners and viewers who must also have actual influence on the programming" (ibid., p. 17). This statement sums up the pivotal argument of *Danmarks Radio 1995–2005*: DR's activities should be guided by the listeners' and viewers' wishes and needs, and therefore it is crucial for DR to enter into dialogue with them (this argument is repeated a number of times; see. pp. 18, 29, 30, 31, 35, 43–44, 70). Thus, as defined in the key internal document of the period "public service" contains the following semantic elements: "strengthen the citizens' ability to act in a democratic society," "increase the number of alternatives," "particular emphasis on Danish culture," "dependent on the wishes and needs of the entire population," "independent of economic and political private interests," "deeply anchored in society and in a lively dialogue with listeners and viewers," and "listeners and viewers must have actual influence on the programming."

The realization of the many ideas proposed in *Danmarks Radio 1995–2005* continued with the establishment of 27 project groups which were formed in the beginning of 1995. Three of these groups were to become important for the future creation of DR Online: "Project: Marketing," "Project: Listener/viewer dialogue," and "Project: DR's commercial opportunities outside the proper broadcasting activities" (in the following referred to as "Project: DR's commercial opportunities").

The Creation and Development of DR Online

Having identified the main semantic components related to the idea of public service within DR in the period, we will now examine what actually happened, as well as how the idea of public service was used as a strategic concept, from the first mention of the possibility of DR going online in July 1994 to the end of the trial period in July 1996. This period can be divided into four distinct phases.[6]

The pre-history of DR Online, July 1994 to January 1995

The first DR staff to suggest that DR should go online was the editorial team of the radio program *Harddisken* (The Harddisk)—DR's high-profile and trendsetting program about new media. During the first months of 1994, *Harddisken* had been in email contact with a number of its listeners, and the staff wanted to extend this service by creating a more permanent online presence. Therefore, in July the team wrote a letter to the management of the radio department (July 19, 3 pages) which outlined what DR's presence on the internet might look like. But apparently nothing happened in response to that correspondence, since they had to write an almost identical letter six months later.

By September–October 1994, three subdivisions of DR's television department (Television Development, Television IT, and Television Archiving and Research) had discovered the new media form, and they launched a joint initiative called "Project Internet" (approved by television management). In the memo titled "Information on Project Internet" (October 10, 5 pages), the group explained their vision, which was basically to clarify how computer networks could be used in DR's television department, especially as a powerful tool in the journalistic research process.

Finally, in December 1994, the *Harddisken* editorial team wrote a memo to the radio department management in which they elaborated on their initial ideas, and began to imagine the possibilities of a website (December 7, 4 pages). Yet, in the present context it is even more interesting to note that this memo was the first document to link the idea of public service and DR's online activities; first by maintaining that, as a PSB, DR is obliged to provide its "customers" with a proper service, and second by arguing that a website will facilitate dialogue and communication between listeners/viewers and DR.

One of the concrete outcomes of the television department's efforts was the organization of an introduction day (November 24) to introduce the internet to a wider audience within DR for the first time. But more importantly, "Project Internet" ultimately became the stepping stone for DR's emerging internet activities, and towards the end of 1994 DR's management decided to support a continued investigation of how DR could go online. The main stakeholders of the project were the three subdivisions of the television department mentioned above, and television's head of administration was made responsible for the project.

Two separate internet projects, February to May 1995

On February 1, 1995, DR's burgeoning interest in going online became more concrete when the Television Archiving and Research Department hired a project manager responsible for driving the project forward. With a colleague from the Television Development, he wrote the memo "The Internet Project" (March 1, 5 pages), which was sent to television's head of administration. An abridged and edited version written by the project manager was published in the staff magazine *DRåben* (April 21, pp. 12–13). This memo can be considered the first formal attestation of how DR's ambitions to establish an internet presence could be realized, and it set the agenda for the discussions which took place in the first six months of 1995. In addition, the project manager tried to arouse interest in the internet project, partly by organizing a number of introduction courses for DR's employees, partly by publishing a small internal newsletter called *NetNews* (from March).

The key argument of the memo "The Internet Project" is that DR's internet activities should be split into two separate parts: an external part for the public and an internal part, a web server exclusively for the employees of DR. In the following, only the development of the public part is addressed, since it became DR Online.

However, as a number of documents from this period indicate, the launch of the public part of the plan dragged out for a number of reasons: The main interest of the primary initiator, Television Archiving and Research, was first and foremost in establishing the internal part, and much time was spent discussing how the two entities were to fit into DR's organization and who should be members of the steering groups.

"The Internet Project" mainly addresses the fundamental question of what to put on the website, proposing the following content: information about DR's programming and DR as a company, and very little program content, such as radio and television news (as written text), excerpts from teletext, charts and entertainment (without further specification). The document does not mention public service and could therefore apply to any media company of the period which intended to go online. Only a single phrase which appears in the version published in *DRåben* refers to the idea of public service: "The initiative is an example of DR turning into action its words about being a radio and television company at the people's service" (April 21, p. 12).

The expression "at the people's service" is taken from *Danmarks Radio 1995–2005*, but the memo does not elaborate on how DR Online would be "at the people's service."

Finally, it is worth noting that the memo suggests that the public part should refer to the Information Department and that it should be led by a steering group headed by the Information Manager (the Information Department refers directly to the Director General).

DR Online is on its way, May to December 1995

In the beginning of this period the problems of organizing and managing the external part were solved, and in June DR's management decided to establish the pilot project "DR Online," aimed at the public. The Information Department was given responsibility for this project along with two of the project groups established in the wake of *Danmarks Radio 1995–2005*: "Project: Marketing" and "Project: Listener/viewer dialogue"; both were headed by the information manager. Furthermore, it became more and more evident which types of content should be put on the website, and DR Online developed rapidly: a pilot version was constructed, and DR Online was introduced, first at a press conference (November 7), and then to the general public at the Bogforum 95 book fair (November 17). The site was launched online in January 1996. Not surprisingly, this intense activity generated a number of important documents related to the creation of DR Online.

In a memo titled "Discussion paper for a plan for the Internet Project in Danmarks Radio. External part" (May 23, 4 pages), which outlines a proposal directed at the steering group of the external part, the project manager adds a few new types of content to the ones already suggested in "The Internet Project," including material to supplement the broadcast programs, an ftp forum for Danish shareware, and a newsgroup about DR. In addition, he suggests that in the long run DR might sell server space and expertise to Danish cultural institutions, political parties, and so forth. However, these initiatives are not related to public service.

When DR's management decided to establish DR Online in June, the basis for their decision was a document titled "Recommendation concerning the establishing of Subproject: DR Online (i.e., DR/Internet—external)" (June 2, 2 pages). In this document, public service is only touched upon indirectly, in the form of an emphasis on the obvious link to "Project: Listener/viewer dialogue."

Even more interesting is the appendix to the recommendation: "Pilot project to establish DR Online service in early 1996" (June 2, 8 pages). This document represents the most thorough and detailed presentation of DR Online to date. The beginning of the document repeats the affiliation of DR Online to "Project: Marketing" and "Project: Listener/viewer dialogue," but suddenly, a few lines further down, it states that DR Online must also be coordinated with "Project: DR's commercial opportunities." The proposed affiliation to this project marks a significant difference between the appendix and the recommendation. As we shall see, this turn of events foreshadowed DR Online's destiny one year later.

The barely discernible indications of a new direction for DR Online which could be read in the appendix were made clearer three months later in the document "Danmarks Radio's commercial opportunities outside the proper broadcasting activities. Sub–report" (September, 4 pages (incomplete)). This document was written by the head of "Project: DR's commercial opportunities," who was also the author of the above–mentioned appendix, and as the title indicates, the sub–report provides a preliminary account of the development of the project. This sub–report is thus not directly related to the establishment of DR Online at that time. Nevertheless it is an important text because it marks the first time public service is clearly emphasized as relevant in relation to DR Online:

> In the long run, if DR is to be able to live up to the mission statement's wording of *strengthening the citizens' ability to act in a democratic society . . . dependent on the wishes and needs of the* entire *population,* we must ensure that the program material we produce for the license fee is not just broadcast to the citizens via radio and television, but is also provided via other media such as books, CD–ROM and the interactive media of the future. (Danmarks Radio's commercial opportunities outside the proper broadcasting activities. Sub–report, p. ii)

As this excerpt shows, the idea of public service does not simply legitimize DR's involvement in new interactive media. The relation is also a kind of double bind: the idea of public service legitimizes DR's move towards the new media, and the new media can help legitimize a particular interpretation of public service in general in the future.

Furthermore, the sub–report argues that if DR wishes to supplement the license fee with other sources of funding, this can be done by increasing the activities which generate revenue (these activities did not play a significant fundraising role at that time). Following this line of thought, the text proposes the establishment of a brand–new unit in DR, DR Publication, which, among other things, would take over the operation of DR Online. However, at the time these ideas remained merely thoughts in a sub–report with no immediate impact on DR Online, which was still anchored in the Information Department.

Finally, in October 1995, DR's board decided to take the last step by allowing the project "DR Online" to create a pilot version to go online.

The trial period, January to July 1996

DR Online was launched on Friday, January 5, 1996, at an event in TV–Byen, the site of DR's television production and administrative headquarters (cf. *DRåben*, January 12, p. 7). As decided by the management, DR Online was given a six–month trial period, and in this period the website provided information about DR as well as experiments such as a "moving message sign," a "back page" (as in a printed newspaper), downloadable sound, and a competition in which users could make a sub–site for the television miniseries *Riget* (The Kingdom) (cf. the *DR Online News* newsletter, January, February and July). Furthermore, from day one a discussion group was established in which listeners and viewers could debate DR's radio and television programs (approximately ten posts per week).[7] The high point was the first live dialogue between the Director of Television and listeners and viewers, an event which took place on April 29 between 6 and 8 p.m. The Director of Television responded to seven comments, which was quite satisfactory, according to DR Online's editorial team (cf. *DRåben*, May 10, p. 16).

At the time, DR Online's organization was both centralized and decentralized: a steering group, headed by the Information Manager, was responsible for the overall management and DR Online's editorial team (three employees) was responsible for the central editing, while the so–called webmasters in DR's many departments managed each individual area of DR Online (there were approximately 50 webmasters as of June 1996; cf. the internal document *Final report on DR Online's trial period*, November, p. 20). Finally, awareness of the internet and DR Online had increased considerably among DR's employees, partly due to the publication of a newsletter, *DR Online News* (from January 16; successor of *NetNews*), partly due to many introductory courses for DR's staff.

Concurrently with DR Online's online existence, work continued on "Project: DR's commercial opportunities," and on March 26, DR's board decided to establish a new business unit: DR Multimedia (called "DR Publication" in the sub–report from September 1995). Along with teletext, DR Online was to constitute one of three subdivisions of this unit, which gained the status of a three–year strategic development project, from July 1, 1996, to June 30, 1999 (the other two subdivisions were "DR Publication" and "DR Consultancy and Production").[8]

The board's decision was based on a number of documents (several recommendations, reports and project descriptions). The letter "To the Board. Forwarding letter from the management" (March 12, 4 pages) sums up the main points of the other documents, and it strongly emphasizes that the initiatives in the new business unit are in line with DR's mission statement:

> Danmarks Radio's ability to meet the mission statement's public service goals will be strengthened significantly in the future if we can combine and supplement radio and television broadcasting with dissemination via interactive multimedia, and in the communication with citizens about Danmarks Radio's activities interactive online media will be an attractive tool. (p. 2)

It is noteworthy that the order of things has been reversed: public service now has the upper hand, at the expense of the dialogue with listeners and viewers. In addition, the letter also stress that "internationally interactive multimedia are considered a potential area of business with great expectations for future revenue." It seems that DR Online was now well on its way to becoming closely linked to the public service remit, as well as to an obligation to generate revenue.

The Role of the Idea of Public Service

Having examined some of the key documents from July 1994 to the end of the trial period in July 1996, I will now summarize the first two years of DR's online activities by identifying the influence of the idea of public service in each of the four phases as well as the major transitions between the phases (cf. the distinction between synchronic/diachronic driving forces in Brügger, 2010, pp. 39–41).

DR Online, 1994–1996

From July 1994 to January 1995, when the idea of DR going online was beginning to take root in DR (phase 1), the main aspiration was simply to get DR on the internet. In addition, radio wanted to provide content and get in contact with its listeners, while television wanted a powerful research tool. Public service and the use of the internet to facilitate dialogue between listeners/viewers and DR are mentioned in passing in one document from this phase, but otherwise public service was not an issue.

From February to May 1995 (phase 2), when the focus was mainly on the internal part of DR's internet project, the predominant driving force was a desire for DR to use the new communication channel in order to provide, on the one hand, information about its activities, and, on the other, very limited content from radio and television. But neither of these two main objectives was related to an idea of public service in the extant documents, with the exception of a vague suggestion in the article about DR Online in *DRåben*. In addition, the external part was not yet clearly anchored in the organization.

Between May and December 1995 (phase 3), DR Online's organization fell into place, and the website began to take shape. This period was also characterized by the most complex constellation of driving forces and an increased use of the concept of public service. As in phase 2, the motivation behind this phase was DR's desire to market itself and provide information about the company online, but DR also wanted to use DR Online as a platform for dialogue with listeners and viewers. Contrary to the casual mention of the latter in the pre–history of DR online, the dialogue with listeners and viewers was now being directly related to the pivotal argument from *Danmarks Radio 1995–2005*: DR must know its listeners' and viewers' wishes and needs, and dialogue with them is a means to this end. In this sense, public service indirectly provided an impetus for the creation of DR Online: although public service was the goal to be achieved, the main impetus in this period was not to achieve this goal in itself but rather to provide one of the means to achieve this goal—specifically, the online involvement of the listeners/viewers. All in all, it is not surprising that in this period DR Online was anchored in the Information Department as well as in "Project: Marketing" and "Project: Listener/viewer dialogue."

But in the same period, two other driving forces were present. First, there was a sense that it was critical for DR to enter the realm of interactive multimedia, since these media would become important tools to help DR achieve the goals of public service in the future. Second, it was felt that DR Online—along with other interactive multimedia—should help fund DR's public service activities by generating revenue. However, the available sources indicate that these thoughts did not yet influence the creation of DR Online.

In the trial period from January to July 1996, DR Online was constantly developing, and the task of making it a permanent activity within DR continued. The impetus behind the development of the website was that DR wanted to provide information about DR as well as to experiment with the new medium. And concerning the future of DR Online, driving forces which were only hinted at earlier became pivotal: DR Online was to help DR live up to its general public service remit in the future, and the online presence was to become an instrument for generating revenue. These new driving forces were anchored in the future DR Multimedia business unit.

The major transformations of DR Online

I will now attempt to identify the role of public service in a diachronic perspective by focusing on what factors drove the transitions from one phase to another. From July 1994 to July 1996, DR Online was characterized by two major transformations.

The first transformation took place in June 1995, when the decision to start work on DR Online was finally taken. DR Online was transformed from a loosely conceived project without any clear direction and management to an integrated part of DR's (future) marketing and information activities, firmly anchored in the Information Department. The change was motivated by DR's desire to establish yet another platform to convey information about DR, as well as to facilitate dialogue with its listeners and viewers as a means of meeting its public service commitments.

The second transformation began in March 1996, when DR's board decided to integrate DR Online into the new DR Multimedia unit in July of that year. DR Online was thus transformed from a marketing and information project to part of a project founded on the idea of public service combined with revenue generation—two functions which the new DR Multimedia united. This transformation was motivated by the idea that DR Online and other interactive multimedia could be used as a lever to help DR develop in the future: on the one hand, by making it possible for DR to meet the public service remit of the future, when new media would become a natural means to reach "the entire population," and, on the other hand, by contributing funding for DR's activities in general.

What Happened When DR Met the Web?

The description of the events of 1996 in DR's 1996 annual report indicate that DR Online was created as an integral part of the public service remit. However, a close analysis of some of the key documents from the first two years of DR Online's creation and existence reveals a somewhat more complex, confusing, and dynamic field of driving forces.

In addition, the following three general tendencies can be identified. First, the closer we get to day–to–day operations (steering group, project manager, webmasters), the more importance is attached to considerations of content and technical solutions, and the less importance is attached to public service. Second, the closer we get to the decision–makers higher in the organization (board and management), the more important becomes the overriding purpose of DR Online for DR, including the relation to public service. Third, as time passed, the relation of DR Online to the idea of public service became increasingly clear. These three tendencies may not seem that surprising, but they can nevertheless now be substantiated.

There are several possible reasons for DR's somewhat vacillating attitude towards the role of public service in relation to DR Online, all of which revolve around the fact that DR Online was created in a context of great uncertainty. It was not clear how DR Online was to fit into DR's organization, neither was it clear how the internet would evolve technologically, both within DR and in general (for instance, would the number of internet users continue to grow?). How DR Online would affect DR's economy was also uncertain: Could the online activities become a new source of revenue at all, or would they simply become yet another expense? And, finally, legal issues were not yet solved: how would the lawmakers respond to the initiative in the long run? Would they include it as an integral part of the public service remit? In brief, in the period 1994 to 1996, it was not at all clear whether and how DR should actually engage in the new online media. But despite these uncertainties and the difficulty of making an informed decision, DR was prepared to leap into this brave new world. By the end of 1996, all these uncertainties had apparently been thrust into the background: Public service had become the natural explanation for DR Online's existence, and it had been reinterpreted so as to include new media.

However, the actual implementation of this new conceptualization online revealed that to a large extent public service online is understood as a continuation of the broadcast history of DR rather than as an effect of the affordances of the web—for instance, with regard to forms of content and user interaction. Although ideas for new ways of involving the users online were presented at DR, only a few of them were realized, among them the competition in which users could make a sub-site for the television miniseries *Riget*. In most cases, either they were not realized on DR Online—for instance, the ftp forum for Danish shareware—or their realization was based on the traditional mindset of a radio and television broadcasting organization. This was true, for example, for the discussion group which was part of DR Online from day one: The broadcaster DR communicated with its listeners and viewers about DR's radio and television programs, but the discussion group was not understood as an open platform for discussion *among* listeners and viewers, or for discussion about *other issues* than DR's programs—a manner of communicating which had been widespread in Bulletin Board Systems, Newsgroups, and Internet Relay Chat for a number of years on the internet.

In summary, when DR met the web in the mid '90s the new medium was by and large understood in line with what DR had been doing as a broadcaster for years, and less in light of the history of the internet. It may therefore be concluded that in DR's online elaboration of its public service remit, traditional broadcast ideas overshadowed what DR could (also) have accomplished with DR Online.

Notes

1. This focus on the actual use and possible impact of public service as a strategic concept within the media organization differs from much of the existing literature (see, for instance, Bardoel & d'Haenens, 2008; Enli, 2008; Syvertsen, 1999, 2004; Søndergaard, 1999).
2. It is very difficult to get an overview of relevant documents from DR, as well as to get access to them. Unlike the BBC Written Archive (cf. Kavanagh, 1999), DR's archives are hermetically closed to the public, including scholars, and the archive's reg-

istry is not very detailed or systematic. However, as an exception I was granted access to certain files related to DR Online. Since DR was promised anonymity to protect individuals, the authors of the sources have been left out. All sources were originally written in Danish, but their titles have been translated to English for the purpose of this chapter. Interviews were conducted with the former director general and the project manager, but since they were made before the writing of this book chapter, the idea of public service was not directly on the agenda, and these interviews have therefore not been used in this context. Nevertheless, on a general level, the statements of the two interviewees support the overall conclusions of the chapter.

3. This framework is presented in more detail in Brügger, 2010, pp. 34–42.
4. Other important driving forces include DR wanting to gain experience with the new medium, to be a first mover, and to sustain its position as prime developer of new technology.
5. An earlier key text is *Program Strategy. What Danmarks Radio Should Stand for in the '90s* (1991, 3 pages).
6. The history of DR Online remaining to be written, this chapter constitutes one of the first historical analyses of DR's online activities between 1994 and 1996, (DR Online's pre–history is described in more detail in Brügger, 2010, pp. 42–51).
7. The entire debate can still be found in The Internet Archive at http://web.archive.org/web/19970209082643/www.dr.dk/debat/drdebat.
8. Instead of being funded by license fees, DR Multimedia was to be run on a purely commercial basis and to be separated financially from the rest of DR.

References

Bardoel, J. & d'Haenens, L. (2008). Reinventing public service broadcasting in Europe: Prospects, promises, and problems. *Media, Culture & Society*, *30*(3), 337–355.

Brügger, N. (2010). Website history: An analytical grid. In N. Brügger (Ed.), *Web history* (pp. 29–59). New York: Peter Lang.

DR. (1994). *Danmarks Radio 1995–2005.* København, Denmark: DR.

DR. (1997). *Beretning og regnskab 1996. Satsninger og resultater.* København, Denmark: DR.

DRåben (1995, April 21). København, Denmark: DR.

DRåben (1996, January 12). København, Denmark: DR.

DRåben (1996, May 10). København, Denmark: DR.

Enli, G.S. (2008). Redefining Public Service Broadcasting: Multi–Platform Participation. *Convergence*, *14*(1), 105–120.

Kavanagh, J. (1999). The BBC's Written Archives as a source for Media History. *Media History*, *5*(1), 81–86.

Syvertsen, T. (1999). The Many Uses of the "Public Service" Concept. *Nordicom Review*, *20*(1), 5–12.

Syvertsen, T. (2004). Citizens, Audiences, Customers and Players: A Conceptual Discussion of the Relationship between Broadcasters and Their Publics. *European Journal of Cultural Studies*, *7*(3), 363–380.

Søndergaard, H. (1999). Some Reflections on Public Service Broadcasting. *Nordicom Review*, *20*(1), 21–28.

8 "...[and] They Formed Themselves into a Single Unit"[1]

The Development of the Israeli Broadcasting Authority Website

Amit M. Schejter & Merav Katz-Kimchi

Introduction

Two noticeable developments characterize Israel since the mid 1980s and following the stabilization of its economy: an ideological transition from a social democracy to a neo–liberal populist regime and an unprecedented and virtually incomparable acquisition of information and communication technologies by its inhabitants. Both changes have had an enduring effect on Israel's national broadcaster, the Israel Broadcasting Authority (IBA). Ideologically, its importance as a public–service broadcaster has diminished and its very need has been questioned, while its dwindling coffers denied it the means to develop technologically. This situation led yet again to the rise of the "tinkering" culture—the bottom–up improvisation of professionals within an organization developing institutional capacities through trial and error—that has been its trademark since its inception. Tinkering was central this time in the activities surrounding the development, design and content of the IBA's presence on the World Wide Web.

This chapter focuses on the history of IBA's web site. After setting the general historical context and introducing IBA's history and structure, the chapter describes the development of computerization in Israel and at IBA and the steps that led to the launch of its website up to its present form. The historical description is based on archival materials accessed at IBA, interviews conducted with the relevant IBA employees, and previously published analyses of

IBA's web site, which helped highlight the changes in its design and content. The description reveals how the culture of "tinkering" that has characterized IBA for decades, led to an irresolute process in which IBA's fractured nature, technological inferiority and succumbing to government pressures, served to hamper the creation of a unified web presence devoted to a public service mission despite the good–willed intentions of the professional brass.

From a Socialist–agrarian to a Neo–liberal Information Society

Founded in 1948 as a socialist–inspired democracy Israel has experienced a "'change from a socialist inspired mixed, highly centralized, highly planned state–centered, protectionist economy to a much more decentralized and internationally oriented neo liberal one'" (Aronoff, 2001).

Nowhere has this transformation been more evident than in the telecommunications and information industries. These industries were solely comprised of government—provided services since the inception of the state. Since the 1990s they morphed into an industry providing universal access to digital landline telephony; mobile services and broadband internet capability over competing networks; as well as a multichannel information and entertainment industry delivered over privately owned and operated digital television, radio and online outlets.

During this period, national policymaking was taken over by key ministers and technocrats (Sharkansky, 1997) who were consequently able to launch a revolutionary neo–liberal change in policy (Plessner, 1994; Rivlin, 1992). The change in policymaking culture was also characterized by improvisation, immortalized in the words of the slain Prime Minister Yitzhak Rabin as the "'rely on me'" culture (Sharkansky, 1999). Thus for both high impact and small–scale initiatives, change in Israel has traditionally been characterized by a culture of improvisation, which can also be referred to as a culture of "tinkering" (Badham & Ehn, 1999).

The Introduction of the Internet in Israel

The internet arrived in Israel early, through two small–scale initiatives of highly motivated individuals in the 1980s. It was a process characteristic of the innovative nature of Israeli society and of the center of such innovativeness—Israeli academia. The first was the establishment in 1982 of a dial–up connection at the Hebrew University of Jerusalem, which was limited to email exchange and was only available to people within the University. It was discontinued as the phone bill charged by Israel's state telecom monopoly became prohibitively high. At the beginning of 1984, the Ministry of Science helped establish the first connection to the American CSNET. Israel then became the first international node on the CSNET. Later that year, and independently, another connection was established between the recently established Inter–University Computation Center (IUCC, known in Israel by its Hebrew acronym MACHBA) and EARN, the European Academic Research Network. At that time, EARN was already connected to the American BITNET. In 1985, Israel was only the third country in the world to be allocated a Country Code Top Level Domain (ccTLD),."il," immediately after the United States (US) and the United Kingdom (UK).

Development in the 1980s was limited to academic institutions as is true with regards to the development of the internet worldwide at that period. The "Israeli" twist of this development was that the institutional action was typically a reaction to individual initiatives. The first institutional decision aimed at expanding access to the internet was the establishment in 1990 of the Israel Research and Education Network (IREN) and of an inter–ministerial committee that set the criteria for adding more institutional users to the net (John, 2008). The government awarded in 1994 the first Internet Service Provider (ISP) licenses to three entrepreneurial companies and MACHBA was entirely cut out of the commercial aspects of the internet by mid 1997. The first 15 years of internet presence in Israel were thus characterized by a slow and cautious government response to academic and private sector initiatives. The liberalization of telecommunications markets in Israel between 1993 and 2001, in which Israel joined a growing international trend, further contributed to the expansive growth of Israel's internet industry.

History of the Israel Broadcasting Authority

In 1965 the Knesset passed the Broadcasting Authority Law, establishing the Israel Broadcasting Authority (IBA), the country's first non–government broadcaster. Private broadcasting was non–existent at that time. The Law stipulated that the IBA would maintain the Israeli Broadcasting Service—until then a government–run radio service.

As one of the first independent authorities created in Israel, the IBA suffered a cumbersome structure from its inception—which was further complicated by the launching of the television service in 1968—and was closely tied to the government, much more so than were the national public service broadcasters of Western Europe (Schejter, 2009).

Since the rise of the nationalist and economically conservative *Likud* to power in 1977, the Israeli media scene has assumed a bifurcated character: IBA was deemed to become more nationalistic, and it was provided with lessening support as the neo–liberal ideology gained further footing. At the same time a vast commercial media industry was erected, which included 2 channels of commercial television, 15 regional–commercial radio stations, and two competing digital multi–channel platforms over cable and satellite with dozens of locally packaged channels. As the 1990s came to a close IBA assumed its current structure, operating one terrestrial television channel, one satellite television service predominantly in Arabic and eight radio networks.

While this may seem a well-planned process and structure, a closer look at the historical events leading to the establishment of different media outlets in Israel, both within IBA and in the private sector, reveals that many of the turning points in this development were either accidental, a reaction of the government to illegal developments in the market, or a result of unofficial informal initiatives that eventually assumed a life of their own. A state comptroller report of 1999 summarizes decades of managerial chaos in which the public bodies of the Authority and its management struggled to control the feeble operation (State Comptroller, 1999).

IBA's difficulties, though, did not manifest identically for its television and radio arms. Exposure studies for both television and radio conducted within the media industry demonstrate that while IBA television's share has dropped from 100 percent of the audience in 1984 to 15% in 2008; on radio it only dropped from 60% in 1988 (when its main "competitor" was the military's station, Galey Tzahal) to 35% in 2008. And while on television the dominance of over–the–air viewing has transferred to the commercial channels, on radio all commercial networks together were still held down to 30% of the market, with the military station, Galey Tzahal, still holding the remaining share. The different performance levels and the different impact commercialization has had on radio and television is just one manifestation of the fact that within IBA the radio and television arms did not traditionally share resources or strategic goals. In addition, chains of command were commonly disregarded, and a culture of improvisation, "tinkering" and "rely on me" characterized the operations of IBA. The introduction of the internet only further exacerbated all these phenomena: the rise of neo–liberalism; the rise of nationalism; the managerial chaos; and the culture of "tinkering."

Mid 1980s: The Computer Arrives at IBA

The history of modern computer usage in Israel adhered closely to its American counterpart in terms of the mainframe—small systems—personal and networked computer transition (Ceruzzi, 1998). With the exception of a few digital computers built in Israel at the Weizmann Institute and at RAFAEL (the armament development authority in the Ministry of Defense) from the mid–1950s to the mid–1960s (Breznitz, 2007), computers were imported from the US starting in the early 1950s with the first International Business Machines (IBM) mainframes, followed by midrange computers in the late 1960s, personal computers in the mid–1970s and various types of networked computers from the mid–1980s on.

In the mid–1980s, as the price of imported computers dropped, the IBA introduced computers first to its Finance, Administrative and Collection departments and later to the radio's newsroom. Computers were also used to monitor and manage the exact timing of ads broadcast. At the same time, computerized teleprinters were extensively used to bring international news to local audiences. During that period, IBA's management established the Computing Department, which at first was placed in the Finance Division. Concurrently, a computerized teletext service was launched in Israel after its success in the UK and elsewhere in Europe (Greenberg & Lin, 1988). The service was managed by the government run Instructional Television but was broadcast de facto by the radio newsroom, using brand new computers. Although a complete failure in terms of its audience share in Israel—as the haphazard plan to introduce the service failed to acknowledge the need for consumers to buy special decryption devices that would allow reading Hebrew text on imported television sets—teletext paved the way for the next steps in the computerization of IBA radio, as those in charge of its operation were the first to show interest in the internet as it was making its way to Israel.

1990s: First Steps in the Internet World

The first transmission of an IBA program over the internet took place in August of 1995. It was the brainchild of a private company named "Artificia," which notified the director of radio at IBA in September 1995 that it had started retransmitting the news programs of IBA's news network, "Network B." Clearly there was some measure of naïveté at both Artificia and IBA at the time. IBA radio personnel were fascinated by the new technology and cooperated with Artificia's initiative by running a promotional jingle on the radio. This activity went mostly unnoticed by IBA's central management for at least two and a half years. It was, however, received enthusiastically by internet users around the world, including Israeli expats, travelling businesspeople, non–Israeli Jews who used it to learn Hebrew, and others who showered the web site with thank you emails. Artificia's operators estimated at the time 100,000 hits a month on the web site, although the accuracy of that number can be questioned. In late 1996 Artificia created an online pay service called "Israel Club" (whose URL was www.artificia.com/html/news/entrance) that offered two tiers of service: a "basic" (and free) limited access and a "Super

User" pay service that allowed full access to radio news and select access to some television programming including news, and as of 1997, including IBA's flagship documentary program produced for Israel's 50th anniversary "Tkuma" ("Ressurection"). IBA radio officials, unaware of this development, at first disassociated themselves from Artificia altogether when they finally learned about it in 1997. IBA television staff was apparently fully unaware of Artificia's existence, let alone the fact that its popular news program was being retransmitted worldwide. However, it was only in early 1998, and as a result of a complaint filed by an operator of a satellite company that had purchased exclusive rights for retransmitting IBA television programs in the U.S., that IBA's management became fully aware of the extent of Artificia's operations. The central management then initiated legal action that led to Artificia's site closing down.

However, by September 1997, IBA radio launched concurrently another website tied to a weekly radio program on internet issues titled Interbet[2] on its news network "B." An informal cooperation agreement with Netvision, Israel's pioneer ISP, included two computers placed by Netvision in the IBA newsroom and a point–to–point dedicated line from IBA's radio studio in Jerusalem to Netvision's headquarters near Haifa. Netvision launched a web site, whose URL interbet.netvision.net.il provided access to a live transmission of IBA radio's network "B."

The website was simple in design. It had both Hebrew and English versions (though not one in Arabic, which is one of Israel's two official languages) and provided a hyperlink to a recorded version of the latest radio program of Interbet. In addition, the home page functioned as an online directory of websites that had been mentioned in the program since it began to be aired in 1996. These websites were grouped together under diverse categories such as "news and media," "education," "computers and internet" and "nature, geography, science and animals."

This initiative too, driven and managed by mid–management level individuals at IBA radio, resulted in legal difficulties. First among them was a claim by music right holders that they deserve extra compensation from IBA for airing their copyrighted materials, now that IBA has added a new "medium" of transmission.

Unrelated to the radio's initiative, IBA central management started studying the issue of the internet in the mid 1990s. A consultant was hired, who provided the management with an elaborate scheme for a web site that would include all of IBA's media. This initiative was clearly antithetical to IBA's corporate culture (in addition to seeming expensive) and never took off. However, now that the management was called in March 1998 to resolve both the

Artificia and Netvision "situations" and as a result of the legal difficulties created by these local initiatives in lower management, it resolved that the best way to go about the chaotic situation, in order to adhere to IBA's contractual duties and obligations under administrative law, was to outsource the expensive effort and publish a public tender. The management decided that only radio content would be distributed over the internet and that television programs should be left out of the website. Netvision sued IBA for apparent breach of contract; however, eventually gave up, the Interbet site was abandoned,[3] and the "Interbet" program was taken off the air.

The new management appointed in 1998 following the change in government of 1996 decided to launch the www.iba.org.il web site, which went live in the spring of 2000. Choosing the .org top–level–domain put IBA at the time alongside the Japanese NHK and the American PBS, NPR and CPB. This in itself made it an interesting choice as IBA as a public broadcaster operated utilizing a model more reminiscent of the British BBC than of either the Japanese or American models. Indeed, top–level domain choices, which more often than not provide an indication regarding the self–identity of the organizations employing them, are not as indicative in differentiating among public broadcasters and the different models they employ (Schejter, 2003).

The new site was managed by the Computing Department, which was housed in the central management building while the content was provided by interested units at IBA at their own initiative—both content units (i.e., the different networks of IBA Radio and IBA Television) and administrative units (i.e., the collection department, the ombudsman, etc.). IBA radio news was the first interested party.

2000s: Launch of the IBA Website

Starting in 2000, the homepage carried headlines of breaking news, originating in the IBA radio newsroom. In addition, it provided information about IBA broadcasting schedules for radio and television, hyperlinks to live radio broadcasting of the different IBA networks, a hyperlink to a recorded version of its television evening newscast, a hyperlink to a recorded version of its television news program in English and a hyperlink to a recorded version of a popular cooking program on television. Thus, the website's main focus was to provide an additional channel for disseminating content originating in IBA's traditional media.

Since its launch and until probably 2007, and loyal to its nationalistic positioning, the IBA website carried links to the Israeli Ministry of Foreign Affairs and to the official press office of the military and placed them at the top left hand corner of its home page. Surfers were not informed of the nature of these external hyperlinks, which appeared as integral components of IBA website.

In 2007, Israel's leading news website, Ynet.co.il, published a review of a study on the IBA's website (Schejter, 2007), in which this nationalistic gesture was questioned and critiqued. As a result, the Computing Department personnel decided at their own initiative to move the links to the bottom right hand side of the page, and changed the link's title from English (in which they were called "Foreign Affairs" and "Defence Force"[4]) to Hebrew.

The process by which content was added to the website was initiated by employees of the different IBA radio channels that were interested in making the broadcasting of their channels serve as sub–domains of the IBA website, and not by IBA's management. The small group of employees working in the Computing Department technically assisted those employees in getting the content online. These sub–domains were grouped separately on the IBA page. Later, when television and administrative services (such as information regarding payment of the license fee and information required under the Freedom of Information Law) were added, they too were grouped under the appropriate sub–headings and laid on the iba.org.il home page.

The selection of television programs offered on the website during this whole period as well was initiated by the producers of the programs themselves. Thus only a few of television channel 1's programs could be accessed over the website while the process for selecting those programs had no clear criteria and the timing of their launch reflected no centralized policy. Still, despite the lack of a guiding hand, the selection of programs on the web site grew steadily and allowed access to a growing number of news, documentaries, current affairs, sports, and cooking programs. While in 2005 the site only offered access to recorded television programs (Schejter, 2007), by 2010 it allowed access to a live feed of television as well.

In its early incarnation, between 2000–2005, the website did not provide any content created especially for internet distribution; neither did it utilize any interactive technologies (such as RSS) or services to mobile or handheld devices. These missing features were even more noticeable when comparing the IBA website to other Israeli websites of media outlets, such as the websites of Israeli daily newspapers, which presented advanced services and dedicated internet content during the same period. The IBA made no effort to attract children or teenagers who are usually considered target audiences for public broadcasting.

Continuing its long neglect of Arab citizens of the State (see Schejter, 2008), the IBA website only provided a hyperlink to recorded versions of the radio newscast in Arabic in the mid–2000s but not to live feeds of programs in Arabic. Other services such as paying the annual IBA fee online were not available in Arabic.

The radio newsroom systematically fed the front page of the IBA website with breaking news stories (text only) in the first five years after the launch of the website. However, starting at the end of 2005 and until the end of 2008, a pay dispute between IBA's management and newsroom employees led to a halt of the daily feed. During these three years the Computing Department fed the IBA front page with occasional breaking news titles delivered directly from the IBA radio director's office, circumventing the newsroom. Managed by an untrained administrator, this initiative led to embarrassing incidents—among them cases in which news items under "embargo" made their way to the website before they were cleared for broadcast on radio.

2000s: Latest Developments

Following the 2007–2008 violent skirmishes along the border with the Gaza Strip, the IBA website received thousands of hits by citizens demanding updated news bulletins on the ongoing bombing. As a result, at the beginning of 2009, and with the appointment of a new director of news at IBA radio, IBA management decided to set up an internet desk that would officially and systematically feed the front page of the IBA website.

The establishment of the internet desk was one example of the growing involvement of IBA's management in the website's content. Another example was its intervention in the carriage of network "C" and the traffic network. Since the first websites went online in 1995 and 1996, IBA officials were of the impression that they needed to rewrite their copyright agreements in order to regularly broadcast music online. As a result, the Israeli music network "C" and the music-heavy traffic network were kept offline. However, in 2005, then acting director general of the IBA attended a meeting of the European Broadcasting Union in Dubrovnik. During a casual conversation with Danish colleagues he learned that they had made all their music programs accessible online and encountered no legal difficulty. Upon returning to Israel he ordered immediate access to live online broadcasts of the two light music networks ("C" and "traffic"). Both these examples demonstrate that even when management was involved in the process, its involvement was not part of a planned effort, but rather a reaction to a suddenly recognized need and opportunity. The same can be said about the appointment in 2003 of a "director of the internet medium." A political move on behalf of the sitting Director General, the appointment was made in order to "free up" the position of News Director at IBA radio. The new "Internet Director" discovered shortly after his appointment that he was awarded no resources to launch a new medium and eventually resigned from the Authority.

Although working on a very tight budget, the Computing Department kept pace with advances in online broadcasting and web applications and managed to broadcast all the joining networks and to add some new web applications like RSS. However, the small budget limited any further development of the website when compared to the capabilities of public service broadcasters in developed Western democracies. In the spring of 2007, for the first time since online broadcasting began in 1995, IBA management appointed a steering committee to oversee internet affairs. The committee included personnel from the Computing Department, ex–managers of the different media and external advisors including leading figures in the Israeli high–tech industry. In the fall of 2009 the steering committee met with the management and presented two options for the website's development. The first was to formally recognize content distribution over the internet as a "medium" separate from radio and television and to deliberately usher the IBA into the new era of online broadcasting. The second option was more realistic and rooted in IBA's limited budget and its declining popularity. It offered that IBA would authorize an outside agency to handle its content in order to recapture its importance in public life and heighten its appeal to younger audiences. IBA's website, at the same time, was to remain in its current form. This second option was the road chosen.

At the time of going to press the IBA website homepage still presents headlines of breaking news. In addition, it provides live access to all IBA radio programs on their respective networks and serves as a gateway to each of the networks' sub–domains, which include textual materials describing each network and its programming. IBA television channel 1's live broadcasts are also accessible and the site provides access to a limited number of recorded television programs in both Hebrew and Arabic.

The site still does not have an Arabic version and does not provide services in Arabic. Paradoxically, there are titles in Arabic on two links on the home page: the link leading to the IBA frequency changes list (as a result of the transition to digital television) and a link to IBA's public tenders and position announcements. However, accessing those links leads to a Hebrew-only web page.

In recent years the website has added traffic reports and weather reports and opened up an online shop that sells CDs of previously broadcast television programs considered "classics." It also added some special features to improve its dialogue capacities with potential audiences, such as "Forums" (online discussion groups for most of the radio programs and some of the television programs). In addition, it has a Facebook site, Twitter and RSS services.

Concluding Remarks

IBA's decentralized culture and mode of operation, and the culture of improvisation and tinkering were behind the establishment of IBA's online presence; however, these apparently were not unique to IBA, but characterized many public broadcasters worldwide as they made a transition to the internet. Toward the end of the first decade of the century, at least the external appearance of the site seemed to indicate professionalization.

Notwithstanding its similarity to the unplanned nature of internet adoption by public broadcasters elsewhere, the process at IBA is indicative and characteristic of the development of media at IBA historically and of IBA's corporate culture. Since computers were present both at the central management offices and in the radio, and as these units were both geographically and organizationally separate, two separate efforts emerged since the mid–1990s to introduce IBA to the internet and vice versa. The haphazard and chaotic growth of the IBA website, improvised by professional tinkerers in the Computing Department, was accentuated by the lack of interest in the internet as a medium on behalf of IBA's management. Mired in conflicting pressures from a government keen at either its dissolution or obedience since the mid 1990s, and managed by appointees unsure of their future due to temporary appointments and threats of removal from office, IBA's management was not equipped with the financial means, technological know how or managerial focus needed to strategically tackle the challenges raised by the internet.

Thus the history of IBA's internet presence is consistent with the history of its other media. Like television and some of its radio services, the development of internet services was more a series of reactions than an outcome of a planned effort. Indeed, similar to other moments in IBA's history, the improvisation, grassroots efforts and tinkering of good–willed public servants created the improbable with limited means and lack of planning. At the same time the service itself, like other IBA services was of low quality and inferior to its Israeli commercial competitors or international equivalents, and remains so.

However, the history of IBA's website can also be seen as a turning point for a new beginning. The decentralized and bottom up nature of the development of the site, has led to a process unseen before at IBA, which stands in contradiction to institutionalized practices: the internet has forced IBA to pull its disparate units, deny its centrifugal forces and work to become a unified cluster. A concerted look at the history we've described herein demonstrates how each individual effort of three separate units—radio, television and administration—has emerged as one uniform entity (albeit admittedly, of limited capabilities). Indeed, the internet carries the potential for enhanced personalization of services and interactivity, which may lead to a contribution to democratization of society and the pursuit of individual autonomy, goals that can be seen within the traditional remit of public broadcasting. For IBA, however, at this under–developed stage it served more as a healer within. While these are all small steps and in no way an indication of major transitions in IBA's culture, as broadband internet becomes the predominant means of communication in society and in Israel specifically, its emergence may mark the beginning of a new and positive era at IBA and its formation into one group.

Notes

1. 2 Samuel 2:25
2. The name "Interbet" is a play on words, as "Bet" is the second letter in the Hebrew alphabet and the nickname of the news network "B."
3. It is still online; however, it has not been updated for content since 2000.
4. The wrong spelling appeared this way on the website.

References

Aronoff, M. J. (2001). Radical change in Israel: A review essay. *Political Science Quarterly, 116,* 447–453.

Badham, R. & Ehn, P. (1999). Tinkering with technology: Human factors, ork redesign, and professionals in workplace innovation. *Human Factors and Ergonomics in Manufacturing & Service Industries, 10*(1), 61–82.

Breznitz, D. (2007). *Innovation and the state: Political choice and strategies for growth in Israel, Taiwan, and Ireland.* New Haven, CT: Yale University Press.

Caspi, D. & Limor, Y. (1999). *The in/outsiders: Mass media in Israel.* Cresskill, NJ: Hampton Press.

Ceruzzi, P. (1998). *A history of modern computing.* Cambridge, MA: MIT Press.

Gil, Z. (1986). *House of diamonds: The history of Israeli television.* Tel Aviv: Sifriyat Poalim. (In Hebrew.)

Greenberg, S. B. & Lin, C. (1988). *Patterns of teletext use in the UK.* London: John Libbey.

John, N. (2008). *The arrival of the Internet in Israel: The local diffusion of a global technology.* (Unpublished doctoral dissertation). Hebrew University, Jerusalem, Israel. Available also at www.sociothink.com.

Plessner, Y. (1994). *The political economy of Israel: From ideology to stagnation.* Albany: State University of New York Press.

Rivlin, P. (1992). *The Israeli Economy.* Boulder, CO: Westview Press.

Schejter, A. (1999). From a tool for national cohesion, to a manifestation of national conflict: The evolution of cable television policy in Israel, 1986–1998. *Communication Law and Policy, 4*(2), 177–200.

Schejter, A. (2003). Public broadcasting, the information society and the Internet: A paradigm shift? In M. McCauley, E. Peterson, L. Artz & D. Halleck (Eds.), *Public Broadcasting and the Public Interest* (pp. 158–174). Armonk, NY: M.E. Sharpe.

Schejter, A. (2007). Online transformation: The Israel Broadcasting Authority on the Internet—What goes, what gets by and what should give. In T. Schwartz–Altschuller (Ed.), *Online Journalism in Israel* (pp. 51–83). Jerusalem: Israel Democracy Institute and Burda Center for Innovative Communications at Ben Gurion University of the Negev. (In Hebrew.)

Schejter, A. (2008) “The stranger that dwelleth with you shall be unto you as one born among you”—Israeli media law and the cultural rights of the Palestinian Israeli minority. *Middle East Journal of Culture and Communication, 1,* 156–179.

Schejter, A. (2009). *Muting Israeli democracy: How media and cultural policy undermine free expression.* Urbana: University of Illinois Press.

Schejter, A. & Elavsky, C.M. (2009). “ . . . and the children of Israel sang this song”: The role of Israeli law and policy in the advancement of Israeli music. *Min–Ad: Israel Studies in Musicology Online, 7*(2), 131–153.

Sharkansky, I. (1997). *Policy making in Israel: Routines for simple problems and coping with the complex.* Pittsburgh, PA: University of Pittsburgh Press.

Sharkansky, I. (1999). *Ambiguity, coping, and governance: Israeli experiences in politics, religion, and policymaking.* Westport, CT: Praeger Publishers.

State Comptroller. (1999). *State Comptroller report,* 1999. (In Hebrew.) Available at http://80.70.129.40/docs/rashot.rtf

Tokatly, O. (2000). *Communication policy in Israel.* Tel Aviv: Open University. (In Hebrew.)

9 *Southern European Public Service Broadcasters Expanding Online*

A Policy Study of RAI and RTVE's Online Activities

Benedetta Brevini

Introduction

Public service broadcasters (PSBs) have played a prominent role in the democratic life of Western European countries for decades. They performed a function that has been recognized and reaffirmed by all European institutions (Brevini, 2010a). For example, the Protocol on Public Service Broadcasting annexed to the 1997 Treaty of Amsterdam clearly states that:

> The system of public broadcasting in the Member States is directly related to the democratic, social and cultural needs of each society and to the need to preserve media pluralism.

It is important to highlight that each PSB system developed according to its nation's peculiar set of historical, cultural and political traditions. Even so, there has been a common rationale behind European PSB aimed to develop a "new kind of access to virtually the whole spectrum of public life" (Scannell, 1989, p. 140).

In the late nineties, several PSBs started expanding into the online world (Brügger, 2010; Brevini, 2010a). In countries like the UK, Germany and Denmark PSBs have been able to seize the new opportunities offered by the internet and establish their supremacy online (Brevini, 2010a, 2010b). The situation in the south of Europe is certainly different, however, where PSB online is a more recent and less explored phenomenon.

This chapter aims to shed light on PSBs' online expansion in the south of Europe. It presents a comparative study of the internet activities of Spain's PSB TVE and Italy's PSB RAI. The study draws on the Hallin & Mancini model (2004) of media systems that identifies Spain and Italy as functioning within the "Mediterranean or polarized pluralistic model" (Hallin & Mancini, 2004, p. 67). The model allows me to attempt generalization of my findings, given the common features of the mediterranean cluster. Among the main traits of the model are a "low circulation of press, high level of political parallelism, weak professionalization, a strong state intervention and politicized public service broadcasting" (ibid., p. 67).

This chapter examines the online expansion of the two PSBs by exploring their historical and political legacy, as well as their regulatory and funding frameworks. On the one hand, it examines the policies adopted by the governments of the two nations regarding the internet activities of TVE and RAI and, on the other it discusses the policies and practices developed by TVE and RAI in the same field. As Hallin and Mancini (2004) have argued, the history of broadcasting policy in the south of Europe has been characterized by a strong political intervention. Hence this analysis can ascertain whether the online expansion of PSB follows the same pattern with an identical limited scope for technocratic decision making.

RTVE Moves Online: From Neglect to a Greater Investment to New Uncertainties

The Spanish provider of public television, Television Española (TVE), was implemented in 1956 during the dictatorship of Francisco Franco (1939–1975). TVE was, since the beginning, characterized by a strong governmental grip, typical of state broadcasting (Pérez Ornia, 1988). Since its foundation, TVE benefited from dual funding: advertisement under monopoly conditions and a small amount of public resources (Bustamante, 1989). After Franco's death in 1975, TVE continued to distinguish itself on the one hand for its strong political control, and on the other for its commercial orientation (Bustamante, 2008). As López-Escobar (1992) explains:

> It was evident that the economic health of public television would depend on its ability to attract as large an audience as possible, and that it could only manage this by showing a popular range of programmes which could compete with the commercial channels. (p. 251)

The reliance of TVE on advertisements also explains why, when the competition of commercial broadcasters was introduced in Spain by Act 10/1988,

TVE began to suffer a crisis of resources. Year by year, the level of accumulated debt became more and more serious. From 1991 to 2006, the debt of Radiotelevisión Española (RTVE)—the public broadcasting corporation that since 1973 incorporated the public radio (RNE) and Television (TVE)—surpassed 9 million euros (RTVE, 2005). For the historical and institutional reasons highlighted—namely for the lack of dedicated resources and the deep structural crisis of TVE—investments in online ventures have been feeble until the new reform brought by Act 17/2006.[1] The reform had an important bearing on the development of the internet activities of RTVE because it readjusted its organization, funding and structure and drove the growth of RTVE online.[2]

As Bustamante (2008), a member of the "council of wise men" that drafted the reform, explained:

> We had to face two issues combined. On one hand the transformation of TVE into a more democratic PSB. On the other hand we had to face the new digital and online scenario. (p. 2)

The turning point in the history of the internet activities of RTVE dates back to the Zapatero reform of 2005–2006. Although RTVE.es started its activities in 1996, before the reform, the online activities were initially very minimal. As demonstrated in an EBU—BBC survey in 2006, RTVE was positioned very last in the European ranking of EBU member websites (EBU and BBC, 2007). According to the survey, 4.9% of the active online audience visited TVE's site in the month of June 2007 (EBU and BBC, 2007). During the same period of 2007, reach of the BBC websites was 59.6%, whereas RAI's online sites attained 11% (EBU and BBC, 2007).

The reasons for this delay in the development of RTVE online and its consequent low ranking among European countries was the grave financial crisis faced by RTVE in the in the 1990s, the mishandling of the budget, the inefficiency of the organization and the continuous turnover of managers according to the different political affiliations in power. From its launch in 1996, the RTVE portal was characterized by a lack of resources, to the extent that the online content was updated just once a week. As Carmen Caffarel, General Manager of RTVE under the first Zapatero government, declared at the time of the first re–launch of the portal in 2004:

> The portal of RTVE was just looked after by three people in the morning and the content was sometimes not updated in weeks. (Diarios, 2004, p. 22)

From Parliamentary discussions of 2004 we can appreciate for the first time what type of online offer was envisaged. A member of Parliament (MP) from the Socialist Group—Rosa Lucia Polonio Contreras—declared:

> The internet portal of RTVE should be not just a complement to public service, but should be itself conceived as a public service, being one of the activities of RTVE as a public entity. Therefore our group considers that RTVE can neither keep being unconnected to the new media scenario, nor can it start integrating into the information society with so many disadvantages in comparison to the private competitors. (Diarios, 2004, p. 22)

This quote is relevant in showing once again the double character of PSB philosophy in Spain that persisted in the online world: on the one hand, the need to deliver classic PSB output (Brevini, 2008) and on the other hand, a strong commercial requirement to be competitive in the market in order to collect advertising revenue.

As mentioned earlier, even though the online activities of RTVE were launched in 1996, it was in 2004 under the direction of Carmen Caffarel that the organization of RTVE's online services started to progress. New streaming contents produced by TVE and by the National Radio (RNE) enriched the platform, and the number of professionals working for the portal reached twelve. In June 2005, the number of pages viewed per month was 1.1 million, and in December of the same year, that figure reached 13.4 million (RTVE, 2005). However, it was the reform of 2005–2006 that brought a radical innovation to the internet department of RTVE. In order to appreciate the contrasting ideas behind the vision of RTVE online within the institution, it is worthwhile to juxtapose the wording of the draft of the reform—the "informe"—with the Annual Report of RTVE of the same year.

According to the draft of the reform:

> The internet of RTVE should offer radio, TV, and multimedia services that are adequate for a two-way communication. That means that it should be strongly participative and democratic for the citizens, according to a vision of public service. (Informe, 2005, p. 127)

This quote certainly illustrates the aspiration—for the "council of wise men" that was asked to reform the public television of Spain—to achieve an authentic public service in the online sphere (Brevini, 2008).

In contrast, the wording of the Annual Report of RTVE 2005 states that:

> The presence of RTVE online becomes crucial both from the point of view of the public service and the business. (RTVE, 2005)

Once again, the debate around PSB online in Spain mirrors the debate about public service television. Even if there is, in the spirit of the reform, the urge to secure the aims of a PSB institution, this idea always clashes with the strong commercial orientation that has traditionally characterized TVE with its prerequisite of obtaining resources through advertising.

The first Mandato Marco signed at the end of 2007 endows a new significance to the internet activities of RTVE.[3] Also, the Agreement on the foundation of RTVE as a corporation establishes a new separate division for the Multimedia and Interactive Services of RTVE.

The Multimedia division launched in 2008 employed seventy professionals, a big change to the previous organization where just twelve people were employed. A new portal—RTVE.es—was launched on the 20th May 2008 under the supervision of the first director of New Interactive Media of RTVE, Rosalia Lloret. It increased unique users from an average of less than 1 million a month in 2007 to an average of almost 2 million in 2008, to 7 million in 2010 (ODJ Interactiva, 2008, 2010).

Since its transformation in 2008, an ambitious plan to upload both radio and broadcasting content produced by TVE and RNE (Radio Nacional de España) was undertaken, with more than one million hours of programs being offered by the archive. Furthermore, the news offer was enhanced by news services produced by a separate online news division. Also, as Rosalia Lloret (2008) explains:

> We have a very similar platform to the BBC I player, Television a la carta. In fact, you can watch everything that is broadcast on TVE for 7 days after the transmission. (Lloret, 2008)

Notwithstanding the reform and the accomplishments of the new division, a strong entertainment and commercial vocation was apparent in the new portal. This trait was explained by the prominent reliance of RTVE on advertisements (accounting for approximately 65% of its total funding) up until the "counter reform" of 2009. Hence, in 2008 Lloret confirmed that:

> We believe that the portal should also spur the online advertisement market that in Spain is still stagnant at 7%. (Lloret, 2008)

However, the abolition of advertisements will have a high impact not only the budget of RTVE.es, but also on its content. The strong commercial orientation that has so far characterized RTVE on the web could diminish and more space could be given to news, public affairs, and educational programs. Although this outcome could be guaranteed just by solid public investment, at the moment the finances of RTVE seem to have been returned to the realm of uncertainties, as in the pre–reform years.[4] If the resources are put in doubt, the recent progress of RTVE.es could be jeopardized. In fact, in April 2010 RTVE reached 7 million unique users per month and surpassed the success of its commercial competitors online by 1 million unique users (ODJ interactiva, 2010). According to ODJ Interactiva, in April 2010 the number of unique users of Antena 3 and Telecinco were both about 6 million (ibid.). This result also confirms that RTVE.es on the web is more a competitor of the commercial broadcasters than of online news providers. Thus, RTVE is still placed in the category of "entertainment media" by OJD Interactiva, being separated from the websites of newspapers such as *El Mundo* or *El Periodico* that are listed as providers of news. *El Mundo* online has enjoyed its supremacy as an online news provider at least until April 2010, when it had 25 million unique users and 377 million page views (OJD Interactiva, 2010).

In a nutshell, RTVE's online expansion has been constrained by a radical institutional and structural crisis that afflicted the Spanish PSB between 1991 up to 2006. The inadequate resources invested by RTVE have delayed the development of its online output until the radical change brought by Act 17/2006. Since then, the Multimedia division launched in 2008 with its seventy professionals has implemented a clear strategy of expansion. The new portal—RTVE.es—has increased unique users from an average of fewer than 1 million a month in 2007 to an average of almost 2 million in 2008, to 7 million in 2010. Still, a strong entertainment and commercial vocation characterizes RTVE's online content. This feature is due to the reliance of RTVE on advertisements (accounting for approximately 65% of its total funding) up until the "counter reform" of 2009 that has once again revolutionized its funding system.

RAI Online Constrained by Political Negligence

RAI (Radio Televisione Italiana) is the provider of Public Service Broadcasting in Italy under a 20–year license convention with the state. The broadcaster started its transmissions in 1954 and maintained its monopoly until the early 80s, when private competitors entered first the local markets and later the national one. During the years of the monopoly, RAI played an important role in the cultural development of the country (Hibberd, 2001, p. 234). It also contributed to the unification of the fragmented Italian public (Monteleone, 2001) through the deployment of successful educational policies. However, in line with the Hallin & Mancini model (2004), the broadcaster never freed itself from control by political elites. In fact, RAI has for many years been subject to "lottizzazione"—the distribution of posts and power according to political affiliation (Hallin & Mancini, 2004; Mazzoleni & Vigevani, 2005)—and subsequent reforms adopted to re–establish RAI's accountability, independence and supervision having in fact never succeeded.

However, with the arrival of competition—and more precisely the commercial television empire of Silvio Berlusconi in the 80s—RAI has unmistakably broken with its tradition by competing with the new commercial rivals for the audience. As Hibberd (2001) puts it "no other European public service broadcaster . . . was forced to break so clearly with its old programming formats" (Hibberd, 2001, p. 237).

Hence, RAI's regulatory framework mixed funding structure and strict links to political majorities are all fundamental elements of the online expansion of RAI.

As can be plainly inferred from the policies developed by the Italian government and RAI itself concerning its online offering, the internet was never considered a crucial part of the public service remit of RAI.

The first policy documents to affirm the importance of RAI exploring new media opportunities were the service contracts[5] signed under the centre–left coalition for the period 1997–99 and 2000–2002.[6] However, the Contract of 2003, signed by the centre–right majority, shifted the main priority to digital television take–up.[7] The same is true for the Gasparri Law (Law 112 of 2004), strongly advocated by Prime Minister Berlusconi to secure his unconstitutional dominance of the television market in Italy (Constitutional Court 1988 and 1994).

It was only when the new service contract of 2007 was signed by the centre–left majority that the new media expansion of RAI became relevant again. Article 6 of the service contract for the period 2007–2009 declares that:

> 1. RAI will define a clear strategy to add value to its own productions and its audiovisual rights on every multimedia platform, from the digital terrestrial and satellite offer to IPTV, mobile and internet;
> 2. RAI will enhance and update the service offered on its portal *www.rai.it* in order to enlarge the actual production with new content for the internet;
> 3. RAI will make available, within the limits of copyright law, every type of content produced by RAI to every internet user. . . . Moreover, RAI will allocate increasing resources to the acquisition of the copyrights of the programs. . . . (RAI, 2007b)

Nevertheless, it is interesting to note that the final draft of the Service Contract 2007 had a more progressive spirit than the official version of the contract. This was perhaps a sign of the resistance encountered inside RAI to implementing the new strategy.

In fact, the final draft of the Service Contract of 2007 stated that:

> RAI will make available on the portal www.rai.it every type of content produced by RAI to every internet user. (RAI, 2007a, art 6(3))

Moreover:

> RAI will negotiate the acquisition of copyrights of programs and it will allocate 7% of all its resources to the production or the acquisition of contents broadcasted by the TV channels . . . and it will offer to the users the opportunity to download every type of content under Creative Commons License. (RAI, 2007a, art 6(3))

As is clear from the text, the two versions showed wide discrepancies. In fact, the official contract took a more restrained approach that failed to secure a clear budget for the online offering, and abandoned the idea of providing free online content under a Creative Commons License.[8]

If the policies developed by the left coalition and the right coalition seemed extremely dissimilar, the lack of a continuous strategy due to scarce resources and a constant turnover of managers demonstrated the insufficient commitment of both the political majorities in power for a strong PSB online. Moreover, the former CEO of RAI NET indicated that one reason for the slow development of an online strategy was the "lack of competence of the leadership of RAI in the field of new media and new technology" (Contri, 2007).

Between 1997 and 1999, in one of several reforms of the Italian PSB of the last decade, RAI was reorganized into five segments, each with a specific remit: RAI NET, responsible for web activities; RAI SAT for satellite channels (and the subsequent agreement with Sky); RAI WAY, for transmissions services; RAI TRADE for the commercialization of RAI production; and RAI CLICK, a joint venture between RAI and Fastweb.[9]

Thus, we can trace the beginning of the online expansion of RAI to 1999, with the creation of RAI NET aimed at "enhancing the brand of RAI on the web" and the launch of the first, official portal, www.rai.it (Contri, 2007). If at that time it was clear that the main internet activities of RAI had to be directed by RAI NET, in 2005 the picture was further complicated by the creation of RAI New Media, a new directorate with the aim of coordinating the five divisions. However, RAI New Media has never performed its harmonizing functions, rather focusing on the Digital terrestrial television transition (ibid).

Interestingly, RAI NET provided the infrastructure for the websites of RAI and other multi–platform services. However, two important divisions of RAI—RAI Educational[10] and RAI International[11]—were completely independent from RAI NET and could " decide by themselves their own online strategy" (Zela, 2007). Besides, many programs and channels are today still running their websites independently (RaiNews24, Trebisonda, to name a few).

This complex organization of the web activities explains in part the lack of a clear and centralized strategy of RAI online. Additionally, the resource allocation for RAI's internet activities seems contradictory. Every year since 1999 when 20 million Euros were invested to establish RAI NET, RAI NET has been assigned 0.2% of the whole budget of RAI, or 6 million euros. Also, the staff employed at RAI NET is very limited, with just "6 journalists and 30 technicians that have to take care of all websites" (Contri, 2008).

The former CEO of RAI NET has surprisingly kept his position from January 2003 to March 2008, despite changes in government, and under his guidance a huge growth in page views and unique users has been achieved.[12] Data from Audiweb—Nielsen Online (2008) shows an increased interest in www.rai.tv, especially after the launch of the new portal rai.tv with an average of 2.8 million unique users every month in 2007, against an average of one million in 2003. However, despite the growth, the internet offering of RAI is still mainly entertainment–oriented with a surprising lack of investment in news and public affairs. The news offering, in the form of text, blogs of the newsrooms and interactive forums, is in its infancy on RAI's portal. Up until 2008, the service offered by RAI Net was not continuous across the week and was suspended during the weekend. Until recently no updates to the news and no upload of programs were made from Friday evening to Monday morning. In 2008 the two most important providers of online news were still enjoying an unchallenged dominance of the online news market with seven million unique users for *La Repubblica* (Nielsen Netratings, 2008) and six million for *Il Corriere della Sera* (ibid.).

Thus, RAI's portal seems the perfect replica of its TV offering, with most of the TV channels' content available online, but with no initiatives catering for the web. Consequently, the offering online mirrors the entertainment–oriented inclination of RAI's broadcasting output. With "scarce resources available to RAI Net," explained Contri (2007), "it is necessary to collect advertisement fees on the web; therefore the entertainment offering seems the only option" (Contri, 2007).

Yet an overview of the online presence of RAI would be incomplete without an analysis of the well–developed web activities by RAI Educational. This division of RAI, dedicated to educational programs that promote history, culture and science, has launched programs on the web since 1997. So far,

> RAI Educational web manages 30 websites of educational programs. The amount of money dedicated to RAI Educational as a whole totals 0.3% of RAI's overall budget, while on average, 20% of the budget of nine million Euros goes to the web activities. (Zela, 2007)

Some of the programs offered on the web by RAI Edu in 2008 were the online editions of successful TV programs, such as the Divertinglese and Divertipc, devoted to the learning of English as a second language and ICT alphabetization,[13] or "La Storia Siamo Noi" ("We Are History"), devoted to history. Others, like Medita were specifically created for the Net. Medita.rai.it, a multimedia project launched under an agreement with the Minister of Education, consisted of a Digital Multimedia Library dedicated to schools, and is "currently the most important online encyclopedia in Italy"(see www.medita.rai.it) and one of the biggest in Europe. In 2008 it comprised 2500 audiovisuals, hundreds of multimedia learning objects and 1100 hours of videos. The material has been designed to act as a complementary didactic activity.

To sum up, the relentless change of government and of its politically controlled management at RAI has thwarted the expansion of RAI on the web. Even though RAI started developing its online output in 1999, the investments were minimal because the internet has never been considered a priority. The growth registered by RAI's portal in 2007—with an increase from 2.8 million unique users per month in 2007, to an average of one million in 2003—was more due to the obstinate work of the isolated management of RAI Net than to a central strategy drawn by the Executive's Board. RAI's presence on the web has since its beginning showed a strong commercial orientation with mostly fictional and reality shows on offer, as a consequence of its high reliance on advertisement and scarcity of funding. Yet, the achievement of the educational department, with its strong focus on the online offer constitutes the exception to the dominant paradigm.

Comparison and Concluding Remarks

This study has detailed substantial differences between the RAI's and RTVE's policies on internet expansion, although the two countries belong to the same Mediterranean model characterized by a "politics over broadcasting system" (Hallin & Mancini, 2004, p. 106). Because of their intense politicization, RAI online and RTVE online have developed different responses to the internet world. At the same time, their strong links to politics confirm once again the validity of the Mediterranean model and its usefulness for attempting generalization on the state of the art of PSBs online in the south of Europe.

I have highlighted in the discussion how Spain embodies a tradition within which its PSB has enjoyed a secondary place in the market, with scarce resources and high commercialization. In contrast, RAI has always benefited from a strong position in the Italian television market, but has developed since the 80s an extremely entertainment-oriented offer, quite similar to that of TVE. However,the recent determination to invest in RTVE online is pushing the two PSB institutions further apart.

Since the first Zapatero reform, and especially after 2007, the development of RTVE has overshadowed RAI's online output. RTVE has not only outperformed the success of its commercial broadcasting competitors online, but has been able to develop a stronger offering of online news and public affairs that represents a remarkable achievement in two years of activities. TVE remains more a competitor to entertainment suppliers online than to news providers and this is certainly due to its funding pressure and history.

By contrast, RAI online, which started its online activities in 1999, much earlier than RTVE and which by 2007 had already a wider range of online activities, never presented a clear vision for its internet department. Clearly, the lack of investment and vision has been sustained by the third Berlusconi government (since 2008), given the unprecedented conflict of interest of the Italian prime minister. RAI online offers an inadequate duplication of its television content, with no plan to exploit the possibilities offered by the features of the internet. The current government has no intention of intensifying the news output of RAI online in fear of undermining the supremacy of television over other media in Italy, therefore weakening Berlusconi's grasp on public opinion. (It should be noted that in Italy just 20% of the population read newspapers, while the other 80% gather news from television) (AGCOM, 2009).

The "counter–reform" of Zapatero (Law 8/2009) that abolished advertisments on RTVE.es could bring the clock back to 2004 in Spain. With no resources invested and no possibility of RTVE.es collecting online advertisements revenues, the quality of the online offering of RTVE is likely to stagnate. The creation of more strictly public service content will ultimately depend on the political willingness of the government to sustain a stronger RTVE. Unfortunately so far Zapatero's government seems more inclined to succumb to private broadcasters' demands to secure profit through advertising revenues than to sustain Spanish PSB. Although for the last two years, RTVE online has moved beyond its historical legacy as a weak PSB, the reform could have a detrimental effect on this achievement.

Southern European PSBs, with their high level of politicization, need a robust political backing to achieve online the social, cultural and political cohesion that they should be aiming for. Unfortunately, the two cases investigated do not show the relentless political support and the desire for renovation that is required.

Notes

1. Act 17/2006, (05/06/2006) on the radios and televisions entitled to the State.
2. After the reform realized by the Zapatero government of 2006, on 1st September 2009 (Law 8/2009), the financial arrangements of RTVE have once again been rev-

olutionized. If the Act of 2006 re–affirmed a mixed funding system based on state funding for 1/3 of the budget and advertisement for 2/3, the new law bans advertising and adopts a pure funding system based on state resources. The funding will be provided by two new fiscal measures and one existing measure, in addition to the existing state funding of RTVE.

3. According to 5th article of the Act 17 of 2006, the objectives of the public service have to be defined by a Mandato Marco emanated by the Parliament every nine years.
4. See note 2.
5. The service contract—"contratto di servizio"—between the Ministry of Communication and RAI indicates the objectives to be achieved by the PSB provider.
6. Art 26th concerning 'multimedia services' stated that "RAI *will* ensure new opportunities and know–how for experimenting new forms of multimedia productions and new audio visual languages, also for the offer abroad (for example, it *will* develop new internet services)" (RAI, 1997)). Art. 25 of Service Contract 2000–2002 reaffirms that "RAI will ensure new opportunities and know–how for experimenting new forms of multimedia productions and new audio visual languages, also for the offer abroad (for example, it will develop new internet services)(RAI, 2000). Art. 23 (1) of the Service Contract 2003 declares "In order to promote the industrial development of the country and the introduction of new techniques of transmission, RAI is obliged to foster the conversion of programmes and services to the digital terrestrial modality" (RAI, 2003).
7. Where in the previous Service Contracts the development of multimedia services, like "internet services" were listed among the new obligations of RAI, art. 25 of the 2003 Services Contract, listed a series of services that RAI *can* develop, placing the investment in the multimedia offer in the realm of possibility. The words "RAI will develop internet services" of the 1997 and 2000 Contract of Service are replaced in the 2003 Contract with the words "RAI can develop internet services" (RAI, 2003). Moreover, in the official version of the Service Contract, 7% indicated in the draft has been substituted for "RAI will allocate increasing resources to the acquisition of the copyrights of the programmes"(RAI, 2007a, Art 6).
8. For more information, see the website http://creativecommons.org/about.
9. The Italian company Fastweb, founded in 1999, is a significant player in the telecommunications sector in Italy.
10. RAI Educational is the directorate in charge of the educational programmes of RAI that deal with arts, history, culture, and science. See the website http://www.educational.rai.it/programmi.asp.
11. RAI International broadcasts throughout the world the programmes of RAI Radio Televisione Italiana, as well as original programmes made for Italians who live abroad.
12. The ex CEO of RAI NET, Alberto Contri, was removed from his position in March 2008, despite the significant results obtained, according to the spoil system logic employed at RAI. Under Contri's direction, from the monetary loss due to structural costs, RAI Net was led into profit in 2005.
13. For more information, see the "D" website http://www.ild.rai.it/index.asp?t=8&pag=faq#a0.

References

AGCOM (2009). Annual report, 2009.

Audiweb-Nielsen Online (2008). Top web parent companies, Italy.

Azurmendi Adarraga, A., Pérez Moriones, A., Rodríguez Pardo, J., Muñoz Saldaña, M. (2007). *La reforma de la television publica expañola.* Valencia: Prosopopea.

Brevini, B. (2008, November 25–29). European Public Service and the Internet: The Idea of PSB 2.0. Presented at ECREA Conference, Barcelona.

Brevini, B. (2010a). Towards PSB 2.0? Applying the PSB ethos to online media in Europe: a comparative study of Spain, Italy and Britain. *European Journal of Communication, 25*(4), 348–365.

Brevini, B. (2010b). Under siege by commercial interests? BBC and DR online between the national and European policy frameworks. *Interactions. Studies in Communication and Culture, 1*(2), 203–215.

Brügger, N. (Ed.) (2010). *Web History.* New York: Peter Lang Publishing.

Bustamante, E. (1989). TV and public service in Spain: A difficult encounter. *Media Culture and Society, 11*(1), 67–87.

Bustamante, E. (2007). *Storia della Radio e della Televisione in Spagna.* Rome: Rai Eri.

Constitutional Court (1988). Sentenza 826/1988. *Giur. Cost.*, 1, 3894.

Constitutional Court (1994). Sentenza 420/1994. *Giur. Cost.*, 5, 3751.

Diarios (2004). Congresos de los Diputados, diarios de sesiones, VIII Legislatura Núm. 172.

EBU and BBC (2007, November). Broadcasting and the Internet. London: Human Capital.

Hallin, D. C. & Mancini, P. (2004). *Comparing media systems: Three models of media and politics.* Cambridge: Cambridge University Press.

Hibberd, M. (2001). The reform of public service broadcasting in Italy. *Media Culture and Society, 23*(2), 233–252.

Humphreys, P. (1996). *Mass media and media policy in Western Europe.* Manchester, UK: Manchester University Press.

Informe (2005, April 23). Informe para la reforma de los medios de comunicación de titularidad del Estado, Elaborado por el Consejo creado al efecto, según Real Decreto 744/2004.

Levy, D. (1997). Regulating digital broadcasting in Europe: the limits of policy convergence. *West European Politics, 20*(4), 24–42.

López-Escobar, E. (1992). Spanish media law: Changes in the landscapes. *European Journal of Communication, 7*(2), 241–259.

Mandato M. (2007). Aprobación por los Plenos del Congreso de los Diputados y del Senado 794/000003 (S) del mandato-marco a la Corporación RTVE, 18 de diciembre de 2007 Núm. 470.

Mazzoleni, G. & Vigevani, G. E. (2005). TV across Europe: Regulation, policies and independence: Italy. In *TV across Europe: regulation, policies and independence.* Budapest: Open Society Institute—EU Monitoring and Advocacy Program.

Monteleone, F. (2001). *Storia della radio e televisione in Italia.* Venice, Italy: Marsilio.

Nielsen NetRatings (2008). Top web parent companies, UK.

OJD Interactiva (2008). Ranking of web companies in Spain.

OJD Interactiva (2010). Ranking of web companies in Spain.
Pérez Ornia, J. R. (1988). *La historia del puritanismo censor en televisión española*. Madrid: El País.
RAI (1997). Service contract between the Minister of Communications and RAI, 1997–1999.
RAI (2000). Service contract between the Minister of Communications and RAI, 2000–2002
RAI (2003). Service contract between the Minister of Communications and RAI, 2003–2005.
RAI (2007a). Final draft of the service contract between the Minister of Communications and RAI, 2007–2009.
RAI (2007b). Service contract between the Minister of Communications and RAI, 2007–2009.
Rodriguez-Pardo, J. (2006, November). Facing challenges through a new legal framework for DTT: Towards are definition of the role of TVE in the Spanish market? Presented at the RIPE conference in Amsterdam.
RTVE (2000). Informe Anual 2000.
RTVE (2005). Informe Anual 2005.
Scannell, P. (1989). Public service broadcasting and modern public life. *Media Culture & Society*, *11*(2), 135–166.

Interviews

Bustamante, E. (2008). Interview with Enrique Bustamante, Madrid, July, 2008.
Contri, A. (2007). Interview with Alberto Contri, CEO RAI Net, July 2007.
Contri, A. (2008). Interview with Alberto Contri, CEO RAI Net, May 2008.
Lloret, R. (2008). Interview with Rosalia Loret, Director of *Interactive Media* at RTVE, July 2008.
Zela, M. (2007). Interview with Marco Zela, Rai Educational, July 2007.

PART FOUR

Local, National, International, Global?

10 *Public Media and the Web in the U.S.*

The Case of Vocalo

Meghan Grosse & David W. Park

Introduction

A familiar narrative in media history involves the promise of democracy being reinvigorated by new media. James Curran describes how it is often "hoped that [new media] will place a powerful means of mass communication in the hands of the people and lead to the democratization of the media" (2003, p. 227). In the context of public service radio, adoptions of new media platforms have brought with them no shortage of high hopes. Internet–based technological developments have led public service radio programmers in the U.S. to re–conceptualize numerous aspects of how public radio should operate. One important example of an attempt to re–conceptualize public service radio via the adoption of internet–based technologies is the case of Vocalo.org (here referred to as "Vocalo"), a locally based online/broadcast outlet launched by Chicago Public Radio (CPR) in 2007.

Vocalo was created in an effort to apply what is thought to be the community–building power of the internet to the context of radio. The internet was taken by Vocalo's creators to be a potentially democratizing force, with the power to erase the boundaries between listeners and producers, allow users to develop their own community, and support a community–based platform for radio/internet content. Here we examine the role of new media as it was imagined during Vocalo's inception, and review the obstacles that Vocalo has faced in its three years online. We conclude with notes regarding how the case of Vocalo illuminates important themes in media history.

Our evidence concerning Vocalo comes from four types of sources. First, we examined CPR documents relating to Vocalo. Second, we conducted qualitative interviews with administrators of Vocalo (including former Vocalo project manager Vanessa Harris, Vocalo content manager Lloyd King, CPR president and CEO Torey Malatia, and former Vocalo general manager Wendy Turner) and drew from the texts of these interviews. Third, we familiarized ourselves with the Vocalo website and audio stream. Fourth, we examined journalism about Vocalo from its 2007 launch to the present.

Public Service Broadcasting in the U.S.

It is difficult to understand the full promise of Vocalo without first considering the shortcomings thought to obtain in public radio in the U.S., for these were the inspiration for the creation of Vocalo. One of the definitive problems found in public radio and public television is a tendency for a lack of federal funding to lead stations to depend on listeners for support, a dilemma that has often led public service broadcasters to neglect much of the public. In this sense, public radio in the U.S. differs from public service broadcasting in much of the rest of the world. Government involvement in public radio in the U.S. today involves relatively less federal government involvement (in the form of funding or of logistical support) than one typically finds in public service broadcasting in much the rest of the world. This difference plays an important role in shaping the form of public broadcasting in the U.S. These kinds of structural arrangements have all taken place under the regulatory guidance of the Federal Communications Commission (FCC), the federal regulatory agency in the U.S. created in 1934, and that was charged with the task of regulating broadcast communication (Barnouw, 1968, p. 26). The role of the FCC was revised after the U.S. government passed the Telecommunications Act of 1996, a law that refocused the FCC to take more thorough account of the internet, while it also reinforced the FCC's observance of free market rules for media regulation (McChesney, 2004, pp. 51–53).

The largest public radio network in the U.S. is National Public Radio (NPR), a project that was founded amidst concerns in the 1960s that radio broadcasting in the U.S. had become overly commercialized and insufficiently diverse (Mitchell, 2005, p. 40). NPR was incorporated in March of 1970, and inaugurated its broadcast operations in 1971. The first NPR program director—William Siemering—insisted that NPR's goals were to "promote personal growth," to celebrate "individual differences" among people, and to "encourage a sense of active constructive participation" (Siemering, 1970). Early NPR broadcasts demonstrated many of these concerns, with broadcasts that were constructed to tell the stories of regular people and to avoid a top–down view of the world.

Though the initial goals for NPR included explicit charges to foster "diversity and excellence" (Mitchell, 2005, p. 33), reaching the "socially disadvantaged" and promoting the "lively discussion of local issues" (Mitchell, 2005, p. 40), these foci have faded. The U.S. Government has become only a vestigial funder of public radio, putting pressure on individual stations to support themselves with pledge drives. Public radio stations in the U.S. have come to depend on listeners "who have disposable income and who give . . . money during pledge drives" (McChesney, 2003, pp. 12–13), resulting in programming that projects an "upper middle–class white view of the world" (Barsamian, 2001, p. 18). Programs targeted specifically to nonwhite or Spanish–speaking audiences make up "less than 3 percent of all public radio listening" (McCauley, 2005, p. 124).

Despite—or perhaps because of—this specialization and homogenization, NPR has developed a growing audience base. In the early 1980s, NPR programs averaged 2 million listeners per week. Less than twenty years later, the average weekly audience had increased to 25 million (Fisher, 2007, p. 260). Still, the public service nature of NPR's earliest programming has faded as the network has moved instead to appeal to the "largest possible audiences," and to develop a sound that is "more mature, more predictable, and less challenging" (Fisher, 2007, p. 253). At Chicago Public Radio, these national tendencies have found local instantiation. One solution developed by CPR administrators was to create and program other stations for the Chicago area, to "provide a different program service and reach additional listeners" (Stavitsky, 1994, p. 42). CPR has attempted to address its critics by dedicating one of its translator stations (WBEW, 89.5, in Chesterton, Indiana) and a companion website to a programming facility called Vocalo.

The Creation of Vocalo

Vocalo is not the only web–based experiment launched in U.S. public radio. NPR has made dramatic strides in absorbing the web into its day–to–day operations. NPR invested heavily in training its staff to develop content for the web, adjusted its website to incorporate more interactive features, incorporated mobile technological applications (Dorroh, 2008), and has enjoyed great success in podcasting (Atkinson, 2006). Unlike many other public radio ventures into an online world, Vocalo was created to address shortcomings experienced in public service media in the U.S. Vocalo is CPR's project to enhance public life in the Chicago area, and to serve audiences under–served by existing public service media outlets.

Vocalo was developed as a project in 2003, and was launched as a web and radio operation in 2007. Vocalo's launch led Torey Malatia to explain that the creation of Vocalo was motivated partly "by the recognition within Chicago Public Radio that the core assumptions on which our work had been based might no longer be valid" (2007, p. 1). He explained that the name "Vocalo" "is an invention, essentially 'Vocal' with an 'o' at the end," a term to rhyme with "'Zocalo,' a Spanish word which in Mexico refers to a town plaza," and "in Colombia refers to the infrastructure that stabilizes the foundation of a large building" (2007, p. 1). Malatia linked this to the FCC's traditional concerns for public service, which he called "a viable, logical foundation" (2007, p. 6) for the Vocalo project. Vocalo was thus dedicated at the outset to re–dedicating public radio to the public and to diversity. Malatia trumpeted that Vocalo would "refashion WBEZ's public radio mission to a target audience formerly unreachable by WBEZ" (2007, p. 1). As Harris observed, public radio in Chicago "tends to speak to people on the North side who happen to be white" (V. Harris, personal communication, February 13, 2010). CPR studied historical non–listeners and found alienation from CPR's programming, particularly among those who were not from the white, middle–class neighborhoods in Chicago. From the point of view of the creators of Vocalo, public radio in Chicago had failed these non–listeners.

Approachability and narrative were crucial factors in how Vocalo would differ from other radio outlets. Malatia envisioned for Vocalo "a kind of uniform power structure" in which listeners "[create] the media themselves, . . . control it themselves, [and] share it with others who also control it, so everyone's equal" (personal communication, March 8, 2010). Vocalo's content was to come from community members who would submit audio via the web or phone. After the community member's submission, Vocalo producers would work with the raw audio, and the material that made it on the stream/broadcast would then be curated by on–air hosts. The listener–supplied narrative was a cornerstone of the initial vision of Vocalo. As King described, the hope was that "we can build a better democracy through narrative, through simultaneous narrative, by having people listening to everybody telling their story at once" (personal communication, February 13, 2010); the idea was not too dissimilar from discussions of public journalism in the U.S. (see Rosen, 1999). A tremendous flow of personal narratives, supplied by community members, would be a way to create an invigorated community in Chicago.

This reliance on community–supplied narratives would require Vocalo staffers to train members of the community in the methods of creating narrative content. King described this outreach as an effort "to get people who aren't normally participating in media participating in media on a big scale" (personal communication, February 13, 2010). Outreach in the form of training in production would be a way to undo the dominant approach to providing news about the Chicago area; by putting the power to create media in the hands of those who had been left out, the hopes for Vocalo were pegged to the potential of new media to erase the differences between audience member and media producer. This was an explicit move away from the "passive" view of audiences in the broadcast model (Willson, 2006, p. 51). Vocalo was envisioned as a kind of public square where audience members would be most active, and would not shed their differences as a cost of entry. The focus would be on the local community. Vocalo was laid out in the hope that locality and the web could have much to do with each other, because without "connection to place," as Malatia explained, "no individual can practice being a citizen. Only place allows us to be political" (2007, p. 10).

The programming envisioned for Vocalo was largely thought of as a negation of historically familiar kinds of public service broadcasting. Malatia initially insisted that Vocalo would "have no shows at all. Like a music station, it will be structured on a continuous, seamless stream. But by no stretch of the imagination would a listener call it a music station" (2007, p. 1). There were to be "no newscasts," and "no branded radio" (2007, p. 1). It was not to "use the Chicago Public Radio brand" and would "not cross-promote WBEZ," nor would it "refer to itself as a public radio station" (2007, p. 1). As one observer described, Vocalo started with "a clean slate" and a "new rule book for radio" (Janssen, 2007).

The goal of programming narratives from community members was and remains central to Vocalo's programming philosophy. Turner described Vocalo as having "a dedication to 24/7 exposure, broad exposure, to the people of our region and their first person stories" (personal communication, February 13, 2010). The ideal Vocalo experience would hail the listener as a potential media creator, so that when you went to the Vocalo website, "you knew that it was about stories and storytelling," and "prompts and assignments" on the site would lead you to "tell your own story" (L. King, personal communication, February 13, 2010). Over time, "you see how these stories connect to each other, and begin to form bigger ideas and threads that contribute to a broader topic" (W. Turner, personal communication, February 13, 2010). Vocalo's focus on narratives emphasizes "relations and informants who are not the usual suspects" (L. King, personal communication, February 13, 2010). The original Vocalo staff consisted of "15 hosts from unconventional [i.e., non-broadcast] backgrounds," called upon to compile user-generated material and "lead the on-air discussions" (Guy, 2007, p. 60). Vocalo's narratives have featured people like "Paris the dreamer calling in and giving his opinion all the time," or "a guy named Speed [who] . . . brings his mom down to the station and they start talking about whatever is the topic of the day" (L. King, personal communication, February 13, 2010). The creators of Vocalo made these locally based narratives that came from community members outside the white middle class central to Vocalo's programming.

New media played a definitive role in Vocalo's efforts to break from past tendencies in public radio programming. The importance of new media to Vocalo was captured in Malatia's remark about Vocalo that "[t]here will be a web site, but it would be wrong to say that it's the station's web site. Really, it is the web site's radio station" (2007, p. 1). It was the ostensible power of new media to empower individuals that occupied the cornerstone of the Vocalo philosophy. As King described it, Vocalo is like "YouTube for radio, but we have a social conscience"; in other words, Vocalo is "crowd-sourcing content . . . through e-media" so that "electronic media becomes both a portal for gathering content, and then an amplifier or mouthpiece for distributing content" (personal communication, February 13, 2010). Turner described how new media make it so that "everybody can record, everybody can broadcast, everybody can write articles and have their say and be part of the conversation in an equal way," giving "anyone . . . an equal space and an equal voice" (personal communication, February 13, 2010).

The creation of Vocalo was predicated on the idea that the Web 2.0 features would allow listeners/users "to become civically engaged, through stories of people making a difference, in their own way, through action" (Malatia, 2007, p. 16). These stories were to be created by users of the Vocalo site. The site "is built to meet the expectations of Web 2.0 regulars" in that it "allows for personal pages or links to them, personal blogs, where one can upload video, audio, photographs, and post text" (Malatia, 2007, p. 17). Non-textual material "that is posted is also housed in a media database that allows people access to all uploaded videos for example, and gives other users an opportunity to critique them" (2007, p. 17). When the Vocalo site is not used to create content, it is used as a "social-networking site where users can blog" and "personalize the site" (Guy, 2007, p. 60). Here we see quite clearly a link between new media and democratic hopes. These visions of Vocalo's potential show how technology was granted the power to allow diverse citizens in a local community to establish a more democratic system.

In sum, Vocalo was pitched from the outset as a way to do more with the web than simply to simulcast material being aired on the broadcast station. One major assumption at work here was that the World Wide Web would act as a kind of salve to the wounds of public service broadcasting. By focusing on the geographic region where the under-served audience lived, and offering to the target audience an opportunity to tell their own stories, there would be a bottom–up cascade of community–based stories, narratives having to do with the life of the community. Throughout the process of getting Vocalo up and running and keeping it together, the focus has been placed firmly on how new technology would make democratic hopes a reality.

Vocalo Encounters Obstacles

Since its launch in 2007, Vocalo has encountered numerous obstacles. These obstacles are relevant to the study of public service broadcasters on the web because they highlight the contexts in which the history of online broadcasting plays out. These obstacles call our attention to how media history is played out not according to the rules of technological potential, but through a relatively more complex interplay between audiences, organizations, institutions, markets, and technology itself.

Just because we are trying to pull the emphasis away from purely technological affairs does not mean that the technical dimension of Vocalo is irrelevant here. Indeed, an important obstacle to Vocalo in the early–going was that its website was, in Harris's words "a bit clunky" (personal communication, February 13, 2010). Additionally, as Turner pointed out, Vocalo's "terrestrial signal . . . has not played out quite to the degree we wish it would," (personal communication, February 13, 2010) making it so that much of the city of Chicago has been unable to tune into Vocalo via terrestrial radio.

Funding has proven to be another obstacle. The economic downturn in 2007–2010 has slowed down website improvement and "marketing, where [Vocalo hasn't] been able to invest the kinds of dollars that might still make a difference in a lot of what we do" (Malatia, personal communication, March 8, 2010). These funding issues were exacerbated by tensions between Vocalo and the rest of CPR. Some of the core audience for WBEZ found it frustrating to learn that their donated money was going to Vocalo without their knowing about the project in the first place (Miner, August 14, 2008). Funding difficulties at Vocalo also resulted in some resentment from other staffers at CPR, who were described by one reporter as "less than happy to be sharing their budget with the wayward kid brother" (Miner, October 21, 2008).

Perhaps the most frustrating obstacle that Vocalo has encountered has been a disappointing number of listeners. Vocalo was created to reach those under–served by existing public radio, and this audience has been "harder to reach" (W. Turner, personal communication, February 13, 2010). "[S]omething close to half" of Vocalo's listeners have had face to face interaction with someone from Vocalo," and that's "a really labor intensive way to expose people" to Vocalo (W. Turner, personal communication, February 13, 2010). The

Chicago Public Radio strategic plan for 2010–2013 acknowledged these problems, stating that "Vocalo must be seen as unsuccessful so far. Great websites exhibit a much steeper growth pattern than we have experienced" (Chicago Public Radio, 2009). The over–riding problem here is simply that without a larger promotional budget, and in the absence of a terrestrial FM signal that can reach more of their mission audience, Vocalo is compelled to seek out a long–neglected audience with new technology they might not have, using a format that involves a new way of participating in the media experience.

Many of Vocalo's problems can be traced to the effort to do something new with Vocalo. The idea of creating a public service audio programming service based more on the web than on terrestrial radio, aimed at an under–served audience, and made largely out of non–professional contributors' narratives, is one that started Vocalo off in an uncomfortable chicken–and–egg situation. Malatia argues that "all radio is so bloody bland and predictable, that there is a hunger for something captivating" (personal communication, March 8, 2010). This hunger for something new has not translated very quickly into a hunger for Vocalo. As King points out, initial "feedback in terms of listeners, myself included," indicated problems: "when I turn to Vocalo, I'm not sure what it is about" (personal communication, February 13, 2010). On top of this, Vocalo's populism clashed with listener expectations for public affairs programming. For many people, "experts are seen as the reason one listens to a news broadcast. . . . And, in fact, common opinion, or the opinion of normal, ordinary folks, is considered to be unimportant" (T. Malatia, personal communication, March 8, 2010). The turn away from expertise has made Vocalo less conventional, and in one sense, less recognizable and thus less listenable, for some potential listeners.

Simply creating a station as devoted to narrative as Vocalo has been has generated challenges. For instance, as Malatia opines, "it actually is harder to listen to a story, even a compelling story, than it is to listen to a piece of music" (T. Malatia, personal communication, March 8, 2010). Because the early versions of Vocalo were experienced as being "not anchored by subject matter, anchored by music genre, or anchored by a personality that you connect with," the station came off as less "sticky" than it would need to be to generate an audience more quickly (W. Turner, personal communication, February 13, 2010). On the production side of the station, Turner added that "doing talk based programming 60 hours a week on the air is extremely resource intensive;" it is "exhausting" to create this much innovative material (personal communication, February 13, 2010). User–generated content requires, in Malatia's words, "a lot of participation on the website, so that there is a sort of rich harvest that could be made to use on air" (T. Malatia, personal communication, March 8, 2010). Lacking this quantity of participation, Vocalo's output has suffered.

The blend of broadcast and web platforms creates new possibilities for generating content and generating an audience, but at the same time, as Turner posited, the broadcast is "the most labor intensive component of what we do because it's live and it happens on the air" (personal communication, February 13, 2010) so there is a great deal of effort that gets pulled away from managing the website and pushed toward managing the broadcast. The two platforms, meant to cross–pollinate, brought with them a tremendous workload. An exclusively web–based station would have allowed Vocalo to "expand much more of [its] resources towards innovation in content mixing, content sharing, [and] aggregating" (W. Turner, personal communication, February 13, 2010). Of course, a dedication solely to web–based audio would also have taken Vocalo away from its hoped–for audience of individuals who lack the kind of broadband access that would make participating in a purely–web–oriented station convenient.

Another area where Vocalo experienced significant difficulties concerned the staffing of the station. Vocalo followed the

> logic . . . that . . . if you hire people from traditional radio, they're just going to recreate traditional radio. You have to get people outside the field. (L. King, personal communication, February 13, 2010)

This has resulted in some problems with how Vocalo sounds. Turner noted that the Vocalo hosts "were not hired for [their] instinct" for on–air presentation "and it's missing . . . from our team" (personal communication, February 13, 2010). Vocalo's staffing generated some tensions between itself and the rest of CPR. Some CPR staffers argued Vocalo had made CPR miss its chance to become the definitive outlet for professional journalism in Chicago, in light of the "near–collapse of traditional media outlets [including the city's two major newspapers] in Chicago" (Miner, November 19, 2009). Some of the same WBEZ staff resented that the Chicago Public Radio strategic plan for 2010–2013 did not include the word journalism at all, though it did have great emphasis on Vocalo. That same strategic report includes an acknowledgement that:

> it must be said that many listeners, staffers and even several CPR Board Members find the content and listening experience of Vocalo to be substandard and unappealing so far. (Chicago Public Radio, 2009, p. 14)

This rather blunt statement points to some of the serious challenges Vocalo faces in terms of garnering an audience and support at CPR.

Finally, the digital divide has been a major challenge for Vocalo. Early experiences with Vocalo demonstrated that the digital divide eroded Vocalo's effectiveness to secure an audience and to develop a steady corps of community members participating in the Vocalo experience. Harris was very explicit about this, pointing out that "there's a digital divide in America that's undeniable," making it necessary for Vocalo staffers to engage in a lot of "ground work" training potential audience members in how to participate (personal communication, February 13, 2010). Malatia offered a slightly more complex picture, acknowledging that "the digital divide does exist," and adding that it "doesn't exist in the way that most people think. . . . A lot of people have access to the internet, but they don't have access to broadband" (personal communication, March 8, 2010). The problem involves "a question of how frequently" those in the community they are trying to reach "actually visit the internet and look at their personal page" (Malatia, personal communication, March 8, 2010). Despite Vocalo's attempts to address the digital divide problem with outreach and with a mobile phone–based method to contribute to the station, the digital divide continues to tamp down on the station's efforts to generate listeners.

Conclusion

Vocalo's three years in operation have highlighted some important themes in media history. First, we see in Vocalo an attempt to use new media to accomplish goals that were envisioned for NPR during its founding in the 1960s and 1970s. NPR's originating impulses involved a fundamental belief in multivocality and an appreciation of the "unfiltered views of people without credentials" (Mitchell, 2005, p. 50). NPR was supposed to generate "greater citizen involvement and a healthier public climate" (Christians & Nordenstreng, 2004, p. 11). At Vocalo, we see an attempt to do this same thing, where "[o]rdinary people" can "have their voices heard" and are given a forum to discuss those issues "considered relevant for the community" (Carpentier, Lie, & Servaes, 2003, p. 55), in an attempt to support a better public life for underserved members of the community. In this sense, Vocalo represents a renewal of traditional hopes for public service broadcasting in the U.S.

Vocalo is more than a reiteration of public radio hopes. It also links up with familiar ideas about how the future and new media operate. James Carey famously described how the future is often thought of as "a participation ritual of technological exorcism" in which "allowing the public to participate in extrapolating trends and making choices is considered a method of cleansing confusion and relieving us from human fallibilities" (1989/1992, p. 174). With Vocalo, we see an instance in which new technology was thought to have the power to finally get us past the limits of the existing system for public broadcasting. The public, it was hoped, would finally be given the power to become the media, via the logic of Web 2.0. The point is not that these hopes were wrong, but that the founding of Vocalo involved a mythic understanding of new media as capable of acting as a solvent for the problems public service broadcasting has experienced in the U.S. It was hoped that new media would finally allow the public to take part in the way it had always wanted to; it was technology that would allow a new measure of democracy into the system of public service broadcasting.

Vocalo also shows us what James Curran refers to when he says that hopes about the democratizing potential of new media are dashed when we find that the new medium "has not fundamentally changed the underlying economic factors that enable large media organizations to maintain their market dominance" (Curran, 2003, p. 227). Vocalo has struggled to find an audience, and this difficulty stems from how radio markets operate. Perhaps the biggest problem it faces is the fact that its innovative "crowd–sourced" content is defined in terms of what it is not. Vocalo's rejection of radio that has come before is intellectually stirring, but has not given Vocalo much of an identity, and this has made it suffer from the functioning of Say's Law: supply creates demand. Robert McChesney describes this law at work in media markets, where in some cases, "the lack of exposure—the low supply—eliminated the basis for demand" (2004, p. 201). Because Vocalo is so new, so different, and is reaching out to a new audience, it suffers for being hard to understand; few actually tune in to Vocalo because its novelty makes it something audiences do not know how to demand, so to speak. It is hard to succeed in a market when the anticipated audience either cannot tune in, due to digital divide issues, or chooses not to tune in, because the programming does not strike them as something they want to hear. Matthew Hindman observes that "when considering political speech online, we must be mindful of the difference between speaking and being heard" (2009, p. 13). Vocalo has succeeded in using the web to open up public service broadcasting for many people. For reasons having to do with the functioning of public radio markets in the U.S., it has yet to make these voices widely heard.

Finally, Vocalo's difficulties point to the possibility that user–generated content may address what audience members wish to say, but may not address what audience members wish to hear. The fact that online media often straddle the borders of the public and the private, the professional and the amateur, and entertainment and information, often makes for new blended forms of media content. One interpretation of Vocalo's problems is that, as a new online form that straddles the internet and the radio through use of innovative, user–generated content, it has outrun whatever audience demand could have existed for it to sustain itself. There is not a pre–existing audience that knows how to listen to Vocalo, meaning that whatever audience Vocalo could attract would need to be cultivated. The fact that Vocalo is such an innovative form requires this cultivation to be performed uphill, as it were. The "reinvention" of radio that was going on with Vocalo made it less attractive to audience members than it needed to be.

In the absence of greater long–term financial support required for making any such audience cultivation possible, experiments like Vocalo may not long survive. Other attempts to make user–generated content part of public service broadcasting might do better, particularly if they take place in a less market–driven approach to public service broadcasting than exists in the U.S., or if they can successfully establish themselves in terms already familiar to their audiences.

Bibliography

Atkinson, C. (2006). *NPR, the new podcasting ruler.* Retrieved May 29, 2010 from http://adage.com/digital/ article?article_id=109970

Barnouw, E. (1968). *The golden web: A history of broadcasting in the United States, 1933–1953.* New York: Oxford University Press.

Barsamian, D. (2001). *The decline and fall of public broadcasting.* Cambridge, MA: South End Press.

Carey, J. W. (1989/1992). *Communication as culture: essays on media and society.* London: Routledge.

Carpentier, N., Lie, R. & Servaes, J. (2003). Community media: Muting the democratic discourse? *Continuum: Journal of Media & Cultural Studies, 17*(1), 51–69.

Chicago Public Radio (2009). *Strategic plan—2010–2013.* Retrieved May 30, 2010 from http://blogs.vocalo.org/ wp-content/uploads/Strategic-Plan-2010–2013.pdf

Christians, C. & Nordenstreng, K. (2004). Social responsibility worldwide. *Journal of Mass Media Ethics, 19*(1), 3–28.

Curran, J. (2003). Global journalism: A case study of the internet. In N. Couldry & J. Curran (Eds.), *Contesting media power: Alternative media in a networked world* (pp. 227–242). Lanham, MD: Rowman & Littlefield.

Dorroh, J. (2008). The transformation of NPR. *American Journalism Review, 30*(5), 24–31.

Fisher, M. (2007). *Something in the air.* New York: Random House.

Guy, S. (2007, September 12). Public radio eyes net gain; internet surfers turn programmers in bold experiment to diversify stations' listening audiences. *Chicago Sun Times.*

Hindman, M. (2009). *The myth of digital democracy.* Princeton, NJ: Princeton University Press.

Janssen, M. (2007). Fresh startup keeps old ideals. *Current.* Retrieved November 1, 2007 from http://www.current.org/radio/radi00708vocalo.shtml

Malatia, T. (2007). Potential difference: redesigning public radio for a changing society. *Current,* 1–23.

McCauley, M. P. (2005). *NPR: The trials and triumphs of national public radio.* New York:

Columbia University Press.
McChesney, R.W. (2003). Public broadcasting: Past, present, and future. In M. P. McCauley, E. E. Peterson, B. L. Artz, & D. Halleck (Eds.), *Public Broadcasting and the Public Interest* (pp. 10–24). Armonk, NY: M.E. Sharpe.
McChesney, R. W. (2004). *The problem of the media.* New York: Monthly Review Press.
Miner, M. (2008, August 14). *Station identification: Should WBEZ donors be told their money might be spent on Vocalo?* Retrieved May 31, 2010 from http://www.chicago reader.com/chicago/station-identification/Content?oid=1109051
Miner, M. (2008, October 21). *Have your made your pledge to Vocalo yet?* Retrieved May 29, 2010 from http://www. chicagoreader.com/TheBlog/archives/2008/10/21/have-you-made-your-pledge-vocalo-yet
Miner, M. (2009, November 19). *WBEZ staffers want to talk turkey: And they think their boss, Torey Malatia, is focusing on the trimmings.* Retrieved May 31, 2010 from http://www.chicagoreader.com/chicago/wbez-stafferstalk-turkey-with-torey-malatia/Content?oid=1236507
Mitchell, J.W. (2005). *Listener supported: The culture and history of public radio.* Westport, CT: Praeger.
Rosen, J. (1999). *What are journalists for?* New Haven, CT: Yale University Press.
Siemering, W. H. (1970). *National public radio purposes.* Retrieved October 17, 2007 from http://www.current. org/pbpb/documents/NPRpurposes.html
Stavitsky, A. G. (1994). The changing conception of localism in U.S. public radio. *Journal of Broadcasting & Electronic Media, 38*(1), 19–34.
Willson, M. A. (2006). *Technically together.* New York: Peter Lang.

11 Regional Radio and Online Media Production

An Australian Broadcasting Corporation Case Study

Anne Dunn

Introduction

This chapter describes and analyses the ways in which some local PSB radio stations have introduced and are using production for the World Wide Web. It uses the Local Radio network of the Australian Broadcasting Corporation (ABC) as a case study. There are at time of writing 52 "local" ABC Radio stations, spread across the six States and two Territories of Australia,[1] the furthest of which is over four thousand kilometres from the Corporation's Sydney headquarters.

From their inception, these often very small radio stations have served and connected populations scattered across great distances. They have always been very lean operations, making do with usually inadequate and sometimes makeshift technical and human resources. Regional radio broadcasters have developed a reputation inside the ABC for resourcefulness and hard work. As part of their public service remit, they are engaged not only in entertaining, informing and educating their audiences, but also in unifying the nation by drawing citizens into issues and debates at the centre as well as reflecting their local concerns.

These stations were among the first output areas of the ABC to take advantage of the possibilities in digital and networked media for a small number of multi-skilled people to produce the same quantity—or more—of content across broadcast and the online media distribution platform of the World Wide Web. Technology, from satellites through ISDN to the internet, has been used in ABC local radio to overcome the constraints of distance and limited resources. The focus of this chapter is to detail how regional radio stations have developed multi–tasked production capacity and turned to new ways of communicating with their audiences. Those audiences have changed in turn; once confined to the transmission footprint of the radio station and its broadcast schedule, now they may join the conversation from any part of the world where an internet connection and open access to the World Wide Web are available. All these changes bring their own challenges, not least to the professional identity and practices of the cross platform producers, in the context of the regulatory and cultural frameworks of public service media.

The chapter begins with a brief outline of ABC Radio's ongoing reliance on technological and organisational change to expand its coverage outside the metropolitan centres to smaller and often remote communities, which was very important to its PSB remit in Australia. Next, the chapter draws on empirical research undertaken at the time cross–media production was first introduced in ABC regional radio, in the early 2000s. Then we consider how this way of working has affected broadcasters' professional identity, production roles, and relationship with their audiences. The chapter concludes with a broadly optimistic view, despite some cautionary notes, of the value of a web presence for regional public service radio and for public service media in general.

Serving Outside the Cities

In 1981 the Australian federal government set up an inquiry into the national broadcaster, *The ABC in Review: National Broadcasting in the 1980s*, known as the Dix Report after its chairman. The picture Dix drew of the ABC was of an organisation that was "technologically and socially backward . . . and very ill–equipped to deal with rapid transformations in broadcasting and cultural landscapes" (Hawkins, 2001, p. 183). One feature of the ABC's radio services to which Dix drew particular attention, was its "bias . . . towards metropolitan audiences at the expense of people in the regional and outback areas" (Dix, 1981b, p. 135).

Listeners outside Australia's six largest cities were offered only ABC Radio 3, a mix of programs first heard on the medium–wave metropolitan networks, Radio 1 and 2. Neither of the city–based networks offered truly local programs, nor ones made specifically for people living in regional centres or remote outposts. Roger Grant, a former ABC Radio senior manager, described how difficult it was to broadcast truly nationally in Australia prior to the advent of broadcast satellites:

> You had State–based breakfast programs [which were] classical music based and a lot of that material was re–circulated by multiple copying. . . . They'd run off 6 or 7 copies [of the tapes], rush them interstate and they put them on the air a couple of days later. . . . There was very little networking . . . *we didn't have the satellite then*, don't forget; it was all done terrestrially. (Grant, personal interview, 1991)

The significance of the first major piece of technology—communications satellites—once put to use by the ABC, was thus a profound one, enabling the distribution of programs to any place in the country with the facility to download from a satellite. It also meant that breaking news, for example, could be transmitted directly from the major cities to remote stations. Alongside technological change, there was structural change to Radio, prompted by the Dix Report. This structural change was also driven by the desire to increase productivity through adoption of digital networked production and information technologies.

The Second Regional Radio Network (SRRN)

The Second Regional Radio Network (SRRN) was officially launched in June 1987. SRRN would enable "an upgraded version of the present Regional Radio . . . specifically focused on the community it serves . . . significantly increasing local programming" (ABC, 1987, p. 44). The intention of the SRRN was to extend both local and national services (the youth network, Triple J, Radio National and the classical music network, ABC FM) to rural listeners, beginning with the FM classical music service, and this happened progressively throughout the last decade of the 20th century and the first few years of the 21st, through a rollout of new transmitters and the opening of new radio stations.

ISDN

The ABC began using communications satellites for news reports from the early 1970s, but satellite time was expensive, so its use outside news was more limited. The next significant technological development for broadcasters working in regional radio stations was the Integrated Services Digital Network (ISDN). This technology (or, more accurately, a set of communications standards, defined in the mid–1980s) uses ordinary (copper wire) telephone lines to transmit voice as digital data. As such, it can also simultaneously transmit video and other digital data. It came to be used heavily by the broadcast industry, as a means of reliably linking two sound sources—such as a live field report and a studio. Used with satellite it can connect reporters anywhere in the world. The ABC connected its Local Radio network stations by means of permanent ISDN lines (some terrestrial, some satellite linked) and still uses these today (regional broadcasters talk about taking and sending stories "down the line" to refer equally to ISDN lines or satellite links). ISDN is also still used for some regular outside broadcasts into local radio stations.

The impact of the Dix Report for listeners and broadcasters of regional ABC radio could not have been as marked without the changes to communications technology outlined above. The result was a rapid expansion of regional radio stations, requiring broadcasters to adapt quickly and without much in the way of assistance and support. The same was true when the first "cross–media producers" were appointed, at the beginning of the 21st century. Meanwhile, the ABC had begun to establish an internet presence on the World Wide Web.

The ABC on the web

The presence of the ABC on the web came about initially not through deliberate management–driven strategy but out of the interest and efforts of a disparate group of program makers. Martin (1999, 2007) has described the development of the ABC's web presence as coming out of more or less conscious resistance by some program makers to a management policy perceived as driven by "commodification of public service broadcasting" (Martin, 2007, p. 63). A number of people were already using the internet for research, and email communication both internally and externally. The availability of networked computers and program makers' increasing confidence with their use were important factors in the eventual creation of the Multimedia Unit in mid–1995. The first web sites were set up by groups of program makers at least a year before any official policy or presence on the web.

But all this was happening largely in the Sydney headquarters of the corporation; regional ABC radio stations did not even have internet connections until 1998 (Martin, 2007, p. 73). In the same year, three years after the first ABC web site was launched, ABC Local Radio's *Backyard* site was established. Local radio managers were always very interested in how the new digital technologies could enable greater productivity and the operation of more services with the same number of people. The web offered the potential to add value to the broadcast output, not only through extending its life and availability, but also through adding images and text to audio, through appealing to a wider range of people within a local community, and extending direct audience participation previously limited to phone–in calls or letters to the station. The *Backyard* meant that members of a local community could connect with each other, with the wider Australian community, indeed with the rest of the world. In order to exploit this potential, the ABC needed a "new breed" of producer.

The New Breed: Online Production in the Regions

The digital world is changing the relations of production (see Deuze, 2007). Tickle and Keshvani (2000) envisaged the journalists of the future: as an "intrepid new breed of broadcast warrior" who "will be expected to move effortlessly at warp speed between radio, television and online news gathering and presenting." While their prediction has come, or is coming true, historically the distinction between the work of journalists, editors and producers in different media was largely imposed by the technological constraints of content production. In public sector broadcasting especially, these differences in work were formalized and entrenched in job classifications and in often union–enforced demarcations.

In the ABC this had begun to change first in the Radio Division at the beginning of the 1990s, with the recognition that digital media technologies would enable very different ways of working, ones which would cut across the existing job classifications. A 1992 restructure amalgamated four separate groups—announcers, producers, production assistants and technical operators—into a single "Broadcaster" classification. By the beginning of the 21st century, Radio was better positioned to introduce multi–media work than was the Television Division, whose employees were still covered by 46 separate awards (compared with Radio's four).

In 2001 the ABC received a "regional initiatives" grant from the federal government of 17 million Australian dollars. One reason for the grant was that the growing networking of commercial radio and changes to radio policy had diminished the truly local content being offered by the non–metropolitan commercial sector. The ABC decided to include in its regional initiatives the appointment of fifty new positions in regional radio of which one third (18) were designated as "cross–media producers." Their roles spanned radio production, online contributions to the ABC World Wide Web site, and digital video production for both the broadband internet and a fledgling digital television channel aimed at youth audiences, called "Fly."

One might ask, why select this particular area of regional radio to introduce cross–media positions? The ABC had plenty of choice, including a growing New Media Division, so why choose local radio? The decision may have been coincidental, the result of the then Head of Radio's convictions about digital media, and her perception of where additional resources were most needed in her Division. If so, it was serendipitous, because there are characteristics of ABC regional radio stations as workplaces that research suggests may make them more likely to be successful sites for the introduction of convergent media practices. Singer (2004) suggests that where "there are fewer folks to convince—and, with greater turnover, fewer entrenched habits," convergence is likely to be incorporated more fully and faster than in larger workplaces (Singer, 2004, p. 15). ABC regional radio stations are small workplaces, typically no more than eight to ten people, and they tend to employ younger broadcasters who stay a few years then seek wider experience elsewhere in the corporation, so these workplaces match Singer's description well. The cross–media broadcaster has physical proximity with other personnel in the radio station as they are mostly designed on open–plan lines, another factor Singer identifies as significant to successful cross–media practice. She refers to the "trust–building benefits of physical proximity" (Singer, 2004, p. 15) and evidence for these emerged from interviews with ABC local radio cross–media producers. In contrast to these advantages, the same factors—a small number of people working side by side in an open–plan workspace—can lead to difficulties for the one person doing cross–media work (radio plus online plus some video) that looks similar but actually has quite different demands from the single medium work (radio) of her or his peers.

The following sections draw on fieldwork conducted from March 2002, which has followed a small group of ABC regional radio cross–media producers from their training and into their workplaces, re–interviewing them and their managers at approximately two yearly intervals. This longitudinal study reveals what were the initial difficulties faced by these broadcasters, and how they and ABC local radio addressed them. The interviews and observations together offer a revealing picture of one area of online work within a public service media organization.

Training for cross–media work

The training of the 18 cross–media recruits began in February 2002. It comprised a one–week course and was very intensive. It covered both editorial and technical issues, with a slightly stronger emphasis on the technical, because there was so much to learn. Editorial issues included ABC–specific policies to do with commercialism, for example, and more general ones, such as copyright in web sites. The technical side of the course covered the capture and editing of still and moving images, using digital media, and production for the ABC's online gateway to local radio, then called The Backyard. For this, they were taught what they needed to know, including advice on writing and a lesson in HTML, to produce and upload stories to those areas of the ABC web site to be made accessible to them, using an in–house developed database and web template system called Wallace.

All the participants had already completed training in radio skills and in most cases had been working in the regional radio stations to which they'd been appointed for periods of time from weeks to months, although one had more than ten years experience in radio. Each person selected appeared to have training and/or experience in at least one of radio, video or web production, sometimes two, but none had experience of working in all three media.

Putting training into practice

Nine months after that week of training, follow–up interviews and observations in November 2002 found the cross–media producers were being used in different ways within their radio stations. All had been assigned some radio production responsibilities in addition to their production work for the web site, as expected. For example, one was providing some radio stories to the weekday Breakfast program but was not its producer (typically, the breakfast presenter is also the producer, in regional radio stations). She also provided web stories to another regional station as well as her own—and this was typical of the expectations of the first group of cross–media producers. The other station would send her the copy (initially just a transcript of the radio piece) and digital pictures by email and she took audio "down the line" (a permanent ISDN line) and compressed it for uploading to the web.

ABC Radio senior management had envisaged that the cross–media producers should divide their time 50:50 between radio and online. This was not often the case once the new producers were placed in their regional radio stations; as one local radio manager put it, radio is "the core business" of their workplace and he considered it should remain the "top priority" for the cross–media broadcasters. Some of the cross–media producers, especially those recruited from radio backgrounds, said in these early months that they saw themselves as primarily radio people.

In practice, the intended 50:50 split of the cross–media producer's duties between production for radio and for the web and digital TV worked well in some radio stations and not so well in others. One participant in the training, who had been working as the breakfast presenter at his radio station in the period between being hired as a cross–media producer and being trained, said he felt "a bit overwhelmed" and wasn't sure how his role would turn out once he returned to his station. He "loved" being on air but could not see how to balance his own desires with the demands of his station manager and those he now realised he had been hired to fulfil.

Another of the cross–media producers had acted as Station Manager for a couple of weeks not long after starting her cross–media job. She appreciated the opportunity but had found it impossible to keep up the same level of output for the online material, which was very frustrating for her.

Another cross–media broadcaster was the producer of the morning show on her radio station, in addition to her role producing text, audio and images for two regional station's web sites, her own and another one. For many people, especially in a capital city station, morning show producer would be a full–time job, so this cross–media producer had to manage her time extremely carefully. The local radio managers appeared very conscious of the time management issues faced by their cross–media producer, but there were other challenges that were harder for them to understand. One of these can be described in terms of professionalism in identity and practice.

Cross–media work and professionalism

The availability of relatively inexpensive digital video cameras, cheaper and more powerful computers, together with access to the internet represent a direct challenge to the historical divide between the amateur and the professional in media production. This is a particularly interesting challenge for a public broadcaster such as the ABC, which is not only funded by taxpayers' money but also has a chartered obligation to provide innovative and "high quality" programs.

Professionalism can be described for the purposes of this chapter with reference to three related elements. It is first characterized by "a work–related affective orientation" (Pollard and Johansen, 1998, p. 356). That is, practitioners in particular occupations think of themselves as—and try to act in ways that they conceive of meaningfully as—professional. Acting professionally for media workers involves "[bringing] to bear on the task in hand a number of known and tried skills that will produce predictable results" (Hood, 1987, n.p.). Finally, professionalism typically involves "developing competence through education or experience and ensuring full, ethical application of that competence" (Pollard and Johansen, 1998, p. 357). The ABC, as a public service broadcaster that enjoys a high degree of respect and affection from the Australian public (Posetti, 2002), expects a high level of professionalism from its employees, and in general its employees think of themselves as professionals (Henningham, 1995).

Professionalism needs cultivation to flourish, and small regional radio stations cannot offer a lot of personal or professional support to someone who arrives to do a job that may look a bit like the existing ones but actually has quite different demands and duties. A trainer pointed out that "these people won't have many people around who understand what they're doing." Two participants talked about not having a clear professional identity. "Sometimes you don't know what you are—radio, web, video," said one. Another said that when she tried to describe what she does, people look at her as though she is "some kind of alien." Participants mentioned the importance of keeping in touch with one another and with the trainers, to build their own network of support.

One of the re–interviewed journalists said she found her role difficult when she first arrived—it was "like, where do you start? There were so many stories"—but nine months down the track it was "a lot easier," although she did still find it difficult to know how to assign time to her various roles within the working day. She dealt with this by adopting the policy of setting herself a specific goal each day and finding satisfaction in accomplishing that. She had kept in touch by email with fellow course participants, sharing how they felt and how they managed their time.

Between the first and second rounds of the research, the ABC had established a mailing list for the cross–media broadcasters, called the BackFence, and had introduced a fortnightly conference call. While the cross–media producers were sometimes too busy to attend each conference call, the sense that there were others doing the same kind of work and they were not alone undoubtedly improved confidence and boosted a sense of professional identity.

Another, related, challenge to this initially fragile sense of professional identity concerned the use of the digital video cameras. When the cross–media producers returned to (or were placed in) regional radio stations after their training, they brought with them computers that were much more powerful than those allocated to other regional broadcasters at that time (2002). In addition, they each had a digital video camera kit, a relative novelty in regional radio stations at that time (digital still cameras had been introduced earlier, before the appointment of cross–media positions, and existing radio staff had been encouraged to learn to use them, specifically to contribute pictures to their local radio web site).

During training some of the trainees had asked whether or not other people in the station should be permitted to use the thousands of dollars–worth of equipment each cross–media producer would be bringing back with him or her, when those others had not received training in how to use it. In some cases, it was clear the station culture would mean that stopping other staff from using the equipment would take a feat of considerable diplomacy on the part of these relatively new employees. Apart from a general sense that the equipment was primarily for their use and that this should be clear to all in the workplace, the trainers laid down no prescriptions about this issue. They did, however, put some emphasis on the cost of the equipment and on the primary responsibility for it, of the individual cross–media producer.

The cross–media producers interviewed in November 2002 felt a strong sense of responsibility for "their" equipment. One said, jokingly, that she felt as though she'd practically have to sell her child to pay for it all, should any of the gear get lost or damaged. Another cross–media producer—and her boss, the station manager—had been persuaded to lend the video camera to a radio news journalist who, as she put it, "didn't respect the equipment." He didn't pack it up properly, took a long time to bring the tripod back and so on, without actually damaging anything. The reporter described herself as nervous the whole time the camera was gone, because her personal responsibility for that equipment had been so firmly impressed on all the course participants. It was clear that this had been a very difficult issue for this journalist and she had only been able to deal with it by referring it to her station manager who, fortunately, was supportive.

This is an issue of professional identity, in the sense that, if this employee had been a television camera operator, for example, no–one employed in a different capacity would dream of asking to use their camera. The role of cross–media producer was insufficiently established and recognized—even by those in the role—as having professional expertise and standards. Rather, the blurring of the distinction between professional and amateur that continues to characterize much digital media work, meant that other regional radio personnel felt "qualified" to at least ask to use the DV camera.

There was evidence that concerns about professional identity and standards were less strong for cross–media producers appointed later than the first group. One of these described what she does as "taking effective radio and turning it into effective online content so that it reaches a wider audience." This interviewee was also quite relaxed about the hybrid role of the cross–media producers, answering the question "What do you call yourself?" with "Online producer and breakfast (radio) producer—half and half." She said there was "not necessarily" any confusion or difficulty about doing both, saying there was a need to be conscious of the specific and distinct requirements of the web. As examples, she cited the permanence of a web posting (as opposed to the transience of live radio) and the web's global audience compared with the very localized radio audience.

New audiences, new relationship

During the first cross–media producer training, senior ABC managers spoke to the trainees about why the ABC was introducing cross–media production. What they said focused on the audience, and the relationship between ABC programs, program makers and audiences. They expressed the rationale for online production in terms of "value adding." Speaking in 2002, these managers saw the web as allowing the ABC to add value to *existing* content in the form of transcripts, text stories, audio files, recipes, photographs and video. They also saw it as providing the opportunity for ABC Radio to develop *new* content, in the form of online forums, feature stories, presenter profiles and listener feedback.

Going beyond listener feedback, the web presents the ABC with opportunities for much greater *local* connection. Localism can be served relatively inexpensively, given the relatively small number of staff in any one regional station and the size of the area they probably cover, through local diaries, sporting results, "what's on" features, and profiles of local characters. Most of this material—not all—can be sourced directly from the local community and is set up so that individual audience members can submit material to the appropriate "pages" of the web site. The ABC saw online content as building awareness of the ABC's services, increasing its profile and increasing the size of the audiences for both media platforms, broadcast and online.

For the cross–media producers in ABC regional radio stations, the concepts of value adding and localism were paramount in their approach to what they chose to put on the web sites for which they were responsible. In the first two years (2002–2004), this resulted predominantly in original radio content minimally re–purposed for online. Nonetheless, some of the cross–media producers could see that the online medium offered opportunities to attract a new audience in addition to their loyal radio listeners, and for a new relationship with these audiences.

In 2002, levels of internet access and use in regional Australia were quite low relative to nationwide use. By the second round of research (in 2004) regional centres had experienced dramatic growth in use of the local ABC web site, in one case, from just 600 to over 2000 hits a day. This was a result not only of better and more widespread internet access becoming available to local communities, but also of vigorous on–air promotion by the radio stations, including competitions promoted on radio but requiring a visit to the web site for participation.

One of the cross–media producers followed in this study was by 2004 using the internet in more innovative ways, to extend the radio material rather than simply re–purposing it for the web. A radio story about an accident on a farm had led to a story online, which had provoked a noticeable and positive response from the local community. The cross–media producer posted a follow–up story about how the injured farmer was faring, using embedded audio from the original radio material and photographs that the reporter had taken with the digital camera in paragraphs she wrote from information supplied by the reporter on the original radio story, and from her own research. The original material was thus given a life beyond the day of the radio broadcast, in a form that combined pictures, words and other sound.

Another example was a story about a local who had planted native trees, re–foresting a degraded bush area. The story on radio could not of course show what the area looked like "before" and "after" the plantings. The radio announcer told listeners they could see this, on the web, where the cross-media producer had produced a pictorial essay, using photographs supplied by the subject of the original radio story. An audio file of the radio interview could also be loaded from the page, and there were hyperlinks for those interested in the environmental issues of bush regeneration raised by the story.

Conclusion

This chapter has used a discussion arising from research in small, regional radio stations of the Australian Broadcasting Corporation to consider a number of important issues and events in the histories of PSB online. ABC regional radio has been traditionally local in its outlook and orientation, its workplaces small and staffed by resourceful and adaptable broadcasters. The introduction of single cross-media producers to a number of these local radio stations illustrates the challenges of online media to broadcast media generally and to PSB in particular.

In this chapter, the emphasis is on the challenges for cross-media producers and their managers, although these inevitably have wider implications. Despite the restructuring that ABC Radio had done to its industrial awards and classifications, the cross-media workers really were a "new breed" and consequently found themselves somewhat confused and isolated in their workplaces initially, in terms of their professional identity. As working across media platforms becomes more common at the ABC—as it already is in many media organisations—this is becoming less of a problem both for the individuals and for those who work alongside them. Nonetheless, the research demonstrates that the question of professionalism is a real one for cross-media workers. A combination of improved training and growth in numbers of such producers is likely to lead to wider recognition and appreciation of their skills within the corporation. However, improved working conditions, in the sense of more realistic demands on their time and better technical resources, may be essential before such recognition is possible.

In local radio, the cross-media producers were instrumental in drawing radio listeners to the ABC's online content. They have also created an audience for the online content that does not listen to the associated local radio station at all, either because they cannot receive it or because they prefer online to radio. This audience has a younger profile than the audience for the radio station, and of course may be accessing the web site from anywhere in the world.[2] This younger and geographically dispersed audience is a very different one from that for local radio, something of which the cross-media producers have had to become acutely conscious.

The period from 2002 has seen rapid growth in internet use in regional Australia and accompanying growth in the number of visitors to ABC Local web sites; in the first two years of the *Backyard* site, the growth was threefold and more at several regional locations. There has been major development in how the web is used by the cross–media producers, from straightforward "shoveling" of radio content onto the site, to more complex and sophisticated re–purposing and enhancing of radio stories into genuinely multimedia narratives. Along with this has come growing solicitation of user–generated content (UGC) and networked social media, such as blogging, Facebook and Twitter. Initially UGC was confined to uncontentious areas of local information sharing such as recipes, school reunions and the like. As blogging and other social media were adopted, audience contribution became potentially much more open and less directed, necessitating the development of policies about how to manage it.

Until 2009, the ABC's default editorial policy was to pre–moderate all audience contributions, a time–consuming and costly process for all concerned. In 2009 a new policy section was added to cover all forms of audience contribution, collectively defined as User Generated Content (UGC) (Section 9, ABC Editorial Policies 2009). Its underlying principles include "the primacy of public service," "providing opportunities for user engagement" and "serving a fragmented audience." It permits pre–moderation, post–moderation or reactive moderation (that is, reacting to alerts from users about particular content), by "appropriately trained staff" (ABC, March 2009, p. 2). Any choice other than pre–moderation has to be approved by a process of "upward referral" to "an appropriately senior ABC person designated for the purpose within the responsible Division" (ABC, March 2009, p. 3).

This is a cautious approach to engagement with the public in the online environment, understandable from an organisation subject to considerable public scrutiny, as well as political and economic accountability. Equally, because the ABC's remit requires it to support innovative content production and in the world of online media, the audience (or "users") is now one source of such content, the corporation must be more open to and less controlling of its audience than the historical ethos of public service broadcasting has allowed. A new venture, ABC Open,[3] which invites online contributions from the audience, produced with the assistance of "ABC Open producers" (the cross–media producers in new guise?), suggests this may be happening.

How this issue, the changed relationship with audiences, will play out for the cross–media producers in regional radio remains to be seen. The form it eventually takes is significant, however. The cooperative efforts of professional media workers and members of local communities, using networked online media, have the potential greatly to enhance the quality and quantity of information resources to once-isolated individuals and groups. Thirty years after the Dix Report, the ABC is poised truly to serve all Australians in equal measure.

Notes

1. The States are New South Wales, Queensland, Victoria, Tasmania, South Australia and Western Australia. The Territories are the Australian Capital Territory and the Northern Territory, both of which now have their own parliaments (the Federal Parliament is based in Canberra, capital of Australia and of the Australian Capital Territory).
2. These changes are as reported by local radio managers, based on internal ABC audience research.
3. http://www.abc.net.au/open.

Bibliography

ABC (1987). *4th Annual Report of the Australian Broadcasting Corporation, 1 July 1986–30 June 1987.* Sydney: ABC.

ABC (2009, March). *User Generated Content (UGC): Amendments to the ABC Editorial Policies.* Sydney: ABC.

Deuze, M. (2007). *Media Work.* Cambridge, UK: Polity Press.

Dix (1981a). [Committee of Review of the Australian Broadcasting Commission] The ABC in Review: National Broadcasting in the 1980s, Volume 1—Summary & Recommendations. Canberra: AGPS.

Dix (1981b). [Committee of Review of the Australian Broadcasting Commission] The ABC in Review: National Broadcasting in the 1980s, Volume 2—Report. Canberra: AGPS.

Hawkins, G. (2001). The ABC and the rhetorics of choice. In T. Bennett & D. Carter (Eds.), *Culture in Australia: Policies, Publics and Programs,*. Cambridge, UK: Cambridge University Press.

Henningham, J. (1995). Australian journalists' reactions to new technology. *Prometheus, 13*(2), 225–238.

Hood, S. (1987). *On television.* London: Plato.

Martin, F. (1999, November). *Digital dilemmas: The Australian Broadcasting Corporation and interactive multimedia publishing.* Master of Arts unpublished thesis, Southern Cross University.

Martin, F. (2007). *Digital dilemmas: The Australian Broadcasting Corporation and interactive multimedia publishing 1992–2002.* PhD Thesis, Southern Cross University.

Pollard, G. & Johansen, P. (1998). Professionalism among Canadian radio announcers: The impact of organizational control and social attributes. *Journal of Broadcasting & Electronic Media,* Summer, 356–370.

Posetti, J. (2002). The politics of bias at the ABC. *Australian Studies in Journalism,* 10/11, 3–32.

Singer, J. (2004). Strange bedfellows? The diffusion of convergence in four news organisations. *Journalism Studies, 5*(1), 3–18.

Tickle, S. & Keshvani, N. (2000). Electronic news futures. *Australian Journalism Review, 22*(1), 68–80.

12 *Canadian Content, Public Broadcasting and the Internet*

CBC's Online Strategy 1995–2000

Brian O'Neill & Michael J. Murphy

Introduction

The Canadian Broadcasting Corporation (CBC) was one among a group of pioneering broadcasters in the mid 1990s to identify the potential of the World Wide Web as a new arm for national public service broadcasting. Its website, www.CBC.ca, first developed in 1995, became a crucial element in the corporation's strategy to build a national and international profile for Canadian news and media content. The CBC's online presence was also technologically pioneering and the corporation was one of the first broadcasters to offer live streaming, downloads and multimedia podcasts of its broadcast services.

One reason for the CBC's early interest in the internet lies in the importance in the Canadian context of ensuring that sufficient Canadian content is available for national audiences. For traditional broadcasting, this has been achieved through a combination of content quotas and production development funding. In this chapter, we present an overview of the early history of the CBC's approach to the web. Looking specifically at the period 1995 to 2000, we locate this strategy within the context of the ongoing financial, organisational and regulatory forces impacting on public broadcasting in Canada. Despite major cutbacks in its own funding and radical changes in the structure of the Canadian broadcast industry, the CBC through this period determined that converged, multiplatform content provision was the best strategy for its long-term survival.

Content Regulation and Broadcasting in Canada

The regulation of Canada's broadcasting and telecommunications sectors falls to the Canada Radio–television and Telecommunications Commission (CRTC), an independent public authority created in 1968. The current Broadcasting Act was first created at that time and most recently amended in 1991. The primary objective of the Act is to protect Canadian culture through preserving access to a wide array of Canadian broadcast programming. The regulatory responsibilities of the CRTC require it to maintain a Canadian-owned and -controlled system of broadcasting, with specific provisions for Canadian content in programming and production. The legislation encourages the development of Canadian expression, and the use of Canadian talent and creative resources. There is also a specific emphasis on reflecting Canada's cultural diversity and a requirement that programming and employment opportunities serve the needs and interests of all Canadians, and reflect their various circumstances.

The protection of the position of Canadian content or "CanCon" is the cornerstone of Canadian broadcasting policy (Petryszak, 1979, p. 23). The Act requires that Canadian expression should be fostered by displaying and broadcasting Canadian talent, maximizing the use of Canadian creativity and the Canadian independent production sector, while also charging the Canadian Broadcasting Corporation, as the national public broadcaster, to actively contribute to the flow and exchange of cultural expression. Under the Act, the CRTC has the power to decide what constitutes a Canadian program and the proportion of time that should be devoted to Canadian programming. A system of quotas is used to regulate the quantity of Canadian programming on radio and television and "Canadian–ness" is measured using a points system based on the number of Canadians involved in its production. For television, public licensees are required to devote not less than 60 per cent, and private broadcasters not less than 50 per cent of evening programming to Canadian content. In its 1998 Commercial Radio Policy, the CRTC increased the Canadian content requirements for AM and FM radio broadcasting from 30 to 35 per cent.

The prominence given to content regulation in Canadian broadcasting stems from the obvious fact that it shares both a border and a common language with the largest producer of cultural products in the world (Johansen, 1973; Collins, 1990). From its earliest days, first in radio and later in television, the US domination of broadcasting in Canada has been evident and public policy has been motivated by an effort to regain control of the airwaves through legislation (Raboy, 1990; Romanow, 2005). Noting that "the majority of the programs heard are from sources outside of Canada," the Aird Commission of 1929 established the first regulator and national broadcasting system and from that time the difficult balance of maintaining popularity and broadcasting distinctive Canadian content has been negotiated (Royal Commission on Radio Broadcasting, 1929). The Caplan–Sauvageau Task Force on Broadcasting Policy of 1986 was particularly critical of Canadian broadcasters' performance in this regard, highlighting that nearly 98 per cent of television drama was foreign–originated and that Canadian programs accounted for only 28 per cent of overall English–language television (Raboy, 1989). Despite their profitability, Canadian broadcasters were criticized for not spending enough on developing new Canadian talent or producing sufficient Canadian content. For its part, the CBC was simply under–funded and not given sufficient support to carry out its mandate. The resulting Broadcasting Act of 1991 and more rigorous approaches to content regulation and monitoring since then have been credited with the development of a thriving independent audio–visual production sector as well as a successful Canadian music industry, reversing the trend and fostering an international profile for Canadian cultural products (Canadian Radio–Television and Telecommunications Commission, 1999).

But how, one may ask, does this relate to the CBC's interests in web–based content? In 1999, the CRTC exempted new media broadcasting, and effectively the internet in Canada, from regulation (Canadian Radio–Television and Telecommunications Commission, 1999). New developments in technology, the Commission acknowledged, had led to a situation where new media, incorporating text, graphics, data, fixed images, audio, full motion video and animation, could be delivered over digital networks to exhibition devices such as personal computers (PCs) or television sets. Accordingly, the CRTC determined that as the majority of internet services consisted predominantly of text–based websites, they did not fall within the scope of the Broadcasting Act or under the Commission's jurisdiction. Equally, digital services with the potential for significant user customization and in which users created their own uniquely tailored content were considered not to involve the transmission of programs for reception by the public and, likewise therefore, did not constitute broadcasting. For those media services that did fall under the definition of broadcasting, including video, audio and still images, it was felt that regulation was not necessary to achieve the objectives of the Broadcasting Act. The Commission argued that the circumstances that led to regulation of Canadian content in traditional broadcasting did not exist in the internet environment at the time and that market forces were providing a sufficient

Canadian presence on the internet supported by a strong demand for Canadian new media content.

The CRTC decision of 1999 effectively drew a line between broadcast services delivered by terrestrial, cable and satellite and those services delivered by the internet, releasing the latter from any form of regulatory control or stimulus for further content development support. The distinction would, of course, be increasingly difficult to draw, and convergence at both the technological and industrial level, as commentators have observed, has been the subject of sustained discussion in Canadian media policy with cyberspace becoming as intensely competitive a field as terrestrial broadcasting (Winseck, 2002). For this reason, CBC prioritization of new media from the mid 1990s arose less from a desire to be a pioneer in new technologies than from a need to build and defend a competitive position for the CBC brand in the only truly unregulated space within the Canadian mediascape and within which consolidation and cross–media ownership was the order of the day.

It is also the case, it should be noted, that Canada's reputation as a world leader—and early adopter—of communications technology provided a very conducive environment in which to promote new media services. In the period in which the CBC was forging its new media policy, home use of the internet grew substantially from 16 per cent in 1997 to 40 per cent in 2000 (Statistics Canada, 2001). A 1996 government–wide Action Plan, titled *Building the Information Society: Moving Canada into the 21st Century* (Information Highway Advisory Council, 1996) led to a policy of close partnership between government and industry in which "industry takes the initiative, and the government watches, stimulates, supports, regulates, creates the needed context" (d'Haenens & Proulx 2000, p. 284). The Broadcasting Act, likewise, requires that the Canadian broadcasting system should be "readily adaptable to scientific and technological change," and that regulation should "not inhibit the development of information technologies and their application or the delivery of resultant services to Canadians." CRTC policy has correspondingly supported a generally laissez–faire approach, responding as required to industry needs, not wishing to impede what has been perceived to be a creative and dynamic sector with significant potential for Canada.

Building the brand: cbc.ca

The building of a CBC presence online had a lengthy gestation period. An early 1980s networking experiment called Project IRIS provided a foundation for the electronic delivery of news and information that would form the basis of online news services (Gorbould, 2006a). This pre–internet joint project of the

CBC and the Federal Department of Communications used a teletext technology called Telidon to deliver data directly to television sets following a trend established elsewhere for new electronic information sources. Projects such as these demonstrated the potential of information applications for broadcasters though typically these underestimated the importance of the home computer, instead privileging the television set as the primary information platform.

It was the CBC's Radio Division that made the first foray into internet delivery. A trial in late 1993 encoded episodes of CBC programs as audio files which were then offered for download via FTP, Gopher and the World Wide Web (Patrick, Black & Whalen, 1996). The project, one of the very first internet–delivered audio experiments, proved extremely popular, encouraging CBC Radio to launch "radio.cbc.ca" in December 1994. Real Audio streams were later added in June 1995.

Further experimental projects developed with the addition of sites for all major aspects of the CBC service including CBC Online News, CBC4kids and dedicated sites for its television and radio channels. There was also an early commitment to other new delivery platforms and digital technologies such as Digital Audio Broadcasting (DAB) since 1999, SMS text news alerts since 2001, interactive TV and video on demand since 2003 (O'Neill, 2007). Subsequently, the CBC's support for legal music downloads and podcasting won it acclaim as one of the first public broadcasters internationally to develop a successful model for harnessing new modes of audio delivery (Hughes, 2005; Newitz, 2005). The principle of being available on all relevant and contemporary distribution platforms was also subsequently used to justify the CBC's participation on the Sirius satellite radio platform launched in December 2005 (O'Neill, 2006).

Yet in its early phase, a coherent strategy for content delivery in the online environment using the CBC.ca brand was noticeably lacking. According to Gorbould—one of CBC.ca's first employees—what eventually became the CBC new media division "was a severely balkanized collection of websites, with constant turf warfare among media lines acting as if they were in competition with each other" (Gorbould, 2006a). These included a collection of websites for CBC Radio, primarily serving the arts as well as children's services (radio.cbc.ca, infoculture.cbc.ca, cbc4kids.ca); the CBC Newsworld–owned breaking news site (newsworld.cbc.ca); a promotional site for CBC Television (tv.cbc.ca); and a corporate information site (cbc.radio–canada.ca). Little attention was given to questions of design or user experience at this point. The resulting CBC.ca brand emerged in the first instance as a framework for quite disparate offerings, many developed by IT departments rather than the primary programming divisions, as sidelines to the primary business of broadcast content.

Gorbould (2006b) reports how journalists, programmers and designers struggled initially with concepts of how to engage audiences through online content. Onscreen metaphors were devised that in the case of radio provided visual navigation cues such as the book stacks concept as links for textual and audio content.

With the growing importance of broadband from 1995 on, and the growing interest in online multimedia entertainment, the CBC began to experiment with more demanding applications and program ideas. Following the introduction of "audio on demand" on CBC Radio, CBC Newsworld introduced live streaming of both audio and video in 1996. These early experiments in webcasting would lead to the development of CBC Home Delivery. This push technology used Flash-based authoring to create a "full screen multimedia magazine" of CBC audio, video and web content delivered directly to a subscriber's computer (McLaughlin, 2003). Hailed by Macromedia (2010) as a groundbreaking site, the Home Delivery package became a core element of the ill-fated Radio 3 project, the CBC's new, youth-oriented, national radio service building on Canada's strong independent music and popular culture scene. Despite building a strong subscriber base, the project was closed in 2003 following a restructuring of CBC priorities (Belanger & Andrecheck, 2005).

New Media, New CBC

As a public service broadcaster, the possibilities for convergence offered the CBC both substantial opportunities and significant challenges to its remit. A key argument supporting an extension of the public service remit to the online space was and is that in order to ensure its continuing relevance and public support, public broadcasters need to publish across a variety of new media platforms and in particular maintain a high-profile presence on the internet (Lowe and Hujanen, 2003). Often against a background of financial cutbacks and uncertain future investment, high risk strategies in the mid-1990s were adopted by organizations such as the BBC in the United Kingdom, Canada's CBC and National Public Radio (NPR) in the United States to invest in new media content and services outside of the traditional modes of public service radio and television broadcasting (Collins, Finn, McFadyen & Hoskins, 2001). The role played by such prominent brand names was often a pioneering and market-leading one, and as such not without controversy, leading to claims about an unfair subsidy or potential distortion to the commercial market for internet services (Hills & Michalis, 2000).

The CBC's approach towards new media was particularly decisive and received strong support from its technophile President, Perrin Beatty. As CBC President during the years 1995 to 1999, he steered the corporation towards an ambitious plan of refashioning the national broadcaster as the primary Canadian content publisher across diverse and broadcasting multimedia platforms. This occurred against a backdrop of major financial cutbacks in the CBC's budget, imposed by the Liberal government in 1994, and a major reduction in its television output and its regional services (Chidley, 1996). The counter argument, in Beatty's view, was to propose a rejuvenated CBC that would be much more Canadian–focused, but would also be smaller. Adopting new media and the internet as one of the areas in which the CBC could flourish, in 1998 he outlined as one of the key goals for the organization: "to create a critical mass of content and services to ensure that Canadians can never be relegated to a back corner of the web" (Beatty, 1998). Following one of the most significant financial crises to affect the CBC with massive downsizing and reductions in local and regional broadcast services, this initiative gambled on success in the online world as a key element of the CBC's future. The stated aim was for the CBC to be the primary source of Canadian news and culture on the web. Beatty outlined four guiding principles underpinning this new media strategy. Firstly, the CBC would serve its audiences wherever they were and on whatever technology they were using. Secondly, the CBC would respond to the demand for increased choice—in particular for specialty and niche interest channels via radio, television and the web. Thirdly, with its special responsibility to preserve and promote Canadian content, the CBC would use its web presence to leverage the CBC's position as the main repository of Canadian audio–visual culture. Finally, Beatty committed the CBC to a path of technological innovation on the premise that Canadian audiences demanded it and would only be retained by innovative and exciting new media content. Acknowledging the plethora of risks involved—not least the CBC's new, leaner economic reality, the dominance of multinationals on the web, the difficulty in developing a realistic revenue model for the internet, the threat of cannibalizing audiences, and the limitations on current bandwidth—Beatty argued that it was precisely for all these reasons that the CBC had to adopt an aggressive approach to new media.

The new media strategy that emerged around 1998 harnessed the corporation's online experience to date and proposed a bolder vision of what the corporation could become in the twenty–first century. In the hearings leading to the CBC's licence renewal in 1999, Beatty proposed that Canada's public broadcaster should imitate the BBC and offer a grand constellation of broadcasting services, "anchored on a traditional network and including distribution, entertainment and a variety of specialty and niche services." Unambiguously committing the CBC to a pioneering role, he argued: "We will play a leadership role in new media and new technology. There is not a shred of doubt that the CBC belongs—indeed, will thrive—in this swiftly growing arena. Without our presence, there is a real risk of Canadian voices being submerged" (Saucier & Beatty, 1999).

In the development of its new media activities, the CBC had to either self-finance or cross-subsidize from other activities, placing a substantial burden on the organization. The CBC's mandate, for which it receives direct federal funding, is to develop radio and television content that is "predominantly and distinctively Canadian" and "made available throughout Canada by the most appropriate and efficient means." By adopting the additional role of being an aggregator of Canadian content on the internet, the CBC was effectively attempting the "Canadianizing" of the web in the same way that media policy had previously sought to counteract US domination of content in Canada's domestic broadcast space. Its goal to be "the most important and popular source of Canadian news, information, and entertainment content on digital networks" set the CBC the task of being the reference point for Canadian content at a global level, against competition from the other major multinational interests beginning to dominate internet traffic (Galipeau, 2003). The objective and the prize, of course, was to extend the reach of the CBC brand, known for "its quality, credibility and Canadian values" (Beatty, 1998) onto a global stage, in much the same way that other major international brands, such as the BBC, were attempting to do.

In 1999, the more pragmatic Robert Rabinovitch succeeded Beatty as CBC President. In the more sober climate following the dot-com bust of 2001, Rabinovitch abandoned what was perceived as Beatty's sometimes overreaching and overly commercial strategy in favor of a more modest approach that would re-focus the CBC on its public service core competencies (Fraser, 2000, p. 43). What this amounted to was a more conservative approach appropriate to the corporation's parlous budgetary position with a concentration on distinctive, home-grown programming in news, current affairs, documentaries, and drama. Moreover, CBC Television would reduce its commercial dependency on advertising revenues, which had been the source of creeping commercialism at the network. A number of major plans were abandoned including the axing of new specialty radio and TV services.

Yet despite this more cautious environment, the CBC's online presence had matured to the extent that convergence and new media publishing had become embedded in the corporation's operational processes. This was particularly evident with the refashioning of CBC.ca in the early 2000s as primarily a news and information site (Fuerst, 2004). This signaled a move away from program-centered online content (and indeed with less emphasis on streaming and downloads) towards well-designed and user-focused breaking news and information services. Part of this strategy arose from internal CBC research that sought to extend the reach of CBC news services to daytime, office–based audiences, cleverly augmenting CBC audience share in ways that radio and television could not. Traffic to the site greatly increased and by early 2004 CBC.ca was Canada's most visited news site.

The parliamentary Standing Committee on Canadian Heritage in 2003, reviewing the provisions of the Broadcasting Act, singled out CBC's new media activities for particular praise. Recognizing that the new landscape required broadcasters to develop cross platform strategies by which their online content could supplement their radio and television activities (Canadian Heritage, 2003, p. 218), it recommended, in the interests of greater clarity and mission focus, that "the Broadcasting Act be amended to recognize the value of new media services as a complementary element of the CBC's overall programming strategy," thus endorsing the CBC's transition to a model of public service media.

Conclusion

The CBC's online strategy and the development of CBC.ca achieved a number of important objectives for the national broadcaster. It made the CBC the number one media/broadcasting company online in Canada, a position it does not maintain in the offline world. It brought the CBC to younger audiences—its online service has the highest proportion of 18–34 year olds of all CBC services. It also succeeded in extending audiences for CBC content in new timeslots where traditional media has had relatively little success.

The CBC's early commitment to new media publishing and diversifying its operations across a variety of digital networks might in retrospect be seen as a far sighted strategic decision that provided the correct response for a public service broadcaster under pressure in a declining market. On previous occasions when broadcasters faced market difficulties through either changing demographics or challenges from competitors, the response has normally been a programming one. The new media strategy was broader in scope and attempted to extend existing services across new networks. Arguing that the decline in radio listenership was indicative of a longer term trend and the result of younger listeners opting out of broadcaster–provided content in favor of self–programmed audio content, the CBC put in place a set of complementary platform solutions that played to user sovereignty and recognized the multi–platform reality of contemporary media consumption. This shift in emphasis had a consequent impact on the production cycle which required that content was produced not for a single medium but was available across all platforms and re–purposed as required for different formats.

Alongside some evident success, CBC.ca as a brand–building exercise highlighted a number of strategically important and difficult issues that face broadcasters in the global competition for market share on the internet. Framed within the parameters of Canadian legislation and broadcast content regulation, the internet is an unregulated space with no carriage or content rules and the task of maintaining and preserving a distinctive Canadian voice in this cultural sphere is challenging. As in the terrestrial world, broadcasters like the CBC operate in an environment dominated by United States–based, transnational interests and the regulatory solutions that Canada has previously pursued in the attempt to enhance Canadianization of media content and to preserve cultural sovereignty may be either inadequate or inappropriate for this new media environment. The Canadian content regulation regime or "CanCon," for instance, does not directly apply to web content. New developments in digital broadcasting including internet radio and satellite broadcasting are likely to place such regulatory measures under increasing pressure raising even more questions about such a cultural policy in the first place.

The review conducted by Canadian Heritage of the Broadcasting Act in 2003 acknowledged the high stakes involved, arguing that "it would take just a few serious mistakes on the part of the regulator, broadcasters or distributors for the entire broadcasting industry to be thrown into economic turmoil" (Canadian Heritage, 2003, p. 442). The CRTC's early decision to exempt new media from regulation stemmed in part from the fact that intervention would serve no positive purpose. There was also a recognition that the future impact of new media on conventional broadcasting was clouded in uncertainty. Digital networks may replace traditional radio and television broadcasting in the future as the dominant means of reaching mass audiences and as such geographic boundaries may become meaningless in the distribution of media content. Alternatively, the internet may continue to play a complementary role to conventional broadcasting and enhance media diversity with fewer restrictions on entry to the system. In either case, the CBC has worked on the assumption that while the mantra "content is king" holds for any discussion of future media scenarios, distribution is the new barrier that entrants to broadcasting will face. And as experience of internet domination in Canada by powerful US interests has illustrated, gatekeeping to distribution channels is only likely to increase in importance in an unregulated or under–regulated digital environment.

Acknowledgments

The assistance of the Government of Canada under its Faculty Research Program (IRL–FRP–632–2–07) is gratefully acknowledged for support in conducting research for this chapter. The cooperation and assistance of the Canadian Broadcasting Corporation and the many professionals who agreed to be interviewed is also gratefully acknowledged.

References

Beatty, P. (1998). New Media, New CBC. Speech to the Canadian Radio–Television and Telecommunications Commission. Retrieved from http://www.cbc.radio-canada.ca/speeches/19981124.shtml

Belanger, P. C. & Andrecheck, P. (2005). CBC's Electronic Radio 3: Connecting with the Elusive Youth. *Journal of Radio Studies, 12*(1), 120–135.

Canadian Broadcasting Corporation (2009). *Annual Report 2008–9.* Retrieved from http://www.cbc.radio-canada.ca/annualreports/2008–2009/index.shtml

Canadian Heritage (2003). *Our Cultural Sovereignty: The Second Century of Canadian Broadcasting.*Ottawa: Standing Committee on Communications and Culture.

Canadian Radio–Television and Telecommunications Commission. *Broadcasting Public Notice CRTC 1999–84 (New Media).* Retrieved from http://www.crtc.gc.ca/archive/eng/Notices/1999/PB99–84.htm

Canadian Radio–Television and Telecommunications Commission (1999). Building on Success—A Policy Framework for Canadian Television. Ottawa, Canadian Radio–television and Telecommunications Commission.

Chidley, J. (1996, September 30). CBC Cuts Announced. *Maclean's.* Retrieved from http://www.encyclopediecanadienne.ca/index.cfm?PgNm=TCE&Params=M1ARTM0011002

Collins, R. (1990). *Culture, Communication, and National Identity: The Case of Canadian Television.* Toronto: University of Toronto Press.

Collins, R., Finn, A., McFadyen, S. & Hoskins, C. (2001). Public Service Broadcasting Beyond 2000: Is There a Future for Public Service Broadcasting? *Canadian Journal of Communication, 26*(1), 3–15.

d'Haenens, L. & Proulx, S. (2000). The Changing Stance of the Canadian Government in an Age of Globalization and Information. *International Communication Gazette, 62*(3–4), 281–299.

Fraser, M. (2000, September). The CBC's Choice: Constellations or Core Competencies? *Policy Options*, 43–49.

Fuerst, M. (2004). We Can Compete on the Web—CBC.ca Does. *Current.* Retrieved from http://www.current.org/web/web0405fuerst.shtml

Galipeau, C. (2003, July 3). New Media at CBC. Paper presented at the Publishing across New Media Platforms Conference. Vancouver, BC: Simon Fraser University.

Gorbould, P. (2006a). CBC.ca Prehistory. *10 Years of CBC.ca.* Retrieved from http://www.cbc.ca/10th/columns/prehistory_gorbould.html

Gorbould, P. (2006b). Seemed Like a Good Idea at the Time . . . and Other Growing Pains. *10 Years of CBC.ca.* Retrieved from http://www.cbc.ca/10th/columns/seemed_gorbould.html

Hills, J. & Michalis, M. (2000). The Internet: A Challenge to Public Service Broadcasting? *Gazette: International Journal for Communication Studies, 62*(6), 477–494.

Hughes, G. (2005). The Future of Radio. *CBC News Viewpoint.* Retrieved from http://www.cbc.ca/news/viewpoint/vp_hughes

Information Highway Advisory Council (1996). *Building the Information Society: Moving Canada into the 21st Century.* Ottawa: Minister of Supply and Services Canada.

Johansen, P. W. (1973). The CRTC and Canadian Content Regulation. *Journal of Broadcasting, 17*, 465–474.

Lowe, G. F. & Hujanen, T. (Eds.) (2003). *Broadcasting & Convergence: New Articulations of the Public Service Remit.* Göteborg, Sweden: Nordiskt Informationscenter.

Macromedia. (2010). *CBC Home Delivery.* Retrieved from http://www.adobe.com/special/inspiration/cbc

McLaughlin, R. (2003). CBC Radio 3. *Communication Arts, 45*(5), 122–123.

Newitz, A. (2005). Adam Curry Wants to Make You an iPod Radio Star. *Wired.com. 13*(03). Retrieved from www.wired.com/wired/archive/13.03/curry.htm

O'Neill, B. (2006). CBC.ca: Broadcast Sovereignty in a Digital Environment. *Convergence, 12*(2), 179–197.

O'Neill, B. (2007). Digital Audio Broadcasting in Canada: Technology and Policy in the Transition to Digital Radio. *Canadian Journal of Communication, 32*(1), 71–90.

Patrick, A., Black, A. & Whalen, T. (1996). CBC Radio on the Internet: An Experiment in Convergence. *Canadian Journal of Communication, 21*(1), 125–140.

Petryszak, N. G. (1979). The Canadian Television Industry: A Study in Contradictions. *Canadian Journal of Communication, 6*(2), 22–42.

Raboy, M. (1989). Two Steps Forward, Three Steps Back: Canadian Broadcasting Policy from Caplan–Sauvageau to Bill C–136. *Canadian Journal of Communication, 14*(1), 70–75.

Raboy, M. (1990). *Missed Opportunities: The Story of Canada's Broadcasting Policy.* Montreal: McGill–Queen's University Press.

Romanow, P. (2005). "The Picture of Democracy We Are Seeking": CBC Radio Forums and the Search for a Canadian Identity, 1930–1950. *Journal of Radio Studies, 12*(1), 104–119.

Royal Commission on Radio Broadcasting (1929). *Report of the Royal Commission on Radio Broadcasting (Aird Commission).* Ottawa: F.A. Acland.

Saucier, G. & Beatty, P. (1999). Presentation to the Senate Committee on Transport and Communications by Guylaine Saucier and the Honourable Perrin Beatty. Retrieved from http://www.cbc.radio-canada.ca/speeches/19990513.shtml

Statistics Canada (2001). *Quarterly Bulletin from the Cultural Statistics Programme, 13*(2). Retrieved from http://www.statscan.ca

Winseck, D. (2002). Netscapes of Power: Convergence, Consolidation and Power in the Canadian Mediascape. *Media, Culture & Society, 24*(6), 795–820.

PART FIVE

Talking Back to Aunty

Interactivity and Public Service Broadcasting Sites

13 *Vox Populi, Vox Dei*

ABC Online and the Risks of Dialogic Interaction

Fiona Martin

Entering the Dialogue

In 1995 the ABC's science broadcasters, inspired by their early research encounters on Usenet and other internet communities, created the organisation's first websites—and later ABC Online's longest-running discussion forum *Self Service Science*. At that time science online founder Ian Allen welcomed the advent of user commentary and critique:

> If someone takes exception to a particular article, we provide the forums and means for them to say instantly so. . . . We don't have to pretend to be the authoritative "Voice of God." Science isn't like that anyway. Debate and dissent is healthy. (Allen in Martin, 2008, p. 127)

Yet pioneer narratives, with their euphoric inflection, have limited use in historicizing online media development. Elsewhere in the ABC staff have been far more cautious about publishing user comments, regarding them as potential threats to institutional credibility and the task of moderating them as an editorially challenging, resource intensive business (Ray, 2003; Debrett, 2009).

This "new gatekeeping" analysis explores how the ABC has responded to the uncertainties posed by the growth of a read/write web and tensions between the institutional Vox Dei and the polyglot Vox Populi in forum, guestbook and blog formats.

Those tensions are not readily evident in the social democratic rhetoric used by PSBs to promote online community building (BBC, 1999) and cultural exchange (CBC, 2002) or, in the ABC's case, the creation of a "virtual town square" where "all Australians can come to listen and learn—to speak and be heard" (Scott, 2009). Equally first decade web scholarship has explored the opportunities for PSB user participation to support media democratisation (Carpentier, 2003; Enli, 2006) an information commons (Murdock, 2004) and collaborative knowledge production (Bruns, 2008), rather than systematically probing hurdles to those outcomes.

Online exchanges between users and broadcasters have become potent symbols of public service broadcasting's increased relevance, inclusiveness and accountability. Yet it is critical to interrogate the limits of those relationships, to understand why the institution might fail to satisfy users' wishes to be heard and its desire to host civil dialogue.

As a first step this chapter analyses how the risks of dialogic encounters have been perceived and managed at the ABC from 1995 to 2010, based on analysis of corporate documents, websites and interviews with ABC Online managers, journalists and moderators. It examines the conditions for dialogic interaction and explores staff responses to the everyday risks encountered there over time, with a focus on three high-profile discussion communities.

ABC Online and Risk

ABC Online emerged from an institution at risk. In 1995 as web publishing moved into its first commercial phase, the largely state–funded ABC was in a poor position to invest in new media. Its real operational funding had been in decline for a decade, it was involved in several loss–making commercial ventures, and it was about to suffer a 12% budget cut from an incoming Conservative Coalition government, focussed on its political reform.

In that climate, and with significant costs looming for broadcast digitalisation, a risk–averse executive gave seed funding to staff lobbying for a web service. ABC Online's early growth then relied on the success of opportunistic or "guerrilla" development initiatives in receptive program areas (Burns, 2008) with staff diverting funds from broadcast to web production and later petitioning federal politicians for science innovation and regional programming grants. Support by successive managing directors saw ABC Online rapidly institutionalised as a third publishing platform, but it has been a difficult object to assimilate into the ABC's organisational structure—not television or radio but integral to the digital re–imagining of both. Its role is yet to be codified in the Charter and its cannibalisation of broadcast budgets has created inter–divisional tensions about the scope of its activities. So ABC Online's policy trajectory has been marked by uncertainty.

Clearly public service broadcasting itself is an agonistic concept, engendering constant upheaval and restructure (Craig, 2000). However ABC Online's growing pains have been overshadowed by more global threats to the ABC—the broader political and existential crisis under neo–liberalism (Tracey, 1998), the pluralisation of digital media channels that may undermine its market failure rationale, and the destabilisation of corporate media authority by DIY publishers and citizen journalists seeking a mediated "conversation" (Gillmor, 2004).

Predictions of catastrophic risk arise, in Ulrich Beck's (1999) classic formulation, from the uncertainties generated by the complex changes of reflexive modernity—in the ABC's case the perceived negative impacts of digitalisation, internetworking and increased audience agency on the institutional legitimacy of PSB and mainstream journalism. Yet as Beck noted risk assessment occupies "a peculiar intermediate state between security and destruction" where the *perception* of risk pre–determines our responses and strategic decision–making (1999, p. 135). So tracking how risk has been perceived over time allows us to better understand the mechanisms of socio–technological change.

This chapter is not concerned with the actuarial, standardised measurement of risk in project management, which became a central part of corporate practice during the 1990s. Instead it aims to reveal broadcasters' varying hopes and fears for a dialogic relationship with users—how they imagined opportunity, protected tradition and acted to shape public exchange, by capitalising on or ameliorating likely threats. This history of risk perception also raises ethical problems around the notion of "public service" as it shifts from a paternal, impartial role to more interlocutory interventions aimed at the self–realising, entrepreneurial individuals of the advanced liberal imagination.

Publicly, ABC executives have supported initiatives that give web users a voice. Early on Managing Director Brian Johns declared ABC Online an important way to network with interest groups and individuals across distance (Johns, 1996). Discussion forums were then promoted to "build ABC audiences and loyalties" (ABC, 1999, p. 31) and reflect cultural diversity. By 2001 the ABC's Chairman's support for "interactivity" sounded like that of a constructivist educator: "The audience's diversity and the depth of knowledge must be regarded as a new asset for program makers. Learning from our audiences improves our work" (McDonald, 2001).

But broadcasters retained doubts about their audiences' editorial and ethical capacities. Years later, when asked whether the ABC's gatekeeping role would be diminished by user generated content and audience collaboration, a senior radio manager invoked Alcuin's eighth-century caution:

> People point to this idea of the wisdom of the crowds and that if you get masses of people together then once they start cooperating they're going to produce something that's worthwhile. I don't think that's always the case—there's also the idiocy of the crowds as well. (Walker, 2007)

The Conditions for Dialogic Interaction

Alcuin's "madness of the crowds" critique, from which this chapter takes its title, is often referenced in warnings about misinformed, populist online media (cf. Barlow, 2008; Lanier, 2010):

> Those who have a habit of saying "The voice of the people is the voice of God" should not be listened to, since the disorderly nature of the common people is invariably the closest thing to madness. (Alcuin, n.d. trans. 2010)

But Alcuin was in fact calling for the teaching of civility through literacy in advice to the Frankish emperor Charlemagne, whose Carolingian Renaissance sought to secure the scholarly knowledge of Europe and educate the populace in order to boost his empire's economy. Alcuin's rarely quoted preface suggested that ordinary people "should be led according to divine decrees, not followed; and for a model honourable individuals are best chosen instead" (ibid.).

This prefiguring of the Reithian ideal, using exemplary broadcasters to deliver "the best in every department of human endeavour and achievement" (Reith in Blumler, 1992, p. 11), is pertinent here because it also foreshadows the difficulties facing ABC staff in governing dialogic environments. Where legal statutes, conceptions of excellence and centralised editorial practices had helped them produce model professional broadcast speech and mostly civilised dialogue between experts, it has been less clear how to apply these strategies to free–flowing written exchanges between individuals online.

Conversation, while idealised in public sphere theory and Socratic learning, has no a priori, natural association with civil, democratic or educational practices (Schudson, 1997). Online exchanges, where relative anonymity, weak social ties and perceived disembodiment disable face to face ethical responses, are even less inclined to civility. So in order to activate audiences as autonomous, dialogic users and to govern their collective exchanges ABC broadcasters have had to experiment with communicative models that reconcile individual and institutional modes of interaction.

Dialogic interactivity may seem an unwieldy term to describe that process. But popular tropes such as user led innovation (von Hippel, 2005) and user–, consumer– or entrepreneurial–generated content, suggest ex–systemic rather than co–creative activity. They also mobilise unhelpful binaries (amateur/professional, low quality/high quality, etc.). The term social media on the other hand ascribes primacy to a generalised relational field rather than situated, culturally resonant acts of engagement.

Dialogic interactivity, following Mikhail Bakhtin, refers to online "utterances," self–contained expressions which nevertheless presuppose an earlier speaker (1986, p. 91). ABC Online user posts react and/or contribute to the ABC's representational processes, are intended to be public and anticipate an implicit, if not explicit and corresponding, response. Theoretically online dialogue might involve any medium of expression from emoticons to video blogging but as written text is the most accessible, persistent, and used means of co–creative interaction on ABC Online it has been the focus of this study.

There are parallels between utterance theory and Rafaeli's (1988) systems definition of interactivity, but Bakhtin's speakers adjust their articulation to specific socio–cultural contexts, speaking:

> with an expectation of a response, agreement, sympathy, objection, execution, and so forth (with various speech genres presupposing various integral orientations and speech plans on the part of speakers or writers). (1986, p. 69)

Predictably the conditions for that articulation—what can be said to who, where, when and how—are already partially defined by the discursive technology and the institutional actors who control that system. ABC Online's "conditions of use," for example, were built on existing public speech, privacy and intellectual property laws and did not invite user input into their development.

However a brief survey of key moments in ABC Online's framing of dialogic risk exposes more unexpected, contested responses to enabling online conversation—including some institutional anxieties that carry into the present.

Dialogic Control and Risk Management

The key unknown in the ABC's early dialogic experiments, apart from user behaviour, was whether ABC Online's jerry–built communications technology would meet demand. This was particularly the case with live "web chats" like those that followed *Frontier*, a television documentary series on Australia's colonial land wars, or which enabled school students from the Pilbara desert to question Antarctic scientists (ABC, 1997).

The chats, later called forums, used modified guestbook software built in–house to avoid the security risks of adopting bulletin board solutions and to allow cheaper customisation. But ABC Online had too few servers to cope with hundreds of simultaneous log–ins and could not queue queries until they were moderated. Live forums would often crash under the weight of incoming posts, locking late users out. ABC Online's marginal political status meant it was 2001 before a risk minimisation review removed all single points of technical failure (Preston, interview 2010). Even so, resource constraints on managing and modifying dialogic interfaces remained a concern for all staff interviewed for this study.

Much of the risk management in ABC Online's experimental phase involved defining boundaries between user self–governance and corporate control. Early forum disclaimers reminded users to be conscious of their legal and ethical speech responsibilities, and they were able to post web and email addresses on guestbook entries. Yet some quickly showed they expected tighter policing of dialogic protocols. When users of the 1998 Constitutional Convention forum were spammed by lobbyists they complained about the ABC's alleged party prejudices and lack of system security, triggering the removal of all personal details from public view.

Users were later advised to adopt a pen name or pseudonym and not reveal personal information in their posts. Anonymity and privacy became co–dependent strategies necessary to protect citizens from unruly others. As a result many users were atomised, unable to connect with each other outside the confines of ABC Online, except via direct appeal to ABC producers. This isolation was reinforced as staff recognised the workload implications of answering user email and removed their own contact details from websites.

Yet as forums and guestbooks multiplied during the first decade of ABC Online, corporate policy was relatively silent on how dialogic interaction should be managed—other than to dictate pre–moderation of all user posts to manage legal risk. Managers were reluctant to move to post–moderation which they saw as "the equivalent of talkback without a seven second delay" regardless of pre–moderation's impact on dialogic spontaneity (Rapley interview, 2010). Curiously though moderation duties were often given to "the most inappropriate people," junior and technical staff without editorial experience and who editorial manager Stephen Rapley argued were more interested in exploring the new medium than "risks to reputation."

As unregulated speech increased, the personal safety of staff and users became a concern. In ongoing community forums moderators encountered the new risks of establishing more individualised, intimate relations with users. All broadcasters interviewed for this study talked guardedly about an instance of "cyberstalking," where a moderator was criminally harassed by a user, resulting in police intervention. Formal moderation training was developed after another incident where a user posted his suicide plans to a post–moderated group during the night, and members' pleas to delete the thread were only acted on when the moderator came to work. In children's communities the threats of paedophile activity and cyberbullying resulted in tighter moderation protocols (Ray interview, 2011).

By the time moderation training was introduced in 2002 the first flush of enthusiasm for direct user contact had dispersed. Many forums were too little used to justify their maintenance, while others were home to a small group of regulars who discouraged newbies (Campbell interview, 2010). Radio National (RN) forum attempts had "fizzled," with little indication whether a lack of publicity, poorly framed invitation or uncontroversial content was to blame (Connors interview, 2009). RN manager Jane Connors suggested that users may even have been deterred from commenting by the narrative closure of specialist radio features, which left little space for debate or reinterpretation.

In 2007 due to ongoing government attacks on the ABC's political impartiality (Jacka, 2005) editorial guidelines were developed for "interactivity involving audience contributions" (ABC, 2007a) and discussion papers commissioned on blogging and user generated content. The latter described critical audience engagement and risk–taking as part of the ABC's innovation roles, but it did raise for debate the view that dialogic interaction could have catastrophic outcomes:

> The ABC cannot afford even one bad incident. The damage to our reputation and to community trust would be too great. Our funding may be threatened, and we may be subjected to greater regulation. (ABC, 2008)

So far the risk perceptions documented here have been defined by institutional concerns, then shaped by dialogic experience. They highlight the technical, ethical and legal difficulties of supporting unrestrained user vocality, and engaging unruly and silent users.

Risk being a sociocultural phenomenon (Tulloch & Lupton, 2003) it is also important to examine how user engagement was also differently understood across ABC Online's decentralised production sites—according to the speech genres and practices of a given program area (e.g., news, science, opinion), the dialogic technologies mobilised and the ritual interactions they enabled.

Three case studies illustrate how distinct those technocultural interpretations of hazard and opportunity could be. The first explores the introduction of live forums to the realm of high journalism, the ABC TV's flagship investigative current affairs program *Four Corners.*

Four Corners

When *Frontier* producer Bruce Belsham became *Four Corners*' executive producer in late 1999, he argued successfully to extend the program's web presence with a guestbook and live, hosted post–broadcast forum, although some journalists were initially reluctant to invite as–live user commentary on their work, fearing the uninformed critique would not be worth the cost of moderation.

After a year of running weekly forums *Four Corners* website accesses jumped from 2,000 to 30,000 per week (Johns, 2000). Journalists would trawl the posts for comments on their work and occasionally passed further leads to daily radio current affairs. Neither the forums nor the impact of user commentary was significant enough to be mentioned in the program's fortieth anniversary speech or its "full, chronological history" (ABC, 2001), but Belsham now argues a key benefit was introducing different, dissident voices to journalists who drew their most regular feedback from managers and peers (interview, 2010).

Forums were a resource intensive, highly interventionist user engagement strategy. ABC News Online journalists pre–moderated comments to minimise legal risks but budget constraints meant forums usually went ahead with only one moderator. Martin Southgate, moderator from 2000–2006, said he would coopt other journalists when they were not busy and sound them out on line–call editorial decisions.

Moderators' concern to ensure legality, balance and civility while working at speed resulted in high post deletion rates. Southgate estimated that in 2000 only 25% of comments received were posted although by 2006, when he says users were more "educated" about editorial expectations, this had risen to 50% (Southgate interview 2010).

Even after forums became routinised they still required intense planning. At 9.30 p.m. EST, after the show had gone to air, journalists and producers or researchers plus as many as five invited experts would log in—generally from home—to discuss the program with users until around midnight or when comments slowed. The late finish targeted West Australia's time zone, nearly four thousand kilometres from the ABC's Ultimo, Sydney headquarters, but added to the cost and strain on staff who had already worked long hours to meet broadcast deadlines.

Web producer Ruth Fogarty noted forums could demonstrate a "strong community spirit" but they also concerned her for logistical reasons. There were occasional technical hiccups working with external hosts, it was difficult to predict the number of contributors and the servers could fail (Fogarty, interview 2010). In turn, pre–moderation delays and the unthreaded, view–by–topic forum software contributed to a sometimes chaotic, confusing experience for irregular users, the bulk of participants.

The difficult logistics and cost of forums led to their gradual decline. In 2000 forums were run after 36 out of 41 programs, with legal concerns constraining their use in the others. By 2006 it was down to twenty forums and by 2009, only seven ran. Between 2006 and 2009, two forums had as few as twenty contributors, and most had less than 200—although overall traffic statistics suggested more users observed than ever posted.

For Belsham forums were justified by a few significant responses, like that following a 2002 documentary on Villawood immigrant detention centre when moderators, were overwhelmed by more than 5,000 posts. But forums were not easily incorporated into broadcast production rhythms. Hierarchical control, technical, temporal and labour constraints had chilling effects on spontaneous conversation between experts and users. The bulk of contributory traffic now goes to the site's guestbook, "Open Letters," where users generally post statements rather than addressing each other and rarely attract a direct editorial response. Increasingly Twitter and Facebook provide more open channels for real–time, emotive exchanges (Fogarty, interview 2010).

The *Four Corners* experience suggests the limitations of event-based, heavily moderated interaction for cultivating recognition or trust between participants, relational qualities that might help constitute a "town square" environment. It stands in contrast to the model of engagement used in *Self Service Science* which was built on principles of asynchronous open access, self–organisation and knowledge sharing.

Self Service Science

For over a decade *Self Service Science (SSS)* has been a discussion hub for scientists and fans of "sleek geek" educator Dr. Karl Kruszelnicki. Site creator Ian Allen argued its collaborative potential was best demonstrated after September 11th 2001. Users immediately debated why New York's World Trade towers collapsed on themselves, rather than sideways, answering the question days before the first newspaper account appeared:

> We had people on the forums who were pilots, who were fire fighters, who were engineers and physicists . . . and that was the first time I'd seen online "group think" solve a problem that quickly. (Allen, interview 2009)

Unlike synchronous broadcast forums *SSS* was supported by Federal government innovation funding. It evolved to enable fan conversations on Kruszelnicki's guestbook, where listeners could answer questions phoned in during his radio talkback program. As users began to address each other,

Allen introduced a threaded discussion board format and left it open so discussion could continue. Kruszelnicki would also divert email queries to the forum, using it to manage his fan response (Kruszelnicki, interview 2010).

The group quickly displayed signs of social bonding and identity performance. Regulars adopted Kruszelnicki's informal, playful address and threads would often digress into banter and rhetorical games. Users became attached to, and protective of, their user names and personas, despite there being no registration process to protect that identity. Face–to–face events, like a lunar eclipse barbeque on the ABC's Ultimo terrace and user–organised gatherings around the country, deepened the relationships between core contributors. Users were invited to suggest forum improvements and together they developed a Frequently Asked Questions section and superforums tackling intriguing or complex topics.

Allen argued his greatest challenge was to identify and control individual behaviours that could destroy that cohesiveness. A series of disruptive impersonations led him to develop a code of conduct and conditions of use which were later implemented across ABC Online. This included a "three strikes" holding policy, where users who repeatedly breached the code had their posts withheld for hours or days.

Controlling abusive behaviour later involved heavier measures. Thread deletion, list filtering for banned users and IP blocking were all used to penalise repeat offenders, some of whom would cycle through identities as each was banned. But in general moderators sought a light touch, negotiable approach in order to respect users' investment in their identities and "to preserve the integrity of the discussion space" (Allen, interview 2010).

To encourage model behaviour registered users were post–moderated. Allen also created an unmoderated, super user category called "avatars" (after the virtual guides in role–playing games) to identify and encourage expert contributors mentioned on Kruszelnicki's show, although some users questioned the imposition of this hierarchy. As one self–deprecating guide observed:

> Avatardom is little more than a means (of recognition) to stroke someone's ego in the hope that they'll stick around and continue to contribute quality material for free. (Dr Ed G, 1999)

SSS has coevolved with such strategic risk management to become a self–sustaining community, producing 1,300 posts per day at last count. Allen conceded there was an editorial risk in not being able to closely monitor its flows, but suggested the greater threat to creative exchange was applying centralised, broadcast–oriented control strategies.

SSS illustrates that the conditions for dialogic exchange are more effectively negotiated and developed with users. Yet in cultivating ties between and with users *SSS* staff have also found it hard to determine appropriate, sustainable levels of intervention and conversation.

The interpersonal complexities of transitioning from old to new editorial models are apparent in the interactions of ABC opinion community *Unleashed,* created a decade later. It was new territory for the ABC, which had traditionally left the insistent subjectivity of opinion to newspapers and talkback radio.

Unleashed

Unleashed was designed to engage audiences in the ethical conflicts of public affairs, either by writing opinion pieces or replying to them. *Gloves off,* its working title, indicated the adversarial rhetoric expected of commissioned authors and user commentary (Rapley, interview 2010).

The concept responded to growing public interest in opinion–sharing technologies, but was also designed to mitigate the continued threat of government censure and to demonstrate the ABC's capacity to represent diversity. Launched in September 2007, prior to a federal election which saw a Labor government returned after twelve years of conservative rule, *Unleashed* addressed ongoing Cabinet allegations of bias in news and current affairs and complaints about the lack of right–wing perspectives. The ABC declared it represented "a firm commitment to present diverse perspectives on issues that will ignite public debate" and would canvas writers from "all political and social spectrums" (ABC, 2007b). Bruce Belsham, by this time ABC Online Managing Editor, said:

> Unleashed gives us the opportunity to further open ABC Online to the Australian public and to present a kaleidoscope of views, from brilliant hypotheses based on years of research to iconoclastic theories concocted over a bottle of budget cabernet. (Ibid.)

In practice its openness to authorial diversity was tempered by normative editorial practices. *Unleashed* adopted a blog format with ABC selected articles followed by pre–moderated user comments. Initially, commissioned authors dominated, but gradually users began to submit their own work. After print op–ed veteran Catherine Taylor was appointed the site editor, more time was spent honing user–generated stories. Taylor still selected these on the basis of timeliness, novelty and relevance, but she gradually moved *Unleashed* to a 50/50 balance between commissioned and unsolicited work, building the site's profile as a participatory vehicle.

Unleashed de–institutionalised dialogic interaction in several respects, with debate freed from broadcast agendas and outsourced moderators working in shifts to monitor ongoing discussion threads which, unlike other news sites, were left open until they petered out or digressed radically. Yet direct dialogue occurred only between commenters, with authors rarely responding to the ensuing debate. This left the conversation open to capture by regular users.

Between 2008 and 2010, posting increased from an average 800 posts a week to several thousand, with some users adopting daily posting routines. Moderators had difficulty ensuring that regulars did not dominate threads with the speed, volume and familiarity of their messages. Some regulars, unhappy with the pace and consistency of moderation, developed a collective fantasy about a pub called "The Pigs Arms" where they could withdraw to debate unfettered (Anonymous, interview, 2010). Eventually they created a blog of that name for "truly unleashed contributors" (James, 2010).

All *Unleashed* interviewees indicated aggressive, hostile commenting was the greatest threat to site inclusiveness:

> It's as if people feel so voiceless in the old media and now they have a voice, now they can express what they think publicly, they want to scream it out—and if anyone questions that or tries to moderate it they respond with this incredible anger. (Taylor, interview 2010)

Post deletions increased from 8–9% in the first year to a peak of 15% of total comments. Users and authors reported the tone of threads was off-putting and some writers declined to contribute again (Rapley, interview 2010). One moderator suggested that the greatest risk of her work might be the cumulative emotional impact of having to adjudicate negative, combative exchanges (Anonymous, interview 2010).

Taylor also attributed some uncivil behaviour to users' sense of personal entitlement to publication by their ABC. Moderators had "no right to reject [user] comments because they pay tax" (Taylor, interview 2010). Posts regularly questioned the organisation's legitimacy, Taylor's right to select opinion writers and staff political prejudices.

The angry user phenomenon is partly an outcome of applying centralised governance to a vocal, critical constituency, rather than engaging them in collective risk management. However at the time of writing ABC Online's elderly content management system did not incorporate the type of flagging, rating or ranking tools that might have enabled more user collaboration in governance (Belsham, interview 2010).

Anger also suggests conflict between individual goals (self-expression, competition, validation) and institutional goals (dialogue, participation, recognition), which has intensified as the size of the community has increased. It signals users' discomfort at a trusted institution, trading in closed narratives, opening up to individualised ethics and critique.

Finally *Unleashed* hosted debate about an absent author, between relatively anonymous users, policed by anonymous moderators. Its architecture of privacy disrupted the conditions for social trust established under less inclusive, broadcast conditions—without substituting effective models for individual accountability. In one sense ABC Online is experiencing an age old dilemma: how institutions might foster productive dialogue among citizens at a moment of rapid social change. The context though is new, with the consequences of increased user agency still to unfold.

Conclusion

The chapter has interrogated ABC staff anxieties about reinterpreting their exemplary broadcast role for an age of self–publishing, self–expression, argument and counterargument. Many of their attempts at dialogic interaction have not been conversational in synchronicity or reciprocity, with forums often resembling a tightly managed town hall debate rather than the familiar encounters of a town square.

Perceptions of risk surfaced in problems of technical delivery, cost and administration, legal and political obligation, moral responsibility and cultural understanding. They were personified with incidents of user "bads," spamming, abuse and privacy breaches. All interviewees saw a risk in pre–moderation stifling debate flow and in resources not meeting user demand for fast, informed moderation.

This chapter has analysed three technocultural responses to those risks, which developed from differing editorial objectives and philosophies. Of these participatory cultures only the decentralised science model seems sustainable. Indeed the failure of hierarchical governance strategies has spurred calls for reactive, community led moderation in *Unleashed* and greater use of real–time, third party channels like Twitter.

Ulrich Beck argued that the global risks from which populations have been insulated by paternalistic government can now only be addressed by new institutional arrangements, tendered by much better informed and engaged publics. In that sense the great challenge for the ABC lies in moving from opening a dialogue with users, to exploring more carefully why they might or might not take part, and how the ABC can facilitate their objectives, as much as its own.

References

ABC (1997, August). *World's first web chat with the Antarctic.* Retrieved January 27 2010 from http://www.abc.net.au/news/features/antarctica/thelab.htm

ABC (1999). *Australian Broadcasting Corporation Annual Report, 1998–1999.*

ABC (2001, August 20). *The big picture.* Retrieved May 28 2010 from http://www.abc.net.au/4corners/4c40/timelines/default.htm

ABC (2007a). *Editorial policies.* Retrieved June 3 2010 from http://www.abc.net.au/corp/pubs/documents/edpol07.htm

ABC (2007b, October 8). *abc.net.au: Presenting a diversity of opinions,* media release. Retrieved from http://www.abc.net.au/corp/pubs/media/s2053275.htm

ABC (2008, June 23). Discussion starter: User–Generated Content. Retrieved from http://www.abc.net.au/corp/pubs/documents/200806_ugc-discussion_starter.pdf

Alcuin (n.d.) *Letter* 166.9 (addressed to Charlemagne). Capitulare admonitionis ad eumdem carolum. Migne column 0438A. Patrologia Latina Database. trans. Dr Anne Rogerson, University of Sydney.

Bakhtin, M. (1986). *Speech genres and other late essays.* Austin: University of Texas Press.

Barlow, J. (2008). The madness of crowds: Recent criticisms of Web 2.0. *The Journal of Education, Community and Values, 8*(6), Retrieved from http://bcis.pacificu.edu/journal/2008/06/article.php?id=7

BBC (1999). *BBC online communities day.* Retrieved April 7 2010 from http://www.partnerships.org.uk/bol/

Beck, U. (1999). *World risk society.* Cambridge, UK: Polity

Blumler, J. G. (1992). *Television and the public interest: Vulnerable values in West European broadcasting.* Newbury Park, CA: Sage.

Bruns, A. (2008, February 22). *Beyond public service broadcasting: Produsage at the ABC.* Retrieved April 19 2010 from http://produsage.org/node/23

Burns, M. (2008). *ABC Online: Becoming the ABC.* Saarbrücken, Germany: VDM Verlag Dr. Muller.

Carpentier, N. (2003). The BBC's Video Nation as a participatory media practice: Signifying everyday life, cultural diversity and participation in an online community. *International Journal of Cultural Studies,* 6, 425–447.

CBC (2002, February 15). *Fact finding inquiry on interactivity,* Comments of the Canadian Broadcasting Corporation, Public Notice CRTC 2001–113. Retrieved March 24 2010 from http://www.cbc.radio-canada.ca/submissions/2002.shtml

Craig, G. (2000). Perpetual Crisis: The politics of saving the ABC. *Media International Australia,* 94, 105–116.

Debrett, M. (2009, July). Leveraging trust: The politics of accountability and risk taking at the ABC. Paper presented at ANZCA *Communication, Creativity and Global Citizenship,* Brisbane. Retrieved May 25 2010 from http://www.cpe.qut.edu.au/conferences/2009/anzca/proceedings/Debrett_ANZCA09.pdf

Dr Ed G. (1999, October 15). Self Service Science forum post, Subject: re: helen for Avatar. Retrieved January 19 2010 at http://www2.abc.net.au/science/k2/stnarchive1/posts/topic44666.shtm

Enli, G. S. (2006). Redefining public service broadcasting: Multi–platform participation,

Convergence: The International Journal of Research into New Media Technologies, 14(1), 105–120.
Gillmor, D. (2004). *We the media: Grassroots journalism by the people, for the people.* Sebastopol, CA: O'Reilly Media.
von Hippel, E. (2005). *Democratizing innovation.* Cambridge, MA: MIT Press
Jacka, E. (2005). The elephant trap: Bias, balance and government–ABC relations during the Second Gulf War,' *Southern Review, 37*(3), 8–28.
James, E. (2010). About, Window Dresser's Arms, Pig & Whistle. Retrieved May 15 2010 from http://pigsarms.com.au/about-the-pigs-arms/
Johns, B. (1996, August 18). Speech to the International Association for Mass Communication Research, Sydney, Australian Broadcasting Corporation, Sydney.
Johns, B. (2000, March 15). Address to the International Institute of Communications, Sydney.
Lanier, J. (2010). *You are not a gadget: A manifesto.* Alfred A. Knopf.
Martin, F. R. (2008). *Digital dilemmas: The Australian Broadcasting Corporation and interactive multimedia publishing, 1992–2002.* PhD thesis, Southern Cross University. Retrieved from http://epubs.scu.edu.au/ theses/66
McDonald, D. (2001, September 22). Taking stock of public broadcasting. Speech to the Public Broadcasters International Conference, Toronto.
Murdock, G. (2004, January 25). Building the digital commons: Public broadcasting in the age of the internet. Spry Memorial Lecture, University of Montreal. Retrieved September 8 2006 from http://www.com.umontreal.ca/ spry/spry-gm-lec.htm
Rafaeli, S. (1988). *Interactivity*: From new media to communication. In R. P. Hawkins, J. M. Wiemann, & S. Pingree (Eds.), *Advancing communication science: Merging mass and interpersonal process* (pp. 110–134). Newbury Park, CA: Sage.
Ray, A. (2003). *Risk assessment for moderators: "Degrassi: The next generation": A case study.* Green College, Oxford: Reuters Foundation.
Schudson, M. (1997). Why conversation is not the soul of democracy, *Critical Studies in Mass Communications, 14*, 297–309.
Scott, M. (2009). Latrobe University annual media lecture, Wednesday April 8 2009. Retrieved October 18 2009 from http://www.abc.net.au/corp/pubs/media/ s2538867.htm
Tracey, M. (1998). *The decline and fall of public broadcasting.* New York: Oxford University Press.
Tulloch, J. & Lupton, D. (2003). *Risk and everyday life.* London: Sage.
Walker, T. (2007, March 21). Manager ABC Digital Radio in Melbourne, interviewed on *Australia Talks Back*, "Wikimania or Fuzziemania?" ABC Radio National.

Interviews:

Allen, Ian. Science Online editor. November 2009 and June 2010.
Anonymous. Moderator *Unleashed.* June 2010.
Belsham, Bruce. Managing editor, ABC Online, May 2010.
Connors, Jane. Manager Radio National, November 2009.
Fogarty, Ruth. Web producer *Four Corners.* June 2010.

Kruszelnicki, Karl. Science broadcaster. June 2010.
Preston, Craig. Technical manager, ABC Online. June 2010.
Rapley, Stephen. Editorial manager, ABC Innovation. May 2010.
Ray, Alison. Former regional online editor 2001–2005. March 2011.
Southgate, Martin. Moderator *Four Corners*. June 2010.
Taylor, Catherine. Editor *Unleashed*. June 2010.

14 *User Participation at the Danish Broadcasting Corporation 1998–2010*

Changing Patterns

Anja Bechmann

Introduction

This chapter examines how the web has provided platforms for various kinds of user participation at the Danish Broadcasting Corporation (DR) from 1998 to 2010 and discusses the requirements of public service in this development.[1]

DR is license funded and this entails requirements and the fundamental obligation to deliver services that represent "quality, diversity and plurality."

The Corporation was founded as a radio corporation in 1925, and became both a radio and a television station in 1951. Experiments with using the web began in DR in the early 90s, partly as a way of creating dialogue with listeners and viewers (Brügger, 2011). The web expanded the lineup of platforms, but it was not until 2002 that the corporation's public service remit became officially independent of platforms, and not only bound to TV and radio: "DR has an obligation towards the entire public, through the platforms of television, radio, the internet and the like, to provide a broad selection of programs and services . . ." (Ministry of Culture, 2002, p. 2).

Before 2002, use of the web could only be justified as an enhancement to radio and TV programming. With the inclusion of "the internet" in the 2002 document, such justification was no longer necessary (Bechmann, 2009).

Seeking to analyze how public service user participation has evolved from

1998 to 2010 in Denmark it is interesting to explore the developments in user participation as a means of meeting its public service remit, and to examine whether the character of user participation in fact profoundly changed in a platform–independent (non–broadcast) direction following the 2002 contract.

Thus, with a focus on web activities the three main questions of the chapter are: How did user participation evolve in the period of 1998 to 2010 and are there significant patterns? How did user participation add to DR's principles of quality, diversity and/or plurality? And did the public service regulative independence of platforms in 2002 make revolutionary changes to participation standards, e.g., towards non–broadcast initiatives or from less to more user participation as suggested in the web 2.0 literature (e.g., Bruns, 2008)?

Following some methodological considerations, this chapter will approach these issues by, firstly, exploring examples of ways in which *DR* designed online activities to facilitate user participation on an interface–related as well as a strategic level. Secondly, the chapter will seek to analyse patterns of user participation in the particular examples and relate them to the principles of quality, diversity and plurality. Thirdly, the chapter will draw parallels between these patterns and the *DR* broadcasting legacy.

Methodological Considerations

In order to examine the role of user participation in depth, three major productions of the DR Youth department will be examined from the periods 1998–1999, 2005–2006, and 2009–2010.

The young people's department at DR, *DR Youth*, has often been used as a corporate lab to test new technological developments and ideas, including user participation and the integration of online activities such as websites and mobile solutions. The reason for this, according to the production team leader, is that the target group of *DR Youth* adapts to technology faster than other target groups, and the team therefore needs to be "innovative" (interview with team leader 2006). Historically, DR Youth's target group (app. 12–20 years), has been of pivotal importance in the must–carry obligation to supply the "quality" specified in DR's public service contracts in contrast to commercial offers. Therefore the department has been a priority area, which has received special attention, both politically and inside DR, but not necessarily economically. However, young people are a special target group for specific genres, which makes this study of patterns of user participation sensitive to the specificity of this particular area, even (or especially) taking into account the status of DR Youth as an experimental lab.[2]

The experimental character of the productions emanating from the department allows them to serve as critical cases when examining whether and how platform-independent solutions are taken on after 2002, and in identifying developments in user participation patterns. The three examples chosen represent, respectively, the first major integration of the web into program production (1998–1999), the first major experiment with user–produced mobile videos in *DR* (2005–2006), and the latest production (at the time of writing: summer 2010).

On a general level, the term "user participation" in this chapter refers to creating "dialogue" and/or engagement with the public.[3] The study is based on official documents such as archived interfaces,[4] press releases, articles and items published in the DR staff magazine, *Dråben*. The study of the mobile video production experiment has moreover relied on extensive observations conducted between 2005–2006, internal papers, and interviews from 2005–2008 with the production team and managers at *DR* and *DR Youth*.

1998–1999: User Participation as Added Digital Value in Cross–Platform Experiments

This section will exemplify how user participation was incorporated in productions from *DR Youth* before 2002.

DR Youth was one of the first departments to actually integrate the web into its existing organizational structure in the summer of 1997. They named the experiment *U.land* and integrated both groups with TV, radio, and the web.[5] In February 1998 *U.land* launched itself as a cross–platform "community":

> As of 4 February 1998, *U.land* will be operating on both radio, TV and the internet . . . with live radio and TV, and a website on the internet where you can test whether you are in tune with the times and check out your knowledge of music in an *Okay Tone Quiz* which is updated every week. (Press release, January 29, 1998, p. 3)

The General Manager of DR saw the cross–platform production groups as an opportunity to unite a somewhat divided organization (DR, 1994), and in 1998 *U.land* received a grant of DKK 8 million (approx. USD 1.3 million) over three years towards a project called *BetaLab* which would run digital experiments. The money was to come from a DKK 9 million pool established to fund "digital programs." The purpose of the lab was to "develop ideas for implementable models" (according to Erik N. Gravesen, in *Dråben,* 1998, p. 8). The board of directors chose this project because it would create "a constant influence and rollout of new knowledge and experience in the rest of DR," "exploit a hitherto unknown degree of digital added value," and turn

Betalab into "the development lab for DR" (DR's board of directors, in *Dråben,* 1998, p. 8). In January 1999, *U.land* became a permanent department under the Director of Radio.

Experiments with "digital added value" as the purpose of the production unit seemed to be interpreted as *adding* various kinds of user participation to the transmission (Jensen, 1998) of programs via the broadcast media: "the viewer is engaged through interactivity in the internet version" (Press Release, January 21, 1999). This interpretation was in line with DR's strategy in the early 90s to create dialogue as a (public service) way of being "deeply anchored in society," meeting viewers' and listeners' "wishes and needs," and allowing them to exert an "actual influence on the programming" (Brügger, 2011).[6] *U.land* aimed to create dialogue with the users and engage them in the concept through discussions and contributions that could influence the program.

The websites employed chat as a central aspect of the interface, and users could influence the programs in various ways. In the "producer's lab," users could create their own brief items for the TV show, or make various kinds of virtual Flash film "greeting cards" to send to their friends.[7] In the program *Plan B,* users could fill out a survey questionnaire at the website on a topic discussed in the TV program, and the results of the survey would be announced in the TV program (Press Release, January 21).

Apart from using the web platform as a means of adding dialogue and user influence to the radio and TV programs, this example shows that participation, in a navigational, consultative (Jensen, 1998) sense, was expected of the users. *U.land* encouraged users to "go to the website," thereby navigating between different media, and one of the purposes of the "added digital value" also seemed to be to offer access to the *U.land* community "whenever you feel like it" (Press Release, January 21).

U.land was launched as a cross–platform initiative with the exploration of "digital added value" as the main focus. The case shows that this added value is interpreted as user engaging digital items on the website, encouraging dialogue with the users, and as free access to productions across time and media platform. The idea of quality through platform plurality (access) and content diversity across platforms with the intention of synergy between media products thereby can be said to drive the development of *U.land.*

2005–2006: User Participation as User–Created Content

This section will analyze user participation in a production from *DR Youth* after the regulative change in 2002 towards public service platform–independency.

In October 2005, *DR Youth* launched *Blokken* as "the first real program in which users supply the content" (Press Release, September 21, 2005). Historically, this is not quite correct, as *DR* had experimented with user–created content on previous occasions, in various programs such as *TV Åben* (TV Open),[8] but this was the first time that DR had attempted to experiment with a program format that incorporated videos recorded on mobile platforms.

Like *U.land*, *Blokken* was financed as an experimental project with the focus on user–created videos and the integration of mobile phones. In 2004, a new Committee for Media Development was created in DR to secure corporate integration of longitudinal media strategies and to create focus areas within product development (interview with Strategic Manager, 2005). The focus areas of development in 2005 were user participation and mobile communication, and *Blokken* was to be an experiment in both areas, not a TV-based format. The Production Manager saw *Blokken* as a convenient experiment with low–budget TV (Production Team Manager, interview 2005). He had proposed the idea of creating an on–line youth TV channel on the website, and saw *Blokken* as a good way to experiment with possible user–created content for this site as well.

User participation now became a question of how much and what type of content the users were able to produce for DR Youth. This idea was heavily inspired by what has been called the "web 2.0" wave. O'Reilly and Battelle (2004) describe the movement of the web from version 1.0 to 2.0 as a shift towards a culture in which users would no longer merely "use" the content created by professionals, but would begin to create the products, communication and content themselves. Flickr and Wikipedia were examples of a "new" kind of website, at which value was created by the community and could be harvested by the organizations hosting them (Surowiecki, 2004; O'Reilly, 2005; Bruns, 2007). Bruns describes the change as a movement from interactivity towards inter*creativity*, characterized by the shifting roles of users and producers (Bruns, 2008, p. 16).

In the case of *Blokken, DR Youth* was especially inspired by the web 2.0 initiatives *Current TV* and *YouTube*. The slogan of *Blokken* was "You supply, we present," and young people could record a video on their mobile phones, edit it in a digital editor, and send it to *DR*. A selection of the videos would then be made accessible on the website, and would together form the TV show, which would later be accessible via mobile phones (Team Leader, interview 2005).

The idea was that users would both create the content and, through the themes of the content, determine what kind of conceptual universe *Blokken* would become. According to the production team, these users ought to be regarded as "members of staff" (Project Leader, interview 2005).

However, the users did not send in sufficient user–created content for the production team to build a TV flow of "high quality." Only a few users contributed, and the editorial staff considered most of the videos submitted for *Blokken* to be of "poor quality," both with regard to the technical quality of recordings made on mobile phones (screen size, sound quality, and editing) and the lack of storytelling principles utilised in the videos recorded by users (interviews with production team member, 2005 and 2006). The production team therefore changed the concept into one of file sharing, called *Spam*.[9]

In this production model, users sent a large amount of file–shared videos to the production team (Bechmann 2010). These were rarely produced by the users themselves, but usually found on the internet or received from friends via mobile phones. The videos were no longer selected by *DR Youth*; instead, users could vote to decide which videos would be used in the TV program. The production team also added the possibility of sharing links on the website, together with a TV item on technical themes which was used as the starting–point for a p2p community on the website discussing technical solutions. The change of concept from *Blokken* to *Spam* revealed a movement away from user participation as video production towards a concept of "sharing"—both video and technical solutions. The users still determined what was going to be on the website and TV program, but for the most part, they did not produce the content.

The case analysis of *Blokken* and *Spam* shows that the initiative arose from the idea of a high degree of user created content as good "quality" and a way to ensure content diversity through niche (user) content. However, the developments of the cases also show that it was the "poor quality" of the TV program and not the website that initially changed the program into one of user file sharing instead of content creation. Despite the regulative change in 2002 and the strategic experiment with user production and mobile phones TV was still the primary platform.

2009–2010: User Participation as Sampling and Networking

To examine whether the regulative change needed some time to make a proper impact in the organization this section will analyze user production four years later.

In the summer of 2009, *DR Youth* abandoned the cross–platform idea, dropped TV as a separate platform (with the exception of a single mainstream music program), and placed all their new videos and 400 archival videos on the website only. According to the editor–in–chief, the reason for this move was the strong presence of the target group on the internet (interview in

Jensen, 2009). The resulting concept, *Pirat TV*, was available in a beta version on 26 June 2009, but was officially launched on 1 September.

The focus on user participation had now changed from being a matter of user production to user filtering or sampling: "TV is something the young people sample themselves . . . they consume it in small chunks. They choose exactly what they want, and in that respect they are their own channel editors" (interview with chief editor Bo Kousgaard, in Hybel, 2009). The idea of participation as sharing and networking, as recognized in *Spam*, was continued in *Pirat TV:* "open–source and networking ideas, in which they [the users] can influence the content, comment on it and pass it on to each other" (Ibid.).

The website was reminiscent of *YouTube*, in that users could rate and comment on videos, embed videos into other websites, and integrate them into their *Twitter*, *Facebook* or other social networking sites.[10] The legal challenge in this strategy of "distributed public service" is copyright law, which restricts the ability of *DR Youth* to distribute content outside of DR's own channels. As the internet department of DR Youth states in its blog:

> We could easily create genuine embedding, but unfortunately we do not have the right to embed our content externally (although we would really like to do so). DR does not dare—in contrast to *YouTube* and others—to operate according to the "opt out" principle. (blogpost at www.flyvergrillen.dk, 1 September, 2009)

In complete contrast to *Blokken* and *YouTube*, however, all (legal) content was either made or chosen by DR, as a means of ensuring the quality of the content (interview with Editor–in–Chief Kousgaard, in Sørensen, 2009). *Pirat TV* re–introduced the editorial staff as the producers and controlling unit, and as the central unit that determined the quality of the content.

Episodes of various programs were grouped, and users could access them through a sorting mechanism along the lines of "most viewed" and "most recommended." Many programs also had their own Facebook group or page where users could display their "membership" of the program and comment on its content, characters or topics, and where the editors could show material from the conceptual universe. A selection of videos with promotional texts was also made available on the *YouTube* channel *"pirattvdk,"* launched on 29 September 2009. However, there was no indication that this was an official channel from *DR Youth* other than the fact that the reporters were recognisable as "Pirat" reporters. Again copyright regulations may be one of the reasons why it is difficult to determine whether *pirattvdk* on YouTube is an official channel or not.

The production was promoted as web only, but some of the videos from the programs were available for download onto mobile phones. However, on 30 April 2010, the conceptual framing of *Pirat TV* took a turn towards TV when *DR Youth* launched a satirical television program with videos from the *Pirat TV* website. This concept was somewhat similar to *Blokken,* in the sense that TV was being created through content from the website, but the content was still produced and/or edited by *DR Youth. DR Youth* was in control of the entire production process.

Pirat TV as a contemporary case study in this chapter addresses "quality" as the disempowerment of the users in relation to production and the strategy of moving away from cross–platform productions and then back again. Despite copyright problems the case also shows renewed interest in platform plurality beyond DR's own website as a kind of distributed public service.

Patterns of User Participation

Having studied the three cases in detail this section will first identify significant patterns in the development of user participation, and second discuss the development in relation to the public service principles of "quality, diversity and/or plurality."

Although this historical analysis shows that DR Youth changed its focus from add–on user influence to user production and user sampling and networking, we cannot conclude that this is a clear trend. The analysis above shows that aspects of all three characteristics are present in all cases in some form, albeit not as the main focus of the production.

To further identify the changes and developments, we must identify and differentiate between the various main topics in user participation that have surfaced repeatedly in the productions studied here. This section will summarize these topics by examining both the disruptive *and* the continuous patterns of user participation as a way of describing the development.

Degree of user production

The analysis does *not* as suggested by Bruns (2008) and O'Reilly (2005) point to a clear trend from interactivity towards intercreativity, or from a lesser degree of user production towards a greater degree of user production in terms of user–produced videos. The analysis shows that the items created by the users in *u.land* played a minor role in the concept as a whole across platforms, in contrast to *Blokken,* while in *Pirat TV* the users were not encouraged to produce videos themselves. This re–introduction of the professional production team to ensure the level of "quality" is consistent with Burgess and Green's (2009) analysis of YouTube, at which almost half of the content registered (41%) is created by professionals working in the traditional media industry (Burgess & Green, 2009, p. 42), despite the YouTube slogan of "broadcast yourself."

Dialogue as conversation and commentary

In all three cases, dialogue was present in the form of conversations between the users in chat, communities and debate forums. However, a changing pattern is discernible in the way in which *DR Youth* integrates these communities. In *U.land*, the chat and debate function was kept separate from the remainder of the content and programs. In *Blokken, DR* used a debate function associated with the program, but which was linked to the overall community (entitled *Skum*), rather than specifically to *Blokken*. This changes in *Spam* with a community with a closer thematic connection with the specific program. In *Pirat TV* a separate community still existed, but users commented on the videos in an associated section linked to the content, as in YouTube, thereby often commenting on both the video and on other users' comments. The cases studied may therefore be tentatively considered to indicate a change towards a more seamless integration of conversation and comments in the overall program universe from 2006 and onwards, despite the fact that the general community of *DR Youth* continues to exist.

Presence of (other) users

In connection with the conversation patterns addressed above, the visibility and identification of other users altered during the period studied. In *U.land* the users were (directly) represented via the results of survey and comments, but remained anonymous. In *Blokken* the producing users were no longer anonymous, but performed in videos as themselves. It was not, however, possible to interact with the productive users; there were no links from their videos to any personal information, or p2p interaction with them. In *Pirat TV*, the users were absent in terms of video production, but present in the form of comments and ratings, and as part of the Facebook network. The sense of the co–presence of other users differed, as the users could see other users' opinions, while in the Facebook group the users could see all other users (via profile pictures with names) and could interact with them through "friendship" or via the user's "wall."

Horton and Wohl (1956) describe how parasocial interaction has been promoted through audience representation in the studios, while interaction researchers (Heath & Luff, 1991; Hutchins, 1991; Dourish & Bly, 1992; Harrison & Dourish, 1996) stress the importance of "passive awareness" of other users for the idea and feeling of a shared community. From a public service perspective, the strengthening of the possibility of "passive awareness" of other identifiable users may indicate a movement away from a dialogue interpretation in which the users are "talking back to auntie." Instead it indicates a movement towards a dialogue structure in which DR encourages engagement (Jenkins, 2006) and dialogue between users, with *DR* activities as conversation pieces, thereby illustrating that *DR* is an important part of society.

Access, sampling, and navigation

Last but not least, the analysis in the chapter calls attention to user participation and influence in the form of various patterns of access to and navigation in the content through different platforms and services (platform plurality).

All three cases reveal a profound strategic interest in providing unlimited access to the content in time and place, accelerating from cross–platform production within *DR*'s own channels (*U.land, Blokken,* and *Spam*) to cross–service structures (*Pirat TV*) in which content is also placed outside of *DR*'s own channels. *Pirat TV* and to some extent *Spam* thereby exemplify a public service definition in which public service products have become diffused into a broader network reaching out to and integrating with other entities competing for user attention, such as YouTube and Facebook. As the analysis showed these access strategies are not without legal obstacles, but political obstacles may also arise as *DR* seek to dodge contemporary allegations of anti–competitive practices (The Media Political Proposal of DR, 2010; Reseke, 2010).

In line with the growing number of access points (platforms and services) for *DR Youth's* productions, *DR* wishes users to participate through actively navigating and consulting (Jensen 1998) content different places. In *U.land* and *Blokken,* program users were for example encouraged to go to the website and obtain more information, take quizzes, upload user–created content, vote or view other user content. In *Pirat TV, DR* encouraged users to sample and share their own video flow. Participation and engagement through navigation is thereby altering from a focus on "platform jumping" towards personally–controlled content flow creation in networks.

In relation to changing patterns of user participation, the chapter has shown that we cannot describe the changes as necessarily indicating an increasing level of user production. However, acknowledging the continuation of aspects of the detailed participation patterns, the study presented here indicates a change toward more integrated dialogue and a dialogue structure between users. The cases studied here also reveal a trend towards more distributed public service structures, which aim to support the remix culture of the internet (Lessig, 2008).

Looking at the identified user participation patterns in the light of the principles of quality, diversity, and plurality it is most striking that multiple content access points and free content sampling have been regarded as a way to increase plurality throughout the cases moving from platform "jumping" towards personally controlled content flows. The niche character of user created content was intended to add to content diversity, but was not consistent with the production team's idea of "good quality." Instead user participation seemed more to add to the idea of quality through the integrated dialogical structure and network visibility moving towards a pattern where peer users not necessarily speak to, but about DR.

Developments in User Participation and the Legacy of the Broadcast Media

The chapter has shown different changing patterns of user participation. As anticipated the user participation did *not* develop from a lesser to a higher degree of user-generated content. Instead significant patterns of change were found in the seamless use of conversation and comments as well as the visibility of other users in the communities of the programs. The study also shows that content becomes much more widespread from different platforms owned by DR to digital network beyond DR as a kind of distributed public service.

However, the principles of diversity and especially plurality and quality seem to have contributed to the ways in which DR has incorporated user participation both on an interface–related and a strategic level. This is especially evident in the choices of opting out of user created videos and including free access to content across services and platforms.

The chapter was also motivated by the question of whether the character of user participation had in fact profoundly changed in a non–broadcast or platform–independent direction following the introduction in 2002 of the liberal regulatory approach to online activities. Examining the cases before and after 2002 reveals a strong will after 2002 to experiment with productions with no specific broadcast program as the centre of the production, whereas this is not the case with production studied before 2002, when the strategy was characterized by *added* user participation.

Nonetheless, the nature of the production changed in 2005 due to the argument that the "quality" of production was inadequate for the TV platform, and although the production in 2010 was purely web–based, *DR Youth* eventually created a broadcast feed for TV. Bearing in mind that DR Youth was acting as an experimental lab in all three cases, this may point to a widespread inertia in the organization in terms of identity, professional skills and knowledge of legal issues and user behaviour on traditional platforms.

In 2011, all initiatives undertaken by DR are required to be subject to market tests, as is the case with the BBC (Ministry of Culture, 2011). A possible conflict with platform independence would be interesting to examine in future historical analyses, as taking on new media platforms also means entering into new competitive markets.

Notes

1. Denmark is a small Scandinavian country with 5.5 million inhabitants, and DR is the only almost fully license–funded broadcasting corporation (over 90%). TV2 (which began broadcasting in 1988) is the other state–owned broadcasting corporation. Its license funding apply only to regional news.
2. One cannot *assume* that the patterns of user participation outlined in this chapter are the same in other areas, such as News, during the same period of time.
3. Historically, this encompasses various interpretations, including dialogue with listeners and viewers and moving from one platform to another, as well as engagement with users through user-generated/-created content, file sharing and communication via peer–to–peer networks, with DR acting as reference point. These characteristics will be elaborated on and discussed as part of the analysis.
4. Due to copyright issues it is not possible to reprint the interfaces in this chapter, but only to reference to the websites made public available on webarchive.org.
5. Back in the early 90s DR had already experimented with bi–medial groups integrating radio and television, and in March/April 1997 a radio program covering technological developments launched an additional website and a TV program, "Harddisken Colour" (*Dråben* 1997, p. 5).
6. Quotes from DR (1994).
7. http://www.dr.dk/skum/_grafik/skum_gennem_tiden/full_ 1998_ulandnet.jpg & http://www.dr.dk/skum/_grafik/skum_ gennem_tiden/full_1999_ulandnet_2.jpg.
8. TV Åben was set up in the early 90s, but throughout the 70s DR ran a similar radio project entitled *Båndværkstedet* (The Tape Workshop). This program was broadcast by DR, but listeners produced the radio items.
9. http://replay.waybackmachine.org/20060410131428/http:// www.dr.dk/dr1/spam. The name was inspired by the more commonly understood usage of "Spam" as something (of more or less value) that is send to you by your network.
10. http://replay.waybackmachine.org/20090629072839/http:// www.dr.dk/pirattv.

References

Bechmann, A. (2009). *Cross–Media: Innovationsnetværk for traditionelle medieorganisationer* [Cross–Media: Innovation Networks for Traditional Media Organizations]. PhD Thesis. Aarhus, Denmark: Aarhus University.

Bechmann, A. (2010). Brugerproduceret underholdning? [User Produced Entertainment?]. In H. Bruun & K. Frandsen (Eds.), *Underholdende tv* [Entertaining TV]. Aarhus, Denmark: Aarhus University Press.

Brügger, N. (2011). The Idea of Public Service in the Early History of DR Online. In M. Burns &. N. Brügger (Eds.), *Histories of Public Service Broadcasters on the Web*. New York: Peter Lang.

Bruns, A. (2007). Produsage: Towards a Broader Framework for User–Led Content Creation. *Creativity and Cognition: Proceedings of the 6th ACM SIGCHI conference on Creativity & cognition*, 13–15 June 2007, Washington, DC.

Bruns, A. (2008). *Blogs, Wikipedia, Second Life and Beyond.* New York: Peter Lang.

Burgess, J. & Green, J. (2009). *YouTube: Online Video and Participatory Culture.* Cambridge, UK: Polity Press.

Dourish, P. & Bly, S. (1992). Portholes: Supporting Awareness in a Distributed Work Group. Human Factors in Computing Systems. *CHI'92 Conference Proceedings*, (Monterey, CA), New York, 541–547.

DR (1994). Danmarks Radio 1995–2005: *En redegørelse om DRs idégrundlag, programpolitik og udvikling* [Danish Broadcasting Corporation 1995–2005: A Report on DR's Philosophy, Program Policy and Development]. Copenhagen: DR.

Dråben (1998, September 11). *Millioner til digital udvikling* [Millions for Digital Development]. Copenhagen: DR.

Dråben (1997, April 4). *Den digitale fremtidsredaktion* [The Digital Editorial Team of the Future]. Copenhagen: DR.

Enli, S.G. (2007). *The Participatory Turn in Broadcast Television: Institutional, Editorial and Textual Challenges and Strategies.* PhD thesis, Oslo University, Oslo.

Harrison, S. & Dourish, P. (1996). Re–Place–ing Space: The Roles of Place and Space in Collaborative Systems, *Proceedings of the 1996 ACM Conference on Computer Supported Cooperative Work*, Boston, MA., 67–76.

Heath, C. & Luff, P. (1991). Collaborative Activity and Technological Design: Task Coordination in London Underground Control Rooms. In *Proceedings of the Second European Conference on Computer–Supported Cooperative Work* (ECSCW '91). Amsterdam: Kluwer Academic Publishers.

Horton, D. & Wohl, R. (1956). Mass Communication and Parasocial Interaction: Observations on Intimacy at a Distance. *Psychiatry*, *19*, 215–229.

Hutchins, E. (1991). The Social Organization of Distributed Cognition. In L. B. Resnick, J. M. Levine, & S. D. Teasley (Eds.), *Perspectives on Socially Shared Cognition* (pp. 283–307). Washington, DC: AP A.

Hybel, K. (2009, August 30). DR's ungdomsredaktion dropper tv [DR's Youth Editorial Staff Ditches TV]. *Politiken.*

Jenkins, H. (2006). *Convergence Culture: Where Old and New Media Collide.* New York: New York University Press.

Jensen, J. F. (1998). Interactivity. Tracking a New Concept in Media and Communication Studies. *Nordicom Review*, *19*, 185–204.

Jensen, T. (2009, September 25). DR dropper provokerende TV [DR Discontinue Provocative TV], *journalisten.dk.*

Lessig, L. (2008). *Remix: Making Art and Commerce Thrive in the Hybrid Economy.* New York: Penguin Press.

Media Political Proposal of DR (2010). Copenhagen: DR.

Ministry of Culture (2002). *Public Service Contract between DR and the Ministry of Culture for the Period of January 1st 2003 to December 31st 2006.* j.nr. 2002–7205–8.

Ministry of Culture (2011). *Ordinance for Approval of DR and the Regional TV2–Business New Services*, Ordinance no. 198 of 2011/03/09.

Moe, H. (2009). *Public Broadcasters, the Internet, and Democracy. Comparing Policy and Exploring Public Service Media Online.* PhD Thesis, University of Bergen, Bergen.

O'Reilly, T. (2005). What Is Web 2.0: Design Patterns and Business Models for the Next Generation of Software. *http://oreilly.com.* Retrieved November 3, 2010.

O'Reilly, T. & Battelle, J. (2004, October 5). Opening Welcome: State of the Internet Industry. *Web 2.0 Conference*, San Francisco, California. Conference website available at http://conferences.oreillynet.com/cs/web2con/view/e_sess/5854. Retrieved November 3, 2010.

Press Release (1998, January 29). *"u"land.* Copenhagen: DR TV Press Centre.

Press Release (1999, January 21). *Plan B fra U.land* [Plan B from U.land]. Copenhagen: DR TV Press Centre.

Press Release (2005, September 21). *Fremtidens tv for unge* [Future TV for Young People], Copenhagen: DR TV Press Centre.

Reseke, L. (2010). Ombudsmand holder øje med DR på Facebook [Ombudsman Keeps an Eye on DR's Facebook Activities]. *www.mediawatch.dk.* Retrieved February 1, 2011.

Surowiecki, J. (2004). *The Wisdom of the Crowds*, New York: Anchors Books.

Sørensen, D. H. (2009, June 26). DR lancerer piratsite for unge [DR Launches Pirat Site for Young People], *Politiken.*

15 *From Broadcast to Networked Journalism*

The Case of Al-Jazeera English

Shawn Powers

Introduction

Launched in November 2006, Al–Jazeera English (AJE) has, to a large extent, been forced to depend on new media platforms to reach its target audiences. Unable to secure access to any substantial cable television market in North America, and anxious to reach out to audiences far and wide, AJE quickly partnered with a number of web–based content providers in order to get its product into the homes and hands of many in non–traditional ways. As a result of its early difficulties in securing access to particular markets, such as the United States, AJE invested heavily in its new media team, hoping that a breakthrough online would demonstrate to skeptics that it was indeed producing high quality journalism and providing a legitimate "voice to the voiceless" (Khanfar, 2007). As of January 2011, the approach has been a success, going from being available via satellite and cable TV in 80 million homes in early 2007 to over 200 million homes.

This chapter outlines the origins of AJE, including its relationship to the Arabic Al–Jazeera, its mission, its concept of public service and the roles in which new media technologies (especially the World Wide Web) play in the Network's operations. After reviewing AJE's transition into digital journalism, this chapter argues that the Network's approach to new media, and its ability to marry its use of new technologies to its organizational priorities and mission, offer an important case study of the potential for public service journalism in the digital era. Far from faultless, AJE's online operations offer some important insights into the difficulties and possibilities of public service news production in the "Age of Information," and in particular, demonstrate the importance and benefits of effectively engaging in online journalism and journalists for the purpose of fulfilling critical public needs regarding one's right to freely receive and impart information.

The Rise of Al–Jazeera English

Al–Jazeera English (AJE) is one branch of the Al–Jazeera Network, an organization that includes the original and now infamous Arabic–language news channel Al–Jazeera, a sports network that spans nine channels, Al–Jazeera Mubasher (an Arabic–language version of America's C–SPAN, a channel dedicated to live coverage of political proceedings and deliberations among politicians and public opinion leaders), the widely popular Al–Jazeera Children's Channel, the Al–Jazeera Documentary Channel, the Al–Jazeera Center for Studies and the Al–Jazeera Center for Training. Importantly, AJE is independent from each of the other constituents of the Network, and uses an entirely different set of journalists, producers, editors and managers from its Arabic–language sister news broadcaster.

While most the of Network's operations and outputs are in Arabic and are centered on the Middle East, AJE has had a distinctly non–Arab feel. In the lead up to its launch in 2006, veteran British newsman Steve Clark was asked to lead the effort, hiring the broadcaster's first 600 employees. The broadcaster's first managing director was another Briton named Nigel Parsons. Starting in 2008, Tony Burman, a Canadian newsman with decades of news and leadership experience from the Canadian Broadcasting Corporation (CBC), was asked to takeover as Managing Director in an effort to move the broadcaster away from being seen as "British Boys Club" (Stebbins, 2008). This is not to say that the broadcaster has been overly Western or not "Arab enough," but rather, multicultural. There have been over 70 ethnicities represented as employees of AJE. Its staff is diverse, and intentionally so in that the news channel hopes to reframe the ways in which news stories are told in parts of the world that are typically ignored or misrepresented by the mainstream Western media. The network's leadership team sees diversity in the newsroom as a means of accessing the local knowledge required to properly contextualize news from Africa, Asia, Latin America and the Middle East. Helal (2008) argues that it is this commitment to diversity and local knowledge that helped AJE stand out when compared to other international media organizations:

> We were in Myanmar exclusively during the tensions last year. We covered Gaza from within Gaza by Gazan correspondents. We looked into why Gazans are united behind Hamas despite the suffering. These kinds of stories are not easily covered by other media. It's not an accusation against other media. It's about the elements of perceiving the knowledge, the know–how when it comes to covering the story and producing it. It's not there in Western media but we have invested in people by bringing more than 60 ethnic backgrounds and nationalities represented in the staff.

AJE, similar to its Arabic–language sister, receives a large grant to support its operations from the government of Qatar. Similar to other state–supported news organizations, while the broadcaster is technically independent from the funder's interests, it is unclear how far that independence stretches in times of political stress or crisis. Yet, four years into the AJE's on–air operations it has shown no consistent bias towards any particular group, country or political interest, except for the station's consistent support for voices of dissent, be they xenophobic political groups in the United States marching in support of Senator John McCain in the 2008 presidential election or voices in favor of the Flotilla protests headed for the Gaza strip in 2010. One could argue that by highlighting voices of dissent towards an American politician and towards the government of Israel that the broadcaster is simply helping to mobilize or sustain opposition to the U.S. and Israel, but AJE has similarly highlighted embarrassing political protests in countries closely aligned to the Qatari government, like in Malaysia December 2007 (Powers and el–Nawawy, 2008).

According to Wadah Khanfar (2007), the Director General of the Al–Jazeera Network, AJE's mission is "to empower the voiceless, rather than empower the pulpit, to tell the news with an alternative voice, putting the human being back at the center of the news agenda." This mission is bolstered by the fact that the broadcaster is the first English–language news network to broadcast from the "global south" to the "global north" (Helal, 2008).

According to Will Stebbins (2008), former head of the America's bureau in Washington, D.C., the launch of AJE cost the Emir more than $1 billion USD and was the largest rollout of a global news network in history. Stebbins predicts, "we'll never see anything like it again, especially given the increasingly bleak outlook for the news business." Indeed, the costs associated with the launching of AJE were justifiably large. AJE was launched with the first global rotating bureau structure, whereby broadcasting responsibilities were passed around the world over the course of each day via the network's four primary broadcast centers in Kuala Lumpur, Doha, London and Washington, D.C. In order to accomplish this task, the Network had to invest in significant infrastructure in each of the broadcasting centers in order to ensure that high-quality journalism could be produced and broadcast from each, while also allowing for seamless transitions between the four bureaux. Adding to the costs, AJE was the first high-definition-ready international newsmaker, requiring significantly more bandwidth and technological investments than most standard news networks. While the structure of the broadcaster is important to its mission, it also added a number of redundant personnel costs, since each of the broadcasting bureaux required a full and well-trained team of editors, producers, journalists and on-air personalities.

There are, naturally, questions regarding whether AJE should be considered a public service broadcaster (PSB). PSBs, according to the United Nations Educational, Scientific and Cultural Organization (UNESCO), are defined as

> broadcasting made, financed and controlled by the public, for the public. It is neither commercial nor state-owned, free from political interference and pressure from commercial forces. Through PSB, citizens are informed, educated and also entertained. When guaranteed with pluralism, programming diversity, editorial independence, appropriate funding, accountability and transparency, public service broadcasting can serve as a cornerstone of democracy. (UNESCO, 2010)

While AJE may not fit into standard preconceptions of what a PSB looks like, a strong case can be made that AJE is, indeed, a PSB. Tony Burman (2009), AJE's managing director, explains that AJE is a PSB in the context of the development of global civil society:

> AJE is a Public Service Broadcaster, but in a different way than the BBC World Service or the Canadian Broadcasting Corporation. We are a global public service broadcaster, covering stories and news that are often under and even misreported by other news outlets, in order to fill a gap in the international public sphere. By rebalancing the flows of international news, we are providing a critical service to development of international civil society.

Moreover, diversity and pluralism are both critical elements of UNESCO's definition of PSB, and both are embodied in AJE's broad range of ethnicities represented in its journalists, as well as the diversity of its stories when compared to other international media, like CNN and the BBC (Schatz, 2007). Additionally, its independence from commercial interests has been clearly demonstrated, as despite continued financial loses, the Qatari Emir remains committed to supporting the Network's costly international operations. And while there are some lingering questions regarding the political agenda behind the Arabic-language news channel's coverage of regional wars and crisis, AJE's programming has been received by critics as among the most in-depth and politically insightful, even when compared to the BBC (el-Nawawy and Powers, 2010). Finally, accountability and transparency, two things that governments and organizations operating in the Persian Gulf are not known for, are actually areas where AJE excels, an issue that this chapter will outline is some detail in the section of AJE's expansion into the World Wide Web and collaborative and generative content.

AJE on the Web: Multimedia, Mobility and Ubiquity

In part due to an effort to ensure that its programming is accessible anywhere in the world, and also in part due to a young organization and staff, AJE's online presence is robust and is even built into its mission. When asked about whom the network is trying to engage, Managing Director Tony Burman (2009) says, "the whole English speaking world, with no exceptions." Thus, compared to more traditional PSBs, whose target audiences typically are defined by their geographical presence and/or national allegiance (i.e., citizens of the United Kingdom, or India, for example), AJE needs to think more broadly about how to reach its target audience. Whereas traditional PSBs have politically and geographically defined target audiences, with identifiable and discernable media consumption habits and capacities to account for, AJE does not. It, indeed, knows little about media consumption habits of its viewers, since the audiences across the world straddle different socio–economic and media capacity and use habits. As a result, the broadcaster has to cast its programming far and wide. In order to meet the needs of as many potential viewers as possible from around the world, "AJE is working to make itself available for free on every possible screen imaginable" (Nanabhay, 2010).

AJE was an early adopter of online technologies for distributing its news and programming. The broadcaster was the first to establish a formal news channel on YouTube, the world's most popular online video website, and continues to redistribute a large majority of its programs online via YouTube.[1] Today, almost every major international news broadcaster has followed suit, creating its own channel on YouTube. Yet AJE is the most popular, with over 20,000 videos uploaded in the first 4 years, and over 8.6 million videos viewed in that same time. By comparison, the Associated Press, which has uploaded twice as much content to YouTube (43,000 videos), has only been viewed 6 million times. As a newcomer to the field of broadcasting, AJE was quicker to adjust to the modern media ecology, and its lead towards and success on YouTube exemplifies this important organizational capacity.

Moreover, AJE was an early adopter of the internet to facilitate the live–streaming of its programming, an idea that was made technologically feasible only within very recent history. While there are several live–streaming websites that host AJE's channel, LiveStation is the most well known and popular, particularly in the West. Importantly, LiveStation is available for free via the World Wide Web, and can also be downloaded onto smart phones such as the iPhone and BlackBerry for free live streaming of AJE's programs on a mobile device.

In addition to its partnerships with YouTube and LiveStation, AJE also launched its own internal group focused on providing its content via the web, as well as developing a robust web 2.0 effort, called "Al–Jazeera Labs." Al–Jazeera Labs webpage features an application for the iPhone, a link to the newly revamped mobile webpage (designed for non–iPhone smartphones), information on how to receive AJE's news via twitter, how to text or tweet in a question for Riz Khan—the host of one of the post popular shows on the network—to question a guest on his interview show, a link to AJE's YouTube page, information on how to receive a RSS feed of AJE's news on your non–internet enabled phone, a link to all of AJE's podcasts (some of which are available through Apple's iTunes), information on how to receive AJE's headlines through your Instant Message client, and, of course, AJE's Facebook application. AJE was also among the first to develop and update applications for the live streaming of the broadcaster's programs on Apple's iPad, and bucked trends pushed by other news organizations by making their Apple applications downloadable for free to all (Bouder, 2010).

While it is impossible to say just how successful these efforts have been in promoting AJE's product, it is hard to deny that they have had an impact in places where AJE has little terrestrial or satellite broadcasting rights, such as in the U.S. For example, in addition to AJE being YouTube's biggest draw in the news genre, its viewership via online sources grew over 600% during the conflict in Gaza in January 2009, the large majority of which were American internet viewers. Also, over a third of all of its YouTube videos are viewed from within the U.S., and over a third of the programs viewed via live streaming on an Apple iPhone or iPad coming from within the U.S. (Bouder, 2010). To put these developments in historical comparison, whereas accessing typical broadcast news required consumers to tune into particular channels at particular times, AJE's approach to disseminating the news—ubiquitous, immediate and multi–media—represents an alternative model for news production and dissemination when compared to many traditional PSBs.

From News Consumption to Co–Production

While AJE's coverage of the 2009 conflict in Gaza drew attention worldwide for its relative depth—AJE was the only international broadcaster that had English–speaking journalists on the ground in Gaza—it also coincided with several new and innovative Labs initiatives. In November 2008, AJE launched its citizen–journalism upload portal, a webpage devoted to "seeking eyewitness news reports from its vast international audience."[2] During the conflict in Gaza, the *Your Media* webpage was flooded with photos and video from Palestinians in the Gaza Strip, many of which made their way to AJE's webpage and some of which were rebroadcast on the network's programs. Other prominent international broadcasters such as the BBC Persian Service and VOA's Persian News Network adopted similar styles of "networked journalism" (Beckett, 2010) months later in their coverage of the June 2009 political protests in Iran.

In addition, the *Mapping the War in Gaza* feature was considered groundbreaking.[3] Using software developed by Kenyan–based Ushahidi, the Al–Jazeera new media team created a map (based on Microsoft's virtual earth program) that integrated information submitted from its citizen journalists into a zoomable layout of Gaza and the surrounding territories. Each bit of submitted information from citizen journalists—be it a tweet, a video or a cell phone picture—was turned into a dot, categorized via color in order to differentiate the different events (dark blue dots noted a death of some sort, while yellow dots were references to news about international aid), and placed on the map. Citizen reports were vetted and verified by experienced journalists to ensure that they were indeed factual, and then integrated into reports from the mainstream media to ensure that the map was providing a comprehensive look at the events taking place (for more on the academic significance of integrating new media technologies into the newsroom, see Beckett, 2008). Later, the same technological platform was adopted by the State Department in the aftermath of the earthquake in Haiti in order to best aggregate and share real–time information and was credited for saving thousands of lives.

Even more innovative was the Al–Jazeera Network's decision to release all of its footage from the 2009 conflict in the Gaza Strip under the Creative Commons 3.0 attribution license (the least restrictive license available), functionally making the footage available for all commercial and non–commercial use, free of charge. By releasing all of its video and programming to the Al–Jazeera Creative Commons Repository, even raw footage that had gone unused and/or was unedited, AJE allowed for other news outlets, filmmakers and bloggers to easily share, remix, subtitle or reuse the footage in any way they saw fit, as long as they credited the Al–Jazeera Network by keeping its logo in the bottom right hand corner of the footage.[4] This was the first time a news organization, public, private or otherwise has released all of its footage, totaling over 1000 hours, with easy access for free use by the general public.

In this particular case, by waiving the rights to control and profit from the footage, the network demonstrated its public service credentials in an innovative way, symbolically suggesting that news and journalism should not be dictated by the market, and that political and cultural efforts to restrict AJE's reach in the West and elsewhere would not stop the images from Gaza from getting out of the region. It is important to note that AJE was the only English–language broadcaster in the world with a full team reporting from within the conflict zone during the war. To put this anecdote in perspective, in 2001, when Al–Jazeera had the only live footage during the U.S.–led invasion of Kabul, the Network was able to profit handsomely—some suspect up into the hundreds of millions—from the royalties it earned from selling its footage to Western news broadcasters. By uploading and disseminating its exclusive footage via a Creative Commons license, the Network sacrificed potential profit for the purpose of providing a public good.

In describing the importance of the Creative Commons Repository, Lawrence Lessig, Professor of Law at Harvard University suggested that AJE is "teaching an important lesson about how free speech gets built and supported. By providing a free resource for the world, the network is encouraging wider debate, and a richer understanding." Joichi Ito, CEO of Creative Commons, agrees, adding:

> Video news footage is an essential part of modern journalism. Providing material under a Creative Commons license to allow commercial and amateur use is an enormous contribution to the global dialog around important events. Al–Jazeera has set the example and the standard that we hope others will follow.

According to Mohamed Nanabhay (2009), Head of New Media at Al–Jazeera,

> We are doing the exact opposite of what everyone else in the business is doing. While they try to find business models to monetize their content, we are giving it away for free to anyone with Wifi. We are opening up the black box of news production process to the scrutiny of the global public.

According to Nanabhay (2009), the Creative Commons experiment with its Gaza footage was a huge success from the perspective of the Network in that it helped get its footage onto a greater number of television and computer screens, thus improving international awareness of the conflict. As a result, Nanabhay and his team started to develop an archival system where they will be able to issue more of their content online with a Creative Common 3.0 attribution license, allowing visitors to search for content based a number of criteria. And, beginning in early 2010, the repository began to grow, as AJE started to upload large amounts of its current programming, including behind the scenes footage and documentaries, for free viewing, use and re–use by anyone with access to the World Wide Web.

During the 2010 elections in Iraq, AJE fully integrated its collaborative and generative journalism initiatives with its traditional media and platforms.

Whereas previously the two journalistic tracks operated independently, though with occasional crossover, the stability of an election—with pre-set dates and with a relatively small set of potential outcomes—allowed for the network to plan ahead to cover the election using a combination of its journalists, Iraqis and new media technologies.[5] Prior to the election, AJE distributed a small number of flip cameras to opinion leaders in neighborhoods throughout the country to facilitate better accountability of the voting process. Knowing that the network could not have its journalists everywhere, especially given security concerns, AJE relied on trusted Iraqis to help document the electoral process. According to the Network:

> Each of these videos features the perspective of a regular Iraqi, whose viewpoints and experiences are rarely shared in the news reports coming out of the country. Through video, we can listen to their voices, see their faces, and gain a better understanding of what it was like inside Iraq on this important day. (AJE Network, 2010)

AJE also created a central website that integrated all of their information that could facilitate a better understanding of the Iraqi elections. Backgrounder reports, with extended information about the election, candidates, and history of democracy in Iraq were made available alongside daily news reports from AJE journalists and citizen videos. There was a section for opinion pieces and blogger contributions to help spark discussion. While progressive, such a fully integrated approach, combining content produced by professional journalists with that of untrained Iraqi citizens, risks obscuring the lines between properly vetted news reports and opinions that, historically, have been important for maintaining the credibility of any news network.

More broadly, the challenge of relying on such citizen accounts of current events is that they inevitably only tell particular sides of the story. While helpful in situations where little professional reporting can be done by journalists (such as in Gaza and Iran in June 2009), it is important to note the risks of such citizen input turning into citizen propaganda, where footage captured by people actively involved in an ongoing event or conflict are able to use citizen journalism portals for the benefit of their particular cause or constituency. The responsibility journalists have to present a balanced curation of important viewpoints on a given issue is increasingly difficult when the 24-hour news cycle pushes traditional news organizations to cover current events live, in progress, with little time to reflect on the larger picture or ensure that a plurality of representative viewpoints are included. While this responsibility has become more and more difficult since the advent of 24-hour satellite news, the rise of citizen journalism portals, such as Al-Jazeera's *Mapping the War in Gaza*, represents an evolution in the news reporting process that may fundamentally challenge the idea of objective, balanced and reflective journalism that so many in the profession have, historically, worked towards (Miller, 2009). Since its inception, AJE has struggled with striking this balance between high-quality reporting presented by trained, experienced journalists and being a conduit for under-represented voices seeking recognition in the global public sphere.

Speaking to this point, Director General of the Al-Jazeera Network, Waddah Khanfar, argues that his network's approach to news differs from other news organizations in that he sees the modern news-making process as one of co-production rather than mere consumption (Khanfar, 2010). Today, audiences are not simply receiving news messages and digesting them accordingly, but rather they are often playing an active role in the news production process, reporting information in real time, commenting on breaking events, and spreading information of interest virally via social networks. And while these habits have always influenced how news stories are shaped and received, the growing ubiquity, speed and access to the World Wide Web fundamentally changes how these habits shape the process of news production and interpretation. Understanding how these changes have altered the social norms and expectations driving the news making process is essential to the future of any news organization. And it is this understanding of the current media ecology that helps explain why AJE has been at the forefront of embracing new media technologies and platforms in order to allow for innovative ways of reaching audiences, but also the means of engaging audience as intelligent elements of the news-making process themselves.

At the same time, the broader consequences of such a model of journalism, particularly if widely adopted, require further study. As audiences and news producers increasingly become one and the same (i.e., virtually connected communities of like-minded citizens), then how do political organizations that disagree on questions of policy-making and nation-states that see the world through different cultural worldviews engage in sustained dialogue? This challenge is particularly important for PSBs to consider given their historically defined mission to serve, according to UNESCO (2010), as the collective cornerstones of democracy.

To summarize, AJE, the first global broadcaster launched in the age of widespread internet access, has been quick to adopt and adapt new technologies and platforms into its mission and web distribution such that its use of the World Wide Web is deeply intertwined with its day-to-day operations. While AJE was officially launched in November 2006, it was first launched four years earlier on the World Wide Web as the English-language website of the Arabic-language broadcaster Al-Jazeera. Since its website's first iterations, the use of the internet for the production and dissemination of the Network's journalism has grown substantially, often pioneering uses of new technologies and platforms ahead of its international competitors. In 2007, AJE was the first international broadcaster to embrace YouTube as a means of global distribution. In 2009, AJE was the first to embrace Ushahidi, an open source platform for news gathering and mapping, a move that has been followed by a number of news organizations, including the *Washington Post* and the Australian Broadcasting Corporation. In 2010, the Network again embraced the open source movement, distributing its Arabic and English–language footage of the Israeli siege on Gaza via the least–restrictive creative commons license on the World Wide Web for use and re–use by other broadcasters and bloggers alike. All together, throughout its brief history, AJE's web presence has been part and parcel of its mission and operations, and its continued investment in new media technologies and robust web presence continues to provide a model for PSB's looking for innovative ways to connect with and reach non–traditional audiences.

From Broadcasting to Networked Journalism

In its current manifestation, the term "broadcasting" is relatively young, arriving only in the 1920s to describe what radio stations popping up across Europe and in the United States were doing. Originally an agricultural term, meaning to "scatter seed over a broad area rather than sowing it in designated places," experts thought that it expressed the proper idea behind radio (Hanson, 2008, p. 24). Yet, today's news media ecology is drastically altered, whereby the directions and origins of news no longer unidirectional, controllable or even "broad," with more and more news being created and consumed within politically and ideologically isolated communities of like–minded individuals (Utley, 1997). The introduction and the adoption of the World Wide Web, and advanced, fast and mobile communications technologies has challenged the news organizations and governments that had previously controlled the construction of news, and as a result, news producing organizations are in crisis, both in terms of a business plan, but also in terms of missions and responsibilities. It is within this environment that the concept of networked journalism has emerged (for more, see Beckett, 2008).

Governments around the world continue to suppress free media. Indeed, the freedom of the press is more in danger in 2011 than it was twenty years ago at the cusp of the fall of the Iron Curtain. Burma, Iran and China offer just a few examples of how effective governments have been at controlling their information environments, despite revolutions in communications technologies (Freedom House, 2010). Against this trend of information suppression, AJE's efforts to promote the freedom of information and the tools for properly expressing information represent an alternative model for public service broadcasting on the web. AJE's mission—perhaps most specifically embodied in their efforts to publicly release news footage, both uncut and edited, to the general public for reuse and scrutiny alike—represents a sensible and important approach to news production in the "age of transparency" (Powers, 2009). AJE's contribution to the global conversation is an important one, and its approach to knowledge production in the digital era is innovative and worthy of further critical and exploratory focus.

Notes

1. For example, see http://www.youtube.com/user/AlJazeeraEnglish.
2. For example, see http://sharek.aljazeera.net.
3. For example, see http://labs.aljazeera.net/warongaza.
4. For example, see http://cc.aljazeera.net.
5. For example, see http://interactive.aljazeera.net/iraqelections.

References

AJE Network (2010). Al-Jazeera Network Annual Report. Manama, Bahrain: Al Waraqoon W.L.L.

Beckett, C. (2008). *SuperMedia: Saving Journalism So It Can Save the World.* London: Wiley-Blackwell.

Bouder, D. (2010, 14 June). Al-Jazeera English tries multi-screen approach. Associated Press.

el-Nawawy, M. & Powers, S. (2010). Al-Jazeera English: A Conciliatory Medium in a Conflict-Driven Environment? *Global Media and Communication*, *6*(1), 61–84.

Freedom House. (2010). Freedom of the Press. Washington, DC. http://www.freedomhouse.org/template.cfm?page=16

Hanson, E. C. (2008). *The Information Revolution and World Politics.* New York: Rowman & Littlefield Publishers.

Miller, C. (2009). *The Future of Journalism: Papers from a Conference Organised by the BBC College of Journalism.* London: BBC College of Journalism.

Powers, S. (2009, July). *Public Diplomacy and Legitimacy in the Age of Transparency.* Los Angeles: Center on Public Diplomacy.

Powers, S. (2010). Author's notes, The Al-Jazeera Forum, Doha, Qatar, May.

Powers, S. & el-Nawawy, M. (2008). New Media and the Politics of Protest: A Case Study of Al-Jazeera English in Malaysia. In M. Kugelman (Ed.), *Kuala Lumpur Calling: Al-Jazeera English in Asia* (pp. 65–82). Washington, DC. Woodrow Wilson International Center for Scholar's Asia Program.

Schatz, R. (2007, 8 March). *Widening the Perspective: Al-Jazeera International Enriches Media Landscape.* Atlanta, GA: Emory University, *Arab Media Center.*

Sparrow, A. & Robinson, J. (2010, Sept. 8). Budget Service Will Face Budget Cuts. *The Guardian.*

UNESCO. (2010). Public Service Broadcasting. http://portal.unesco.org/ci/en/ev.php-URL_ID=1525&URL_DO=DO_TOPIC&URL_SECTION=201.html. Consulted Jan. 15, 2010.
Utley, G. (1997). The Shrinking of Foreign News: From Broadcast to Narrowcast. *Foreign Affairs*, *76*(2), 2–10.

Interviews

Burman, T. (2009). Interview with the author, Doha, Qatar, March.
Clark, S. (2010). Interview with the author, London, UK, January.
Helal, I. (2008). Interview with the author, Doha, Qatar, March.
Khanfar, W. (2007). Interview with the author, London, UK, November.
Khanfar, W. (2010). Interview with the author, Doha, Qatar, May.
Nanabhay, M. (2009). Interview with the author, Doha, Qatar, March.
Nanabhay, M. (2010). Interview with the author, Doha, Qatar, May.
Stebbins, W. (2008). Interview with the author, Washington, D.C., March.

Contributors

ANJA BECHMANN is an assistant professor at Aarhus University, Faculty of Arts and a board member of Centre for Internet Research in Denmark. Her PhD thesis was titled *Crossmedia: Innovation networks for traditional media organizations* and explores cross–media as a digital transition in established media companies, as business and market strategies, cultural negotiations, professional skills, and conceptual designs. Her current research focuses on participation culture, and user relevance as a business strategy for internet companies. Her recent work has been published in *Making Online News, volume II* (2011) and *New Media and Society* (2012).

BENEDETTA BREVINI is Lecturer in Media policy in the Department of Journalism of Brunel University in London. Her research addresses a range of current issues in European and international media policy and regulation. Her PhD research, entitled *Towards PSB 2.0: applying PSB ethos to online media in Europe* has investigated the policies developed by European Member States and PSBs institutions to bring public service broadcasting ethos online. Her work has appeared in international publications like the *European Journal of Communication* and *Interaction: Studies in Communication and Culture.* She also writes on *The Guardian's* Comment Is Free and is contributing to a number of publications including *Index of Censorship* and *Political Communication Polcom.*

NIELS BRÜGGER is an associate professor and head of the Centre for Internet Research, Aarhus University, Denmark. His primary research interest is web history, and he is writing a history of the Danish Broadcasting Corporation's website dr.dk. He has published a number of articles, monographs, and edited books, including *Archiving Websites: General Considerations and Strategies* (The Centre for Internet Research, 2005), *Media History: Theories, Methods, Analysis* (Ed. with S. Kolstrup, Aarhus University Press, 2002), and *Web History* (Ed., Peter Lang, 2010).

MAUREEN BURNS is the Convenor of the Media Studies Major, and Lecturer in Cultural and Media Studies, at the University of Queensland. Her book *ABC Online: Becoming the ABC* traces the history of the first five years of the Australian Broadcasting Corporation on the web. She has published on the history of ABC Online in *Television and New Media*, *Media International Australia*, *Southern Review*, and *Continuum*. She is also currently working on a history of science popularisation in Australia.

ANNE DUNN is Associate Professor in the Department of Media and Communications at the University of Sydney. She spent more than 20 years working as a presenter, media researcher, journalist, producer and director for commercial television, for SBS, the ABC and the BBC. Anne's research interests are public broadcasting, the impact of new media on journalism, media ethics, and broadcast journalism education. Her most recent research project was working with ABC News to look at the impact of digital convergence on broadcast journalism training. Anne is co–author (with Fulton, Huisman and Murphet) of *Narrative and Media* (Cambridge University Press, 2005), and of *Media, Markets, and Morals* (Wiley-Blackwell, 2011), with Spence, Alexander and Quinn.

ALBERTO N. GARCÍA is an associate professor of Film and Television Studies at the School of Communication, University of Navarra, Spain. He has been Visiting Scholar at Fordham University (New York) and Visiting Professor at the University of Stirling (United Kingdom). He has published his work in journals such as *Post Script*, *Comunicación y Sociedad*, *Zer* or *Analisi*. His current research interests include online journalism, media convergence, and new media trends.

MEGHAN GROSSE is currently pursuing her master's degree in communication at the University of Illinois at Chicago. Her research interests include media history, cultural formations, media institutions, and new media.

NICHOLAS W. JANKOWSKI is Visiting Fellow at the e–Humanities Group of the Royal Netherlands Academy of Arts and Sciences. He has been researching forms of community and new media since the mid–1970s. During this period, he has prepared studies about community media, research methodology and new media. Recent co–edited volumes include *Internet and National Elections: A Comparative Study of Web Campaigning* (Routledge, 2007), *e–Research: Transformation in Scholarly Practice* (Routledge, 2009), and *The Long History of New Media* (Peter Lang, 2011). Jankowski is co–editor of *New Media & Society* and edits the Hampton Press book series *Euricom Monographs: New Media and Democracy.*

MERAV KATZ–KIMCHI (PhD, Bar Ilan University) is a visiting scholar at the Office for History of Science and Technology at UC Berkeley. Her research interests include histories of communication technologies and socio–technological change.

FIONA MARTIN lectures in Convergent and Online Media at the University of Sydney. She has a background in public service broadcasting, as a journalist and producer with ABC Radio, and has also worked in print and online media. For the past decade she has been a journalism and media educator, with an interest in online and cross–media publishing. She has contributed to *Virtual Nation: The Internet in Australia* (2004) and *Media and Communications in Australia* (2006) as well as journals such as *Convergence*, *Media International Australia*, *Southern Review* and *Broadcast Engineering News.* She is currently researching legal and ethical shifts in print journalism for the Australian Press Council. She blogs at mediarepublik.com.au.

HALLVARD MOE is associate professor of media studies at the Department of Information Science and Media Studies, University of Bergen. He has researched the transformation of public service broadcasting into public service media. In 2010 he co–edited *The Digital Public Sphere: Challenges for Media Policy* (Nordicom) with Jostein Gripsrud, and *The Idea of the Public Sphere: A Reader* (Lexington) and *The Public Sphere Vol. I–IV* (SAGE) with Jostein Gripsrud, Anders Molander and Graham Murdock.

KENNETH MURPHY (PHD) is an assistant lecturer in the School of Media at the Dublin Institute of Technology. He has previously published on issues of media policy, public media and technological change in *Trends in Communications*, *Irish Studies Review*, *International Journal of Media and Cultural Politics* and *International Journal of Digital Television*. He has just completed a comparative research project on the funding of Community radio broadcasting under the Broadcasting Authority of Ireland's media research scheme.

MICHAEL J. MURPHY (PhD, Ryerson University) is a professor in Ryerson's School of Radio and Television Arts and former academic director of the Rogers Communications Centre. Prof. Murphy's research includes the CoMedia Project—an international collaborative project to provide high–bandwidth shared production services for the media industry—as well as a project to define the future of interactive television.

AN NGUYEN is Senior Lecturer in Journalism in The Media School, Bournemouth University, England. A former Vietnamese journalist and an Australian–educated scholar, he specialises in online journalism, citizen journalism, news audience, journalism professionalism and science journalism. He is the author of *The Penetration of Online News: Past, Present and Future* and many papers in journals and books, including world–leading titles. Dr. Nguyen serves on the Editorial Board of *Journalism Education*, the recently launched journal of the UK Association for Journalism Education.

BRIAN O'NEILL (PhD, Dublin Institute of Technology) researches on media literacy, media policy and information society issues. He is co–editor of *Digital Radio in Europe: Technologies, Industries and Cultures* (Intellect, 2010) and has written on digital radio developments for *New Media & Society, Journal of Radio and Audio Media* and *Convergence*. He is a member of the DRACE (Digital Radio Cultures in Europe) research group: www.drace.org.

DAVID W. PARK is Associate Professor of Communication at Lake Forest College. He is the founder and past chair of the International Communication Association's Communication History Interest Group. He is the co–editor of two volumes: *The History of Media and Communication Research: Contested Memories* (Peter Lang, 2008, edited with Jefferson Pooley), and *The Long History of New Media: Technology, Historiography, and Contextualizing Newness* (Peter Lang, 2011, edited with Nicholas W. Jankowski and Steve Jones). His research interests include intellectuals and the media, the history of the study of communication, media history, and internet studies.

VIKKI PORTER is Director of the Knight Digital Media Center and supervises Professional Development Programs for New Media journalists at USC Annenberg School for Communication & Journalism in Los Angeles. She was the founding director of the Western Knight Center for Specialized Journalism at the Annenberg School for Communication at the University of Southern California. During her 30–year journalism career, Porter worked in five Western states, started a newspaper, served as top editor for three community newspapers, and shared a 1986 Pulitzer Prize Gold Medal as part of a five–person team while city editor of the *Denver Post*. Most recently, she was executive editor of the *Desert Sun* newspaper in Palm Springs, CA.

SHAWN POWERS, PhD, is an assistant professor of Communication and the associate director of the Center for International Media Education at Georgia State University (USA). Previously, Powers has been a fellow at the London School of Economics and Political Science, Oxford University, and at both the Annenberg Schools for Communication at the University of Pennsylvania and the University of Southern California. Powers is also the president of the MountainRunner Institute, a non–profit organization that provides support for public diplomacy and strategic communications campaigns to organizations and governments around the world.

PATRICIA RILEY is a specialist in organizational communication and internationally known for her work on institutional politics and organizational culture change. Her most recent research focuses on the role of communication infrastructure in knowledge management processes and on the role of communication and information technologies in organizational change and transformation. Her interests are wide ranging, from the military, to the UN to the media going through transformation.

AMIT M. SCHEJTER (PhD, Rutgers) is associate professor of Communications and co–director of the Institute for Information Policy at the Pennsylvania State University. His scholarship integrates a comprehensive and critical approach to communication policy. His studies have been widely published in leading communication and law journals, and cited in congressional and Knesset hearings. He has held senior executive positions in the communications industry in Israel, among them general counsel for Israeli public broadcasting. His most recent book is *Muting Israeli Democracy: How Media and Cultural Policies Undermine Freedom of Expression* (2009).

EINAR THORSEN is Lecturer in Journalism and Communication, Bournemouth University. Einar has written several articles on BBC News Online and the inflection of public service media in an online environment. Other research projects include a co–edited book (with Stuart Allan) *Citizen Journalism:*

Global Perspectives published by Peter Lang in 2009, for which he also contributed a chapter on the news reporting of climate change. He has also published articles on the media politics of WikiLeaks, and Wikinews and the neutral point of view.

NIKKI USHER received her PhD from the University of Southern California's Annenberg School of Communication. She focuses on how news is transforming in the digital age. Nikki's specialty is the study of media production, and she has conducted field research both in the US and internationally. She is an assistant professor at George Washington University's School of Media and Public Affairs.

Index

www.ingramcontent.com/pod-product-compliance
Ingram Content Group UK Ltd.
Pitfield, Milton Keynes, MK11 3LW, UK
UKHW021837100926
8556IPUK00004B/392

9 781433 11175